Corazón Abierto

John and Robin Dickson Series in Texas Music

Sponsored by the Center for Texas Music History,
Texas State University

JASON MELLARD, General Editor

Corazón Abierto

MEXICAN AMERICAN VOICES
IN TEXAS MUSIC

Kathleen Hudson

Texas A&M University Press
College Station

This paper meets the requirements of ANSI/NISO Z39.48-1992
    (Permanence of Paper).
Binding materials have been chosen for durability.
Manufactured in the United States of America.

Library of Congress Cataloging-in-Publication Data
Names: Hudson, Kathleen, 1945– interviewer.
Title: Corazón abierto: Mexican American voices in Texas music / Kathleen
    Hudson.
Other titles: Mexican American voices in Texas music | John and Robin
    Dickson series in Texas music.
Description: First edition. | College Station: Texas A&M University Press,
    [2022] | Series: John and Robin Dickson series in Texas music | Includes
    index.
Identifiers: LCCN 2021040877 (print) | LCCN 2021040878 (ebook) | ISBN
    9781623499020 (cloth) | ISBN 9781623499037 (ebook)
Subjects: LCSH: Mexican American musicians—Texas—Interviews. | Mexican
    Americans—Texas—Music—History and criticism. | Tejano music—History
    and criticism. | Texas—Social life and customs. | LCGFT: Oral histories.
Classification: LCC ML3481 .C67 2022 (print) | LCC ML3481 (ebook) | DDC
    781.64089/68073—dc23
LC record available at https://lccn.loc.gov/2021040877
LC ebook record available at https://lccn.loc.gov/2021040878

Que lejos estoy del suelo donde nacido.
(How far I am from the land where I was born.)
—Mexican folk song performed by José López Alavez

He not busy being born is busy dyin'
—"It's Alright, Ma (I'm Only Bleeding)," written
and performed by Bob Dylan

To my muses, companions, loves, memories of people
and places, and the music!

Contents

A gallery of images follows page 118.

ix Acknowledgments

I Introduction

Part 1 Oral Histories

7 **Armando Arciniega** *Music for Fun*

11 **Josh Baca** *Sharing His Passion*

25 **Max Baca** *Bringing the Groove*

32 **Rick del Castillo** *Rich in Spirit*

51 **Ernie Durawa** *It Takes the Drummer*

56 **Linda Escobar** *A Woman of Family*

65 **Rosie Flores** *A Rockabilly Filly*

72 **David Garza** *Talking Texas Music in Mexico*

75 **Henry Gomez** *Mariachi Voice*

78 **Michael Guerra** *A Man with a Mission*

84 **Ruben Gutierrez** *Talking on a Border*

88 **Tish Hinojosa** *Dreaming in the Labyrinth*

97 **Flaco Jiménez** *A Lifetime of Achievement*

103 **Gill Jiménez** *His Father's Son*

109 **Santiago Jiménez Jr.** *He Carries His Father*

114 **Stephanie Urbina Jones** *Mariachis Make Me Cry*

119 **Esteban Jordan III** *The Family River of Jordan*

128 **Billy Mata** *Time to Dance*

138 **Marisa Rose Mejia** *The Joy of Youth*

140   **Fritz Morquecho** *You Can Call Me "Boxcar Fritz"*

143   **Junior Pruneda** *Grace on the Bass*

146   **Tomás Ramirez** *Jazzmanian Devil*

152   **Roberto Sontoya Ramos** *It's My World*

160   **Gilbert Reyes** *A Fount of Knowledge and Experience*

164   **Lesly Reynaga** *Dual Passport*

176   **Frank Rodarte** *Speaking the Truth*

181   **Florin Sanchez** *Subtlety Speaking Volumes*

189   **Poncho Sanchez** *The Heartbeat Is the Drumbeat*

195   **Patsy Torres** *Educating and Entertaining with Grace and Style*

207   **Ruben V** *Life on the Line*

210   **Patricia Vonne** *The Gypsy Dances and Sings*

Part 2 Other Voices

223   Flaco's Eightieth Birthday: A Reminder of How Far Conjunto Can Go *by Hector Saldaña*

226   Freddy Fender's Voice Could Console and Comfort *by Christine Granados*

228   Pride *by Dagoberto Gilb*

231   Having Recently Escaped from the Maws of a Deathly Life, but Not That Life Sentence Called Death, I Am Ready to Begin the Year Anew *by Sandra Cisneros*

232   Manuel's Destiny *by Stephanie Urbina Jones*

235   Conclusion

237   Index

Acknowledgments

Where to begin! It does take a village to raise a book. This one was four years in the making, and so many have stepped up: Mindy Reed, the Authors' Assistant in Austin, was invaluable (our third book together); Schreiner University, for support, release time, Texas studies class and Mexican American film class, and work/study students and interns (Alyssa Cole, Carlos Escobedo, Samara Roberts, Heather McCain, Madeline Zerr, Brittany Smith, Jade Manchaca); Sally Hannay, head of the English Department, who always helped me with a class schedule that supported the book; Charlie McCormick and Diana Comuzzie, president and provost, who shared my vision both for the book and for Schreiner; Chumbe Salinas, for video, travel, and friendship; all the artists willing to give time and friendship; Harold Eggers, for his friendship and prayers; Tamara Saviano, for last-minute coaching; David Gaines, for his friendly and careful read of the manuscript; my friends and family (you know who you are), who tolerated and supported me through this project; Max Baca y Los Texmaniacs, for the ongoing friendship, a steady thread throughout this project and other projects at Schreiner University; and Texas A&M University Press, for sharing the vision and making it available to the world.

Corazón Abierto

.

INTRODUCTION

This third volume of voices of Texas musicians brings my writing, teaching, and fan life full circle. The first book, published in 2001, *Telling Stories, Writing Songs: An Album of Texas Songwriters*, was followed in 2007 with *Women in Texas Music: Stories and Songs* (both published by the University of Texas Press). My love of music and Mexico has always been there, and I embrace the opportunity to share and teach about my passion with this third collection of voices featuring Mexican American musicians.

You are about to read a series of interviews and firsthand accounts given by performers ranging in age from twelve to eighty. They crisscross Texas and Mexico to Europe and other spots around the world. In part 1, "Oral Histories," each performer offers his/her spin on a variety of themes. Part 2, titled "Other Voices," follows the interviews and enriches the conversation about what it means to be an American artist with deep connections to Mexico. My own voice, as a writer and music lover, provides supporting backup vocals in what I have come to view as an accordion-rich conjunto. My hope is that you will read and listen, and perhaps even add your voices to ours, rich with the joy that drives this collective effort.

The conversations that are the heart of this book took place over the past five years behind stages, in restaurants, and over the phone. Although a few questions recurred (about self-labeling, early and ongoing influences, family stories), most took their own shape. I strived to be a listener who encouraged and honored the voices I heard. Different readers will no doubt hear and see different figures in the tapestry—echoes in the hall that, unlike with a quantitative study, have always been foremost in my methodology.

This collection of voices is deliberately varied and textured. What is not deliberate is the exclusion of anyone. Time and space dictate, and these voices showed up in my life, returned calls, and made themselves available for this collection. I was honored to be present as hearts opened in the exchange. The title, *Corazón Abierto*, came to me as I spent time in San Miguel de Allende, the *corazón* of Mexico. I received a heart-shaped pan dulce there in March 2019 from an old friend. When I retired from the Texas Heritage Music Foundation in 2017, Bill Worrell donated a design for our celebration—a silver heart with a treble staff. Again, I saw this collection through the heart of music, *corazón de la musica*. As you read through these stories, some common threads emerge. Yes, everything connects—but the synchronicity still surprises me no matter how often it appears.

The threads include conversations about family, borders, creativity, music, food, history, and community. The artists I talked with have become family to me. I want to invite you to read this as one story told by many voices. I do identify with John Lomax, a collector of cowboy songs. We both stood outside a culture and collected and shared voices, with profound love and respect in our hearts.

Some excerpts from my personal journal during the interview process provide insight into my deep love of Mexico, which I am humbled to share with you and the world:

December 13, 2017:
I drive down 35 into Laredo Texas several times a year, heading to my apartment in San Miguel de Allende Guanajuato. I love the language. I love the way it feels in my mouth. I love the culture. I love the way the food feels. I discovered *chiles toreados* in Mexico. The rubbing together of two cultures on the border creates a certain kind of energy.

I am heading to Laredo again to catch a bus from Nuevo Laredo and continue heading south on the first-class *ejecutivo* tomorrow night. I am called by Mexico, the romance, the stories: Frida Kahlo and Diego. Pancho Villa and Zapata. Padre Miguel Hidalgo y Costilla's cry of "*El grito!*" in Hidalgo. The beginning of the war for independence in San Miguel de Allende. The conspiracy, the stories, the cobblestone streets always call me.

December 19, 2017
I am torn between my two homes: Texas and Mexico. I am present to my love for this culture, and I love knowing that the land I have in Texas was once Mexico.

My Don Quixote cup sits by my computer, awaiting the next cup of coffee my old friend Larry Gunn will bring me from Oxxo. My red horse, another token that traveled from the Nobel awards in Sweden, sits on the other side of the computer. Candles are lit, and the tarot cards are showing my daily story. What else does a writer need?

This collection of interviews I am compiling is a mere sampling of the many voices and stories in the legacy of Tex Mex music of this state. Some self-identify as Mexican American, while others still feel Chicano/a. Most do not feel Hispanic—a word that connotes routes in Spain. I love the mixture of Spanish and Aztec that lives in the culture south of the 2017 border. I am here on the 2017 winter solstice, and I am aware that we are coming out of darkness into more light as 2018 begins.

March 30, 2018

T. S. Eliot said, "April is the cruelest month." I hope not! The sun is shining and all living things around me at the Dancing Star Ranchita are blooming. I am heading up to New Art, Texas, tomorrow to the Bill Worrell studio. We will hear music from bluesman Johnny Nicholas outside on the Llano River. Then I will drive down to my beloved border town, Laredo, to pick up Larry Gunn. I will be immersed, again, in the blending of cultures on a border. Bill was telling me about his life, and he said, "I was born in El Paso six blocks from the river. What a difference a river makes." That became an important distinction for me. Rivers as borders.

I have walked across the bridge many times in Laredo, avoiding customs and airports and long lines. I always stop in the middle of that bridge and gaze down at the river, the Rio Grande. I begin to think about rivers and memories of my youth camping at El Tesoro on the Brazos River outside of Granbury, then recently releasing a turtle on the Llano River at Worrell's studio spot, and then I inevitably find myself filled with inspiration, meditating on the two cultures I love dearly: Texas and Mexico.

The musician interviews that follow serve to express this affinity and honor the spirit of music that transcends borders.

Part 1

Oral Histories

Armando Arciniega

I was at Carnitas Uruapan on a Sunday morning in October of 2017, listening to Santiago Jiménez Jr. at his weekly show there. I noticed a gentleman from across the room, *muy guapo*, tall in a black hat. I watched him carefully. We ended up talking, and I found out that not only does he have a PhD in mathematics and a teaching job; he also plays music. His name was Armando, and we set up an interview on a Sunday afternoon after a show he did at the Tejano Conjunto Festival flea market. The music played throughout the interview—a great atmosphere for talking. I also saw Linda Escobar, Eva Ybarra, Santiago Jiménez Jr., and Gill Jiménez at the festival—all in about twenty minutes of walking up. This event is about culture, heritage, family, and dancing. Oh . . . and food.

HUDSON: The very first thing I want to talk about is the music playing in the background.

ARCINIEGA: This is a band that just started up and wanted to come play at intermission. I don't know who they are.

HUDSON: So you are giving someone else a chance. What is it about this Sunday afternoon event that makes it a cultural phenomenon?

ARCINIEGA: I think that the flea market is a base where people can have Sunday family time. People come to shop, to eat, to listen to music, to drink a beer. But mostly, people come to hear the music. For some of them, it is like exercising. They dance all afternoon.

HUDSON: I love all the different ages here.

ARCINIEGA: From kindergarten to eighty years old. That couple there is eighty years old, and they come every Sunday to dance. They have music here from one to five thirty each Sunday. It is a cultural thing, and most of it is Tejano music—music from Texas. We do some Tex Mex too, and we do *norteño* . . . Mexican regional music. Pan Am Plaza, Bandera Flea Market, Poteet Flea Market, and several more. About four big ones.

They call the Poteet flea market a Mexico mall. In Mexico on Sunday, people go to the park and go out.

HUDSON: I love the parks in Mexico on Sunday. So, tell me your story.

ARCINIEGA: I was born in Durango, in Mexico, and I came to the United States when I was about fourteen years old. I do music for a hobby, not for a job. I am a professor of mathematics at UTSA [the University of Texas at San Antonio], and I do music for fun. I came from Mexico in 1990 and did my high school in New Mexico; I got my bachelor's, master's, and PhD from Texas Tech University. I graduated in 2003, came to San Antonio, and started singing here. I started going downtown, and there is music everywhere. It was something I always wanted to do. It was in my blood. I used to sing at home, but it took San Antonio to bring that out. In fact, in 2005, that was the first time I sang on a microphone. That's where I come from, and this is what I have achieved. I teach for a living and do music for fun. I enjoy teaching too.

HUDSON: I teach and love it. Two teachers here.

ARCINIEGA: Two teachers who love music. People ask me why do I teach math and sing, thinking they do not go together. Well, I like to do both.

HUDSON: And some of the current research on the brain does connect music and math.

ARCINIEGA: Right. Some of the musical notes have mathematical meaning. There's math in music for sure. Probably not music in math. They do complement each other.

HUDSON: Let's talk about Santiago Jiménez Jr.

ARCINIEGA: I met him in 2004, at an accordion school. He used to teach at Heritage Taller. I wanted to learn how, so he started teaching me. After a while, I decided to also sing. I asked him to do a recording of me. I actually have a few CDs I recorded with Santiago Jiménez Jr. He was actually the first person I started singing with. I did the Conjunto Festival in May with him—in 2005, I think. KEDA [radio station] was owned by the Davila family for thirty years, and they play mostly local music. It took my music to a lot of people. Then I decided to go solo and do my own stuff. I wanted to do *norteño*.

HUDSON: Educate me on *norteño*.

ARCINIEGA: Conjunto music had a start with Santiago Sr. The difference in *norteño* and conjunto is mostly that *norteño* uses the saxophone. But there is regional *norteño*, and we don't use the saxophone. It actually comes from the north part of Mexico . . . Nuevo Leon and Monterrey. The rhythm is a little faster in *norteño*, and that is the only difference. Another thing is in *norteño* they only play the three bottom strings in the *bajo sexto*, and in conjunto they play everything.

HUDSON: I will be at the Conjunto Festival and plan on seeing the Chris Strachwitz movie. He tracked down this music years ago. Any recommendations for the show?

ARCINIEGA: Everybody comes to the Conjunto Festival. Linda Escobar from Corpus Christi is very good. She has been in this business for a long time. Fifty years. She started playing when she was a child. She and Lydia Mendoza are both important women. Eva Ybarra too. Not that many women. And there is a difference between conjunto and Tejano. In Tejano they use the keyboard and the trumpet. I believe there is one afternoon with a focus on women. That music [playing] behind me is not *norteña* or conjunto; it is *cumbia*. That is a rhythm for dancing. It's like distinguishing between rock and country.

HUDSON: In Texas, we mix all these things together, it seems. Let's talk about the Frontera and the relationship between Mexico and Texas. I love borders.

ARCINIEGA: I think the music is pretty much the same. You can go to Piedras Negras in Mexico and you can go to Eagle Pass, and the music is the same. In the Frontera, the music is regional. I got myself legal in 1992 or something like that. When I came, it was not as hard as it is right now. Going to school was not easy, because I did not speak English. I wrote an essay when I was a freshman at the university, and it is about coming from another nation and studying the United States. I was able to surmount those obstacles and get an education. Mathematics is a universal language we can all understand. And music is universal too. You are dancing to that music, and you probably can't understand it all.

HUDSON: I would love to see that essay you wrote. Please send it to me.

ARCINIEGA: What I write is because I come from a small village in Mexico where automobiles were rare—only one or two trucks. Mostly you ride your horse. Only one teacher for all the grades in elementary school—two or three teach each grade. That one teacher taught us the basic stuff about life. She was a good one. I want to add that in Mexico sixth grade was the graduation; that was the top. You did not have to go to high school. People would come to the United States to make money and send it back to their families. I came here to have a better life. I was able to do a lot here. My father only went to second grade. My mom went to fourth grade. They know how to write their names. My parents now live in the United States. My father worked in construction. I used to be a mechanic and worked in the fields. You name it.

HUDSON: Thank you very much, Armando.

ARMANDO ARCINIEGA is not only a musician; he is a mathematician and PhD whose research has been published in several scholarly journals.

Josh Baca

Sharing His Passion

Josh, the young nephew of Max Baca, has played at Schreiner University (where I teach) many times with the Los Texmaniacs. His passionate expression with the accordion has always engaged the audience. Whether he is in China; in Bangladesh; at Roddy Tree Cantina in Ingram, Texas; or at the coffeehouse at Schreiner University, he excites the audience. I have watched him mature. On February 15, 2019, he was lined up in Los Angeles for the Grammy Award Ceremony with Los Texmaniacs. Their album *Cruzando Borders* was nominated for (and eventually won) the award for Best Regional Mexican Music Album. We first met up to talk one afternoon in 2014 at Max Baca's house. First I talked with Max, and then I caught up with Josh. Texmaniac fan and videographer Chumbe Salinas had the video camera going, and a yellow Hohner was on the table.

HUDSON: I showed my students a YouTube of you playing that gorgeous yellow Hohner with Los Texmaniacs. Tell me about that.

BACA: Max ordered it and designed it with Hohner. And then we were on tour—I think we were in Washington, DC, or Richmond, Virginia—it was just right there. And I guess that's where one of the main factories for Hohner is in the United States—or the only factory. And a good friend of ours called us. And Max was like, "Hey, we're gonna go down and check out the shop." And I was like "OK, cool." So, I didn't expect anything. At that time, we were going to go and see some accordions and Hohner instruments. So, we got there. And he was like, "Come check this out." Then Max showed it to me, and I was like, "Oh my God, it's amazing." Like, "Wow, man." I was checking it out and then I saw my name on it. And I said, "Oh, man." So, it was kind of a gift from my uncle and from Hohner to endorse me with this accordion—the Texmaniac signature accordion, Josh Baca signature accordion. It was an honor and a real special feeling to have this accordion made for me, because I'm originally from Albuquerque, New Mexico.

And I love where I come from. That's where I grew up. Of course, everybody does. And to be playing this accordion and representing where I come from—I'm representing Tex Mex music, which is what I was raised with—is an honor.

HUDSON: That's just beautiful. I found this beautiful New Mexico flag at the flea market one time. In my kitchen, where the western sun comes through, I put the flag up because of the symbol—the four directions.

BACA: Do you know what the four directions stand for?

HUDSON: Tell me.

BACA: In New Mexico, the Native Americans believed that the four rays going up are dawn, daylight, dusk, and dark. The four rays going to the left are north, east, south, and west. The four rays going down are spring, summer, fall, and winter. And the four rays going the other way are infancy, youth, adulthood, and old age. And the circle in the middle is the sun. That's what they would tell me when I was growing up.

HUDSON: Well, when you talk about Hispanic heritage, some people say, "Well, that's a connection with Spain." We talk about Tex Mex. We know that the American Indian cultures that were already here can't clearly be separated from the Mexican influence, and they overlap. And so, Tex-Mex-Indio—it's a lot of overlapping and integration. I know Max came from Albuquerque. But how did you end up here?

BACA: Well, when I was younger, I'd come back and forth to play music. I'd come to the Conjunto Festival in San Antonio. I was also hanging out with my Uncle Max, and he would come and show me different musicians, give me CDs, and take home a different accordion every time I came. We'd play certain songs. So, I loved Tex Mex music. And where I come from—Tex Mex music isn't very common or big around that part of Albuquerque and New Mexico. So, a guy from San Antonio gave me a call and he was like, "Hey, our accordion player left, and we're looking for an accordion player. Max Baca recommended you. He said that you can play a style and do this music." And I said, " Send me the music."

"Well, we need an accordion player for this Friday." And it was on a Wednesday they called me. And I was, "OK. Well, send me the CDs. Let me learn the song." I had an uncle of mine from New Mexico who said he would drive me to San Antonio. It turned into a road trip. We left Thursday night.

And I never received the CDs because about the time that he mailed them off and they got to Albuquerque, I was already in San Antonio. And I didn't know any of the songs. So, I went on the tour bus with them, and we took off. I didn't know the songs, but I was familiar with their music due to the fact that I would listen to it. Being younger, I would listen to that young style of music—like modern Tejano music or whatever. . . . And I would just learn the songs on the fly on the bus. And the accordion I had—oh my God, it was horrible. It was beat up. It was leaking air. It was three different accordions. The middle piece was from another accordion. It was out of tune, and I was trying to make the gear up like, "Oh man." So, they were like "OK, cool. We liked the one you played, but can you get a working instrument?" I guess they asked me. So, I got here, and I came back home. I said, "Uncle, I need an accordion." He has a signature Flaco accordion and loaned it to me.

And I toured with them for about four to five years. It was a Tejano group from here in Texas: Grupo Vida. They do all the dancing and light shows and all this stuff they used to do back a long time ago before I was even born, I think. So, I made that gig. And then right around that time, Max had his own accordion player, which was one of my favorite accordion players as well, David Farias. He was doing some stuff with his brothers, and he was going to reunite with them and try something new, I guess. And at the same time, me and Grupo Vida had a falling out, and it wasn't working out between us very well. So, right at that same time, I left Vida and Max needed an accordion player. And then Max was like, "Wow. We're going to China. I'm gonna need an accordion player for China because David is not gonna be able to make it." I go, "Well, let me see what I can do."

"You need a passport. You need a passport right now." He's always on me like "Right now, you need to be here right now, and you need to do this right now. Right now." And so, I went and got a passport one day. It cost me an arm and leg, but I got it. We came back and then Max said, "Oh, it didn't go through. We're gonna go next year."

I told the band I was with that my uncle needed my help. We went our separate ways and then Max called. And I was like, "Yeah. Uncle, I need a gig, man. Let's play. I'll play with you. I'll help out until you find somebody here or whatever." He said like, "All right. All right." So, I came in. We actually went in Max's studio. And it was me, Oscar, a drummer, and Max. We started, and I thought, "Oh man, it's gonna be an easy gig, easy gig here." So, I started playing the first few notes. "Oh, no, no, no." Max stops. "No, no, no." I was like, "Oh, well, what's going on?" He's like, "That's wrong. That's not the right note. You're not hitting the right notes there." I was like, "OK, let's try it again." "No. That's wrong. That's wrong." We didn't go through and finish one song. He put his *bajo* down. He said, "Well, practice the songs, and learn 'em the right way and then come back, and we will see." I was like, "Oh man." So, the pressure was on me even more. I came back thanks to Oscar, who was one of Max's bass players. I was with him at that time. And he was an accordion player as well. He helped me out and showed me some of the songs and how things were supposed to go. I'd call David over, and David would tell me to hum some of the songs like he played them on the album, 'cause at first when I first came here, Max wanted me to play the songs like the album—the way David would play. And then he said once you learn the song, eventually you could do your own style or whatever.

The first six months I was doing that. And then after that, he just said, "All right, go ahead and do your thing. Just feel it. Play from your heart and do whatever you're doing." So, the next time, I was hanging out with Flaco a lot. Flaco repairs and tunes all my accordions. I was living in Houston at that time. And when I joined Los Texmaniacs, I bought a house out here and moved down to San Antonio and moved my family out here. So, anyway, I was hanging with Flaco, and Flaco was telling me, "Oh, play like this, and it comes from the heart. You feel this and however you wanna stand or the way you wanna hold your accordion. You wanna play it upside down? If you feel it, you're gonna play it. Comfortably. You can play it like that." And after that, it clicked. It clicked in my head. OK, I get it. It's just feelings. Just play whatever comes to mind at the moment. Whatever is coming on at that moment and you wanna play it, just play it. And that's kind of how I learned to play this.

HUDSON: Well, Friday, when I saw you play with Max, it was very clear to me you were in that space where what we were seeing was what was in you and ready to come out. Passion.

BACA: Yes. An older uncle of mine always tells me, "Play music according to the laws of the art." He says, "According to the laws of the art." The rules can be broken in the art of music if I play the music according to the laws of the art and be authentic. Because if you remember and play where you come from, that's who you are. Flaco told me one time, he said, "Everyday what would you eat? What would your family make? Beans, tortillas, papas. Everyday. And chili. And that's who you are, and that's what you feel when you play. That's authentic. It comes from you." I'm like, "Yeah, he's right."

HUDSON: I teach writing and a lot of that is the same. There's a place where you just become who you are on the page and see if that happens. I'm imagining that given your perspective at your age, you probably see things that Flaco doesn't see; you see things that Max doesn't see. You're coming in with fresh eyes just from being the age you are. Now, you've had a lot of influence. And as you said, you spent time with Flaco and with Max as an uncle. Have you ever been aware that you're seeing things differently, historically?

BACA: Coming from Albuquerque, it's a little different. I wasn't raised over here in Texas. Like there's other accordionists and other kids from Texas here that were raised with this music, and they heard this music every day on the radio. No, that's a standard. Oh, that song we learned when we were younger. Me coming over here, and I hear it like, "Oh man, that's neat. That's fresh." To me, it's fresh. I had never really heard this stuff. And in all reality, to be honest, I never really listened to a lot of Tejano or conjunto music ever. I've always listened to country, rock and roll, or blues, or polka, or Cajun, or zydeco. Music that's not real common, I guess you would say, with instruments that you never really hear. . . . You listen to a Chinese cello—and it's like, "Man, it's the cello, but it sounds—there's something different about it or odd, or some flutes or drumming." Exotic music is what I like to really listen to.

HUDSON: Really? World music.

BACA: World music. Yes. All over. And Max was the one who introduced me to opening my mind—broaden my horizon to listen to that kind of music and start creating stuff on the spot as far as like creating music with instruments that haven't been invented yet. For example, Max was recording a conga a while back some time, and he needed a shaker. He couldn't find one. And he got a bottle of vitamins, and he went back in the studio, and he used it as a shaker. It didn't sound quite like a shaker, but it sounded cool. It was different. I do that as far as when I'm playing traditional music and stuff. But when we have stuff that we're creating—new music and new ideas, and we're coming up with all kinds of different ideas and stuff like this, Max is like, "Oh, come up with something for this part right here, like a little jingle or something that's gonna be remembered every day." When they hear that song, they'll remember that certain part, and that's the kind of stuff I like. I'll do something a little more poppy than so traditional.

HUDSON: Who are some artists that you listen to?

BACA: Oh man. Like I said, I'm a young guy, but I love old music. So, I would listen to a lot of old Creedence Clearwater. When I was younger, I wanted to be like Ritchie Valens and Buddy Holly. And then I got into the modern-day stuff, and I would listen to Metallica. They're pretty old but always stay modern. Adam Levine—he's one of the judges on *The Voice*—and I love the way he sings. I love Willie, of course. He's the ultimate, but I've actually been listening to Willie's son, Lukas. And the amazing thing is I heard this guy singing one time on like YouTube or somebody had a phone. I remember he's playing it. I was like, "Woah, that's young Willie Nelson right there." And I looked. And I go, "No. It's Lukas Nelson. It's his son. I've been listening to his stuff, and he has stuff like his dad, but he does like a more modern thing. So, I've been listening to him a lot because of his ideas and . . . and this time, it's Willie's son.

HUDSON: What do you think about all the terms? You've already used the word *Tejano* and then used *Tex Mex*. I used *Hispanic* just because there's this big umbrella, but the truth is what I'm actually looking at is Hispanic music in Texas. So, that would be Tex Mex. Right? And the word *Tejano* means living in Texas, right?

BACA: How I found that out is when I first joined Los Texmaniacs. They went on tour to Elko, Nevada, and we did the Cowboy Poetry gathering out there in Elko. Yeah. Cowboys and poetry together. Yeah. They had poets that take poems and comedian stuff, and then they had Texas country music and cowboy music. Bob Wills kind of stuff. And us—Los Texmaniacs. It was this traditional folk music. I went out there the first time, and I was talking to some guy, some cowboy that was out there. I asked him something about his hat. I asked, "Are you from Texas too?" He goes, "No. I'm from Montana." I was like, "Oh. I'm sorry, man." This guy was a tall, big cowboy. I was like, "All right. Cool." He was like, "What kind of music do you play?" I'm like, "We play *Tejano* music." He just kind of looked at me. He was waiting for me. There was a quiet pause, and I was like, "Yeah. We play Tejano music." He goes, "Well, *Tejano* what? You play Texas country? You play Texas blues music? Texas rock and roll? What kind of music do you play?" And I said, "Oh." You know, that kind of shocked me. I said, "Well, we play conjunto music." He says, "Conjunto. What's conjunto? What is that? Is that like a group or a band, or is it the name of your band?" "Well, it's like a Tex—" And then our drummer says, "Tex Mex." We played Tex Mex music with Lorenzo Martínez, who was the drummer at that time. He still is, but he's off and on. The guy goes, "Oh, Tex Mex."

HUDSON: But here, it has connotations. When you say *Tejano*, you know you're gonna hear some Spanish.

BACA: You would say Tex Mex. Because if you ever go to California, and then you listen to those guys playing *bajo sexto* and accordion, you're gonna go, "It sounds twisted. It sounds different. Oh, that's the Cali Mex." That's how they play out there like Cali Mex style. And then you go to New Mexico, and you hear some guys who are playing it from New Mexico and it's sounding more different. You come into Texas, and you hear one of the guys play from South Texas, you're like, "All right. Yeah. OK. It's Tex Mex music. Yup." According to Max, if it's rock, blues, country, hip-hop, ska music, or whatever kind of music it is, and it has a button accordion and a *bajo sexto*, it's conjunto Tex Mex music.

HUDSON: And I want to talk a little bit about your background from New Mexico.

BACA: My family was born and raised there in Albuquerque, New Mexico.

HUDSON: So, there's American Indian blood?

BACA: There's American Indian blood. Yes. My grandfather is from Spain, I think. Uncle Max knows more than I do. I haven't really done any research, but I should. But according to a brother of mine, he was telling me that there's a lot of Native American slaves that were in our family way back in the day. It was my father who taught me how to play the accordion. And my mom's side, they come all the way from Durango, Mexico. My grandpa lived out here for about fifty years. I would say about fifty years and never spoke a word of English ever in his life.

HUDSON: Did you know him?

BACA: Oh yeah. I knew him very well. I would go and stay with him. He lived a little south of Albuquerque in the middle of the town. He never picked up English ever in his life. It's funny. I don't understand how he got by, but he never ever picked up English. And he knew my grandmother on my father's side—my grandmother's father who was named Pat Lucero. They were drinking buddies back in the day before my dad and before my grandma. Before everybody. They were best friends. I guess my great-grandpa was a sheriff, and my grandpa would always go to jail or whatever from drinking, and they ended up being best friends, and then they kind of just drifted apart. I remember about maybe twenty-five years later, my dad met my mother, and my mom had me.

HUDSON: So, the two families were connected.

BACA: They were connected before that, and a generation went by, and then back again they were reconnected when my father met my mother, and then my grandfather would say he didn't know anybody named BACA. And when he found out who my grandmother was and my grandmother's last name, he goes, "Yes. I knew a—he was a sheriff or a deputy or something like that." And my grandma was like, "Yeah. He was my dad." He said they used call him in. Rough guy. He was real white, white complexion. White, white complexion, blue eyes, but he was a Mexicano. He spoke perfect Spanish.

HUDSON: So, do you speak Spanish?

BACA: I'm not fluent in it because growing up not a lot of kids would speak Spanish, along with school. And my parents never really spoke Spanish to me, and school never spoke Spanish to me. Or around the house, everybody would always speak English, but I would always see my grandparents speak Spanish. When they didn't want us to know something, then they would speak among each other in Spanish. Yeah. And the music I listened to then. There was rock, hip-hop, and pop, and all that stuff. I had my hip-hop era where I wore my hat backwards, baggy pants and stuff, and a big shirt.

HUDSON: Did you do hip-hop accordion?

BACA: I did hip-hop accordion. I did.

HUDSON: That would be fun.

BACA: Yeah. It's a little different. It's more I guess Latin hip-hop.

HUDSON: Actually, I like the rhythm of hip-hop. Its kind of beat is poetic. It's fun.

BACA: When it's done right, it's fun. It is. I've done some tracks of hip-hop with accordion. There's not really a lot of stuff like that, but I used to play with a lot of hip-hop groups over in Mexico because I used to play keyboards, and I make beats and I would make songs for them. I make the beat. I played keyboards or guitar with them. And sometimes I throw the accordion in there because like I've always noticed—I've been playing at a hip-hop club [and] I'll play a traditional Mexican mariachi song or something. They go crazy. They love it. They love it when you take them back to where they come from.

HUDSON: So, what do you see ahead?

BACA: I don't know. I wanna just live life, just taking it one day at a time, and see what tomorrow brings. I've always been raised that you're never promised tomorrow. You know what I mean? But you also, you gotta be smart to say, "Well, if I am promised tomorrow, this is what I would do." I hope that Los Texmaniacs and everything goes according to plan as well as it should. And I really believe that it's going to be because my Uncle Max—he knows what he's doing. He's done this for years. And I just hope that everybody is in good health—myself, Max, and the guys—because the unit that Los Texmaniacs have right now . . . this chemistry with four men (Noel Hernández on the bass, Max Baca on the *bajo sexto*, and either Danny Martínez on the drums and Lorenzo Martínez with us, and myself), the chemistry in that group is just phenomenal. It's like we all connect not just onstage, but at home just hanging out. We're all best friends because we've all known each other for years. And Noel Hernández, our bass player. I've only known him for a few years, but that guy is so heartfelt, and that guy will give you the shirt off his back.

HUDSON: Let's talk about the China trip.

BACA: It gives me chills thinking about it because we're all so close. And going to China, man, we went to this little valley. We were playing in the city. We were playing in the city and played a big theater. And it's like, "Man, China. Cool, man." Mopeds everywhere and cars, and then we drove for four hours out toward a little village in China. After we started getting into the village, and I started looking around, and I started thinking, "What the hell? What the hell am I doing? What am I doing in the middle of China with my accordions?" We started to keep going and keep going. A little more. Driving the van. This is like on the edge of a cliff.

This cabin and this house that we stayed in, they were all built just by hand. There were no nails or screws involved in the whole structure of this place. And this thing was massive. Everything was made of wood—the sinks, the faucets. It was so amazing that you turned on the sink to wash your hand, and then you smell the wood from the water hitting the wood. Beautiful. And that feeling right there was just like . . . [sigh] It was just clean fresh water straight from the ground and from the river. When I felt it, I said, "Man, this is gonna be a real strange place."

And then the little kids when we drove up, they were peeking and whispering like, "Who are these people; my God, where do they come from? Look at them." Freaking out on us. And then one of the guides went up, and she called a couple of people down to come get our bags and take 'em up to our cabins for us. After that, I thought they'd come with a cart to put it on a cart. No. They came with a big stick. Boom! Little person about this big and skinny, skinny, skinny, and she put one bag on one side, and she holds it, one bag on the other side, and then just took 'em up—walked all these stairs. Came back down and got another one.

And so I realized that the people who live there in that village just live for that day. They wake up about seven or six in the morning, and they walk up to the rice fields, and they pick their rice for their family just to eat breakfast. They leave the breakfast table and go back up and pick some more rice just to eat lunch. I believe that's the way we're supposed to live life. We live so luxurious and all this, and there was an older man that was sitting there, and he was smoking a pipe. I was just sitting there, and I was taking a picture of him, and he was sitting there.

One of the tour guides was sitting next to him. "Well, what do you think of this place that you come to?" And I said, "Well, I think it's so beautiful. It's like a dream. This is a dream." And she told him, and he said, "Well, where you come from is a dream. Where I come from is reality." And right there, I was like, "Wow. That's awesome." Do you know what I mean? He's right. You know, Baca, this is a dream. This is a dream where I live. He's right. Where he comes from is reality. So like, "Wow, man, it's crazy." It's amazing. So, right there, I grew a connection with him. I took a picture of him, and I smoked some of his pipe. And so, we walked all around the village just to check out everything, and I saw these things like in the corners underneath the houses. They're underneath houses, and I asked what they were. "That's coffins." "Oh my God, wow. Are there people in there?" "No, no, there's no people in there, but they're coffins. There's three things in a man's life that they have to do here in the village: it's have their own son, the firstborn son; build their own home for their wives and their family, but build it by hand by themselves, no help, by themselves build it; and build their own coffin." I mean, lay down and build your own coffin. Woah, this is crazy. That's the three major things they have to do in life there.

HUDSON: It's so different from how we live.

BACA: That's amazing when you can live like that, and you live at peace, where not everything is, "No. No. This is my car." We need to just walk out and just live natural. I mean, I guess, unfortunately, this is how it is now. We gotta just keep going with it. There's another experience I had there on these little rice fields. They go up the mountain, and they go like this, and like this, and like this, and like this [stacks hands] on top of the mountain—all the way up, there are rice fields. And at the bottom of every rice field, there's a pit of water, and that's where they grow the rice, in the water. And these little tiny paths, and I am one of the biggest guys around. So, all the kids are freaking out. I mean, they were looking. So, I'm trying to walk. This tour guide is taking us on this path—a winding path up where it's grass and dirt.

So, I'm walking. Noel is in front of me, and then the tour guide is behind me. And I'm taking pictures, and I'm now just walking, trying to concentrate on not falling. So, I'm walking, and I saw Noel. He put his foot down on the front of a rock and pushed it to make sure that it was stable. And so, I saw what he did; I put my left foot down on the rock to make it stable. Then when I put my right foot down, I fell about a five-foot drop down the cliff in China. So, I'm hanging. I'm hanging like this, and I'm pulling myself up. And Noel is grabbing my arms. And he helps me. And he pulls me back up on the cliff. And I got back up, and I was freaking out. And I was standing up there, and I look over off from the cliff. There's another trail down there. And there were two little old ladies who were working in the rice field, and they're pointing and laughing at me. It's just water in a rice field. I would have just rolled over a little bit or fell. They were laughing like, in other words, "Watch it," you know. Crazy Americans. And I was kinda "Woah. Woah." It was a shock.

And then, on the flight home, my knee was killing me. I popped my knee out of place 'cause I have a bad knee. But other than that, that was a fine experience. It was crazy. Then there was another one that we had where we walked on the other side of the village, and we walked and walked to this trail. We went to the biggest drum tower they had there. And the drum tower is like this place of—a sanctuary place they make where they sing and play music inside there and clap their hands. You literally hear the gong all the way up.

And you sing again, and you literally hear it bouncing all the way up to the very top. They would use it to call for meetings or to come and eat. It would ring throughout the whole village. But anyways, toward the last day before we left, we went off to this little spring. It was a natural spring. It's been there for over five hundred years. And we walked and walked and walked all this way, man. We went up to this natural spring water. It was just one tree—one big trunk on the ground and the hole in the tree. There was a rock. It's a natural rock that somebody put there five hundred years ago. The water was running down the stream. I mean, clear, clear water. It's beautiful clear water. And they say it's a spiritual place. And the workers that walk on that trail go stop and get some water, drink it, pull back up, come back down the water, and drink it. I went to feel the water 'cause they say it cleanses your body. And it was humid hot in China.

We were sweating all the time. So, I go down there, and I wash my hands a little bit. I drink water, and my whole body just went cold. And it was amazing. And then, I looked off toward the top of the rest of the mountain, and I felt a light breeze. You see the grass just kinda flowing, and it got silent. The whole place got silent. It's just quiet. And we all did this at the same time, and we were just kicking back and chilling. And my uncle had his own personal experience, and I had just like this cleansing where I was like, "Wow." It is a place where I would love to go back and write. Just sit there and write, and write, and write. I'd live there if I had a choice.

HUDSON: Wow.

BACA: The water was so natural, and it was like a blessing. Like I was baptized or something. It was crazy. It's like a cleansing. It's just the water. I stood up and then I wet my hands, and I wet the back of my neck and then I drank the water.

I was like "Wow." The whole place got quiet, and I'm looking up in the mountain and people were walking and we're sitting down underneath the benches. Everything is natural. The wood is natural. So, these are all naturally made stuff. They're handcrafted stuff. Beautiful. They're sitting there, and everything just got quiet. Silence. Somebody was telling me to just keep running and doing what you're doing, and everything is gonna be OK for you in the future 'cause you ask me about the future. I have time. And it just keeps going, and everything will come to you if you do what you gotta do, listen to all these elders and your uncles that talk to you. I have another uncle in Albuquerque. He tells me if you treat the music right, then the music will treat you right. But I mean, you prostitute it and you start getting involved in doing the commercial to just sell it and don't even care about creating or making music anymore—there's a right and wrong way to do things in life. That's what I learned at that moment right there. It clicked that there's a right and wrong way to do things in life. There's black. There's white. There's up. There's down. There's in. There's out. There's left. There's right. There's north. There's south. There's only one way to do things in life, and it's either the right way or the wrong way. At that moment, I said, "Wow. Yeah. He's right."

And it's all about the power of the creator. I'm a religious guy, and I believe in that. I was raised a Catholic, but I don't really pay attention to any of that. I like to believe that there's a creator out there. We're all connected in one because this world goes round. It doesn't go just left or it doesn't just go right. It's not a box. Please stop. It's round, and we're all just connected by one thing.

HUDSON: Well, I think that would be a great way to end this session. Your conversation has really inspired me and interested me. Thank you. And I look forward to talking to you again.

I saw Los Texmaniacs many times the next four years, and they always please the crowd. I watched them grow in friendship with Johnny Nicholas as they played the Hilltop Café on the Mason Highway outside of Fredericksburg, and then they toured together. In 2019, I found them in Los Angeles attending the Grammy's. Johnny was up for the design on a collection of his work, created by the Dodd Sisters and their design company. Schreiner University, a thread in this story, was the home of these girls at one time. Yes, everything connects, and it's all round. Thanks, Josh.

JOSH BACA, Max Baca's nephew, has recorded and toured worldwide with both Los Texmaniacs and Grupo Vida. The accordionist is active with the Smithsonian Folklife Festival.

Max Baca

Max Baca and Los Texmaniacs have been part of my many music projects, including an annual coffeehouse at Schreiner, a September tribute
to Texas Heritage Music, educational programs in the classroom, and
even as part of an assignment for my freshman composition classes creating a digital essay on Texas music. I decided to start this project by interviewing him on July 31, 2014. Chumbe Salinas, Texmaniac fan and videographer for the Texas Heritage Music Foundation at the time, brought
along her video camera to document our conversation. We met up at
Max's house and sat in the living room, surrounded by awards and music.

Josh and I had just sat at the kitchen table to talk. (Two Bacas at one
time.) They had just returned from a tour in China. Josh was a primary
influence on my work with this project. All the audiences I round up
love him, and he loves us. It seems like when I go to his show, I am
always moved to dance and smile. My heart is always opened by the
song "Cancion Mixteca," a favorite now of mine, and a favorite of Becky
Patterson, my soul sister in love with Mexico.

I went to one Los Texmaniacs show in San Antonio, and two members of Los Lobos sat in: David Hidalgo and Steve Berlin. Steve produced
their album *American Groove*, and he always adds groove. I heard Los
Lobos in 2015 in Madrid, Spain, opening for Bob Dylan. I was on the
Dylan quest then and followed to Granada. (That story is for another
time.) I do know Dylan loves Flaco, and so do Los Texmaniacs. He is a
primary influence in the conjunto music they do. Everything connects.
Max and Los Texmaniacs played the Hilltop Café at the end of December 2018. It was full circle as I talked with Noel and Daniel, both Texmaniacs, and then received a warm, encouraging hug from Max.

HUDSON: I am excited to hear more of your story right now. I was in Blue
Cat Studio once with our dear friend Terri Sharp (RIP), and I saw your
photo with the Rolling Stones. Joe Trevino (the owner) also has so many

stories to tell from that studio. And many include you. What have you been doing?

BACA: Throughout the years, you go through different phases and different musicians. I've had so many drummers and accordion players. I am where I am supposed to me. My nephew Josh on accordion, Noel Hernández on bass . . .

Chumbe speaks up, asking, "Have you started yet?" We laugh and give a formal introduction as she works on lighting for the video. Then Max asks us if we want water or tea. Max asks about my beads, and we talk about my time at Naropa University, contemplative education, and China. Max reminds me that they just got back from China. He tells me Josh has the good photos.

HUDSON: Intro for the video: I'm Kathleen Hudson, the director of the THMF [Texas Heritage Music Foundation], which I started in 1987. It's 2014, and I am excited to begin this new phase of my oral history project. We are talking with Max Baca. . . . Let's talk about the band you are playing with.

BACA: Josh Baca, my nephew, is on accordion. He started playing when he was five years old. He just turned twenty-two last week. He's still learning because you never stop learning. By the time he was eleven, he was playing professionally. He moved to Texas when he was seventeen. He played with a local Tejano Band from Texas. David Farias was playing with me, and Michael Guerra before that. But now we are going to do another Smithsonian Folkway Album with this unit. Noel Hernández plays bass and is my compadre in singing. We do duets.

In conjunto music, there is no lead singer; always duets—that high harmony voice singing with you. That is a characteristic of conjunto. *Conjunto* means "together." It started, back then, at the turn of the century with influence from the German settlers here in Texas. Valerio Longria Sr. was one of the first. And Santiago Jiménez, Santiago Jr.'s father. They introduced the button accordion. The old-timers started off with the accordion and the *bajo*, which was designed to take the place of the left-hand side of the accordion. There are accordion players who accompany themselves while they play. *Bajo* is kind of like Cajun music, where you have the one-row accordion and the fiddle. Kind of like that. Later on, they incorporated the trio and then the upright bass. Back then, there was no name for this. Valerio Longoria is credited with adding the drum set. Then standing up instead of performing sitting down. This was music in the barn for dances at the end of a week of work. The musicians started singing too. Santiago started with the trio. He was credited with singing and lyrics. The word *conjunto* means a band, a group. I have a *conjunto*.

HUDSON: Is this also a name for a rhythm?

BACA: No, a polka is the primary rhythm for a conjunto, but *conjunto* is the group. When it first started with Narciso Martínez, it was instrumentals. No *cumbias* or *huapangos* then. *Conjunto* stayed on as a word for a band. So that is how all accordion four-piece bands are described. I like to say Tex Mex so people can understand. I use Tex Mex.

HUDSON: How did you come up with Los Texmaniacs?

BACA: I was on the road since 1990 with the Texas Tornados, with Doug Sahm. He passed away in 1999. We still played with Freddy, Flaco, and Augie as the Texas Tornadoes. The time I played with Doug, he taught me so much about the business and the music. I came from Albuquerque, New Mexico. I played with my dad as his bass player when I was about nine. We would play for the Native Americans in New Mexico. My father was an accordion player who also played for the Native American crowd. He is a pioneer with music called "chicken scratch" music, with Native Americans playing accordion and *bajo sexto*. The same songs we play, but all instrumental. His name is Max Baca Sr. My father in the 1960s had his own conjunto *norteño*.

We were close to El Paso and Juarez growing up in New Mexico. My dad was a big fan of Narciso Martínez. That is where it started in Texas. It spread out through the years to the southwestern part of the states, but a lot of people think it came from Mexico. But it didn't. You don't see Tex Mex musicians wearing a sombrero. The Mexicans from Mexico would hear this music and play it, so it became the music of the north: *norteño*. They put their own signature on the music, but they heard it from the north. And they incorporated a sax. That is *norteño* music. Beautiful. They harmonize beautifully. My father, in the sixties, started hearing *norteño* music too, and he created a blending of this. Of course, mariachi music is from Mexico and the trio music—the romantic music. The songwriters were from Mexico . . . José Alfredo Jiménez and so many beautiful poets. That's where we got the Mexican folk songs. The Tex Mex from Texas stayed true to the polka. We incorporated all the different styles and took it in our direction.

HUDSON: And that is what we find in Texas—a rich amalgamation of influences. Look at Willie Nelson and his songs. Then Bob Wills and the hard-core Texas swing. Then other bands with his influence. Miles and miles of Texas.

BACA: Back to the Texmaniac name, which we got from Doug Sahm. He had written a song about a Texas tornado, so later on he used that name. I always said that since I was in *that* band and lived *in* Texas, we have to have a Texas name. So I started thinking Texas Twisters . . . and 10,000 Maniacs was popular . . . so I came up with Los Texmaniacs. Not that we are a bunch of maniacs. [Laughter]

HUDSON: I have seen you at a folk festival rocking the crowd, as a duo at a coffeehouse, and a conjunto festival with thousands dancing.

BACA: When we recorded for Smithsonian, I was asked how to describe our music. I grew up with Doug Sahm, so *Borders y Bailes* was our first album with Smithsonian—music that everybody can relate to. It was cool to play at so many different places.

Texas Tornadoes was such a big band—at one time we had fifteen guys onstage. The band was always a big band, and I played *bajo sexto*. Sometimes we had a horn section and a steel guitar. Doug could move between all genres easily, so I said to myself, "I want to put together a smaller package of that." Why not play some music that can use the traditional instruments and then play blues and jazz too? Make it different.

HUDSON: You have made it your own by weaving all these threads together. You have a very unique sound. How did the Smithsonian connection come about?

BACA: Throughout the years, before joining the Tornadoes, I had the BACA brothers out of New Mexico. I attended the Folk Life Festival. I played with Flaco at times. Every time I would talk to Dan Sheehy of the Smithsonian, I would give him a CD and ask him what he thought. Maybe 1992 was the first time. Several months later, he reported that it was good, but he had some questions. I did not know about creating an identity and about traditional music. He would say to work on a concept. "What the hell is he talking about?" I wondered. Five to six years later, I would give him another CD. That went on for fifteen to twenty years.

When I formed Los Texmaniacs in 1997, I got involved with Texas Folklife and Pat Jasper. She called us and commented on our "buzz," our press. We were invited to play for the troops in Iraq. We got a lot of press for that in 2006. Pat Jasper was director at that time, and she asked us to be a member of a program called The Folk Alliance. We played the convention, and people in festivals would come see us. Dalis Allen saw us there and asked us to play at the Kerrville Folk Festival.

We also played the Folk Alliance in Memphis. Then we were invited to the Smithsonian Folk Life Festival. Dan Sheehy is the director, and for years he was telling us to develop a concept—he directed me by telling me this. I wanted to record with Folkways so bad, but I did not understand his reference to a concept. After we performed onstage, he came up saying, "Now you have a concept." We did *Borders y Bailes* in 2009, and that won us an American Grammy in the category Best Tejano Album. The second recording we did with Smithsonian Folkways was the original idea I had: songs of Texas. There are so many songs that mention Texas and towns, so we ended up entitling the album *Texas Towns and Tex-Mex Sounds*. That got us a Latin Grammy nomination. That is a cool album because we had one of my heroes, Ray Benson, singing "San Antonio Rose" with us. All these beautiful songs I have heard all my life—like Marty Robbins's "El Paso"—they called to me. The Smithsonian is known for preserving the original culture of that music. Ray Benson had asked me to be a guest a while back, so it was cool to do this.

HUDSON: What does *Tejano* mean?

BACA: It is a hybrid name for Tex Mex.

HUDSON: I know you are asked to represent Texas in many places and festivals. You just got back from China, so let's talk about that experience.

BACA: Prior to China, we had an invitation to do our third appearance on *Prairie Home Companion* for the fortieth anniversary. Then we were asked to do a tour representing Texas music and the Texas culture in China. We were there for a week—a four-day festival. Three of the festivals we played were at a performing arts theater south of Beijing. And they had a man from Iraq playing the oud. They brought in a man from India and the Mongolian throat singers and then the local acts, many of them dancers—beautiful and colorful from the different provinces in China.

HUDSON: Who chose you to do this?

BACA: They were doing a program through Smithsonian Folkways to do this concert. That is their objective—to preserve and record music in our culture.

HUDSON: It is really an honor that you are part of this. It is so much more than entertaining a crowd in a bar.

BACA: Conjunto has always been part of the dance hall / cantina culture. Even though I was born and raised in New Mexico, my father was an accordion player, and he showed me the history of the music. I have always been playing this music.

HUDSON: Well, this project is not about birth certificates—rather, about the spirit. Let's talk about the history of San Antonio.

BACA: We have received several proclamations and appreciation awards from both San Antonio and New Mexico. We are sometimes considered the ambassador of the Tex Mex sound. And that is a great honor. Through all the years of performing, everything just evolved and fell right into place, and here I am.

HUDSON: I would love other recommendations from you for this project.

BACA: The Westside Horns, of course. Al Gomez would be great. Tish Hinojosa of course. As a matter of fact, she just called me about playing on a new album with her. Mingo Saldívar is a pioneering performer, but he added the country stuff to it—he was influenced by Johnny Cash.

HUDSON: And Tish has a chapter in my first book—my oral history on Texas songwriters.

BACA: Linda Escobar is in the conjunto field. And Santiago Jiménez Jr.—a good one. Funny story with Chris Strachwitz. Arhoolie Records is his own Smithsonian—a label that preserves. Chris was at the Memphis Folklife Festival, and he said, "Max, you guys are a new generation of music. You are conjunto, but I want to hear the old school stuff. You are bringing this to a new audience." I thought about it and decided to add a little maniac flavor to one of the older songs. He stood and watched the entire set. He liked it. That made me feel good.

HUDSON: Interesting about influences, evolution, and new voices. Are there venues that make a difference to you?

BACA: That's a good question. A lot of people will ask me about playing in other countries, often asking if Tejanos are there. I tell them that we play in theaters in other places. We have played the traditional dance hall venues. The first gig back from China, we played at a dance hall in San Antonio. In China we did theaters, so you have people seeing you for the first time, just sitting there, watching and admiring. What music do you play to this audience? You have to learn to adjust your sets to the audience. We play the traditional folk music to this crowd.

HUDSON: A lot of bands get stuck in a dance hall, and you guys get to play many venues.

BACA: There are three venues: the dance hall, the theater, and the festival. We just played the Jazz Fest in New Orleans with twelve thousand people standing there. We played the maniac stuff there. A harder beat.

HUDSON: What a range of audiences for you!

MAX BACA founded Los Texmaniacs. The Grammy recipient has been playing accordion for almost five decades.

Rick del Castillo

Rich in Spirit

I attended a reunion of Del Castillo at the intimate Townsend Theater in Austin in September 2018. I was blown away by the passionate music—the guitar work of Rick and his brother, Mark, and the voice and presentation of Alex Ruiz. My earlier conversation with Rick enhanced my appreciation for this show. Patricia Vonne, a close friend of the band and the woman who told me to talk with Rick, entered the room wearing a red silk dress, black castanets in hand. I knew we were in for a treat. I was not disappointed as flamenco dancing, the accents of castanets, and another vocalist added a layer of texture to this show. In 2019 Patricia Vonne and Rick del Castillo toured in Italy. One Facebook post showed Patricia and Rick dancing in front of the cathedral in Milan.

HUDSON: In June 2016 we met in the studio with Rick del Castillo. I asked him about the origins of his family name.

DEL CASTILLO: Del Castillo means "of the castle." What's classic—we always know when somebody thinks they know the band and they're trying to get backstage. One time, my guitar tech, this guy came up to him and goes, "Hey, man, I want to go say hi to Del. He's a good friend of mine."

My guitar tech was like, "Yeah, right. I'll go get him." They think Del like Led Zeppelin; he's great. *Castillo* means "castle." Well, and see also, technically, with the name del Castillo, the D is supposed to be lowercase because it means anything that's from the, of the, like de Leon. But as our band, Del Castillo, we capitalize it so it's just easier—it looks really weird to have one little D and then all the others are capped.

HUDSON: So that was an aesthetic choice. . . . That's a perfect segue to some conversations I'd like to have about words and language. Today, I drove over on the back road from Kerrville through Comfort and had a spectacular drive to this place.

DEL CASTILLO: She's in good spirits.

HUDSON: I've arrived with all that beauty in me. I have just discovered how to use Prime Music on Amazon and Bluetooth, so that means I can listen to any album I want in the car. So I was coming over here dancing and moving, to say the least. So that's the frame of mind I'm in.

DEL CASTILLO: Listening to "I Never Cared for You."

HUDSON: Yes. We could start off talking about that as I sit here in my Willie-Bobbie shirt (sort of accidentally). I remember the first time I heard it, and I believe I was standing in Panther Hall in Fort Worth. I was just riveted. Well, I've been in Panther Hall many times. I was first there from '63 to '67. Most of my memories of Willie are playing with Ray Price and that real good ol' country sound where he had this little black suit on and this short hair. Those are my first real memories. But I somehow can feel myself standing at the back of that hall, which means I may have gone later because I lived in Fort Worth until 1984. So it could have been any time frame.

DEL CASTILLO: He wrote that song in 1964. That's what I was telling you earlier. It's kind of full circle because that was the year I was born.

HUDSON: And the year I was listening to Willie Nelson. Well, I went to TCU and wanted to barrel race. I had my first horse. I heard Peter, Paul, and Mary, Willie Nelson . . .

DEL CASTILLO: Dylan.

HUDSON: Dylan, of course, and Judy Collins singing "Suzanne," which introduced me to Leonard. I am listening to all those people today. But I wanted to give you a little more context about where I'm coming from with my love and appreciation for the music. I also have a place in San Miguel de Allende, Mexico.

DEL CASTILLO: Oh, I've never been but everybody tells me it's fantastic.

HUDSON: So, everything's connected, right?

DEL CASTILLO: Absolutely.

HUDSON: So we're weaving this together. I think we're going to find, or at least I'm going to find, even more connections as we talk. For example, Florin Sanchez told me to tell you hello. I was with him at the Kerrville Folk Festival. We were listening to David Amram and Judy Collins.

I said, "Well, Wednesday I'm going to go drive and talk to Rick." "Oh, tell him I said hello."

DEL CASTILLO: That is awesome.

HUDSON: So tell me about knowing him, because he's our first recipient of a scholarship for my music foundation.

DEL CASTILLO: I was in a rock band in the eighties called Bad Habit—very unique name. But we later changed our name to Akasha. From the Akashic records. I'm from Brownsville. In 1985, in tenth grade, I started playing professionally. I used to play out on the island, right when the whole spring break thing started happening in 1980, 1981. We were the house band at a pool hall called Sammy's. It was packed every weekend because back then kids could drink without getting in trouble.

HUDSON: And you were a wild rock band.

DEL CASTILLO: We were a rock-and-roll band just having fun. I remember in 1980, our band—we were called Rage back then. This is my high school band. We took a break, and down the street was this amazing Austin guitarist named Eric Johnson that I wanted to go see, and they wouldn't let us in to go see him. But I could hear him playing outside because he was playing really loud. Just to get a little backstory on Rage, in 1981 we opened for Van Wilks at a summer concert on South Padre Island called Tent City. That's the first time I met Van Wilks.

So anyway, back to Florin. Rage, my high school band, broke up, and I formed a band with others—some of the original members of Rage and other local Brownsville musicians. We were called Bad Habit. Our first touring show was in Kerrville at a pub at the mall. I'd never toured outside of Brownsville. The first person I met, I was like, "Who's that guy who looks like Ian Gillan?"—the lead singer from Deep Purple. He has this really long hair, really cool-looking guy. It turns out to be Florin. So, after we played, we ended up at the Purple Sage. We went back to the hotel, and we just jammed and jammed. I thought, God, this is the first guitar player that I met outside of Brownsville. The rest of the world is like this guy. I got a lot of competition because he's great. He had this very amazing unique style. So that's where I met Florin. And then just here and there we kept in touch, and it's just really amazing that's one of the first things you asked me or told me—that Florin said hello.

HUDSON: Well, I moved to Kerrville in 1984. I was working for Rod Kennedy and his music foundation. And I loved rock; I loved rhythm. I was so excited that there was a place to go hear that—the pub in the mall. I started my music foundation in '87. We did not have a scholarship firm for quite a few years. And then we started doing some things. The biggest thing we did was '96. Merle Haggard helped us in an afternoon show. He'd already played the night before. And then the next year, as fate would have it, I had Willie Nelson in town. He did our tribute to Jimmie Rodgers, and Little Joe y la Familia opened for him. That scholarship money—we've been giving it away ever since.

DEL CASTILLO: Wow. So you said Florin was the first recipient. Talking about full circle.

HUDSON: We sat and talked about his life. We produced the only tribute to Jimmie Rodgers in the state. His uncle Percy Bowles played with Jimmie Rodgers. Jimmie Rodgers lived in Kerrville for two years, from 1929 to 1931. And then he moved away; he died in 1933.

DEL CASTILLO: That is another full circle, yeah.

HUDSON: But back to your story, I did want to be sure that we talked about family, culture, language, and words—kind of what we call things. I've read some really interesting descriptions of your music, very interesting. Driving here I listened to *"Corazón Loco."*

DEL CASTILLO: *"Corazón Loco"*—yeah, it's a cool song.

HUDSON: I'm hearing *"Gritos."* I'm hearing *"Pancho Villa!"* at the end of it. And I'm wondering if I'm sitting in the middle of a big Mexican crowd. I mean that doesn't fall under Latin rock. That is definitely a beautiful flavor.

DEL CASTILLO: What's interesting is the whole band is from Brownsville, Texas, but we have Spanish ancestry. Talking about words and stuff—my parents both were educators. My dad was a principal for thirty-three years. My mom taught in the Brownsville School District for forty-two years. So talk about being corrected with my grammar and speech daily—we grew up with that.

It's interesting that we all grew up rock-and-roll guys: AC/DC, Deep Purple, Black Sabbath, but as I grew older, I started listening to classical music. It's amazing what was available down there—this is pre-internet, how word of mouth reached down there, like Jimi Hendrix. My uncle used to play with Jimi Hendrix in the sixties out in California. That's another chapter. Maybe you can interview him. He's a character. He had a band called Aum, A-U-M. He played with all the greats. Anyway, that's another story.

HUDSON: What's his name?

DEL CASTILLO: He went by Wayne the Heart back then. Just take a real quick look at my scrapbook, and it says, "Tonight, Aum, with special guest Carlos Santana, Elvin Bishop, Grateful Dead, and Jefferson Airplane." They all opened for him. But the sad irony of life—they all went on to be amazing and he didn't.

The reason I mention him is because he was an influence on me. He would come in from California with his wild hair and the Fu Manchu thing. We'd go like, "Wow! He's cool. He's pretty crazy." But going into how Del Castillo started, it's funny. I toured as a rock musician throughout the eighties. I always had a classical guitar with me. My dad, on weekends, every now and again—he's visiting right now and he's here at the house—he would play these Mexican songs from Javier Solís and Vicente Fernández. On Saturday nights, he would just blast the stereo and sing along with it. It turns out he also played the piano, but he never was a professional musician, where my uncle, his half-brother, went on to much greater heights and stuff.

So music was always in our family from day one. However, it was very frowned upon to pursue a musical career with my parents. All my siblings went to school—one's a doctor and my brother is a dentist. So they wanted me to *not* do music, but I just had to do it. So after high school, that's when I just left and came back. What's interesting is my younger brother Mark, who's the other guitarist in Del Castillo; he's eight years younger than me. So if you imagine growing up, when I'm fifteen playing in bars, he's eight or seven. So we had no connection, really. By the time I left on the road, I was twenty; he was twelve. It wasn't until I moved—after touring for years, I lived in Memphis for a while, which is a great blues education. And then I moved to Seattle, ironically at the height of the grunge era, to go play blues and rock.

HUDSON: Was there a Latin flavor with what you were doing then in Seattle?

DEL CASTILLO: No. I was doing more blues stuff. And see, what's interesting is the whole sound of Del Castillo was always like a side note of sorts. My brother, unbeknownst to me, was writing that kind of music. He met up—talk about another full-circle story—he met up with the singer Alex Ruiz for Del Castillo. He met him at a party. Alex was at this party. He was interested in this girl from Brownsville who invited my brother. My brother and this girl were really good friends. Well, Alex, eventually they got married. So they said, "Hey, do you play?" "Yeah, I play." And he said, "Well, let's do '*Cancion del Mariachi*,'" the song from *Desperado*. Do you know that song I'm talking about?

HUDSON: Yeah.

DEL CASTILLO: "Ay-ay-ay-ay!" the song that Los Lobos did?

HUDSON: Yes.

DEL CASTILLO: That was the first song that my brother and Alex jammed together on a whim. So while all that's happening, I'm writing—

HUDSON: In Brownsville?

DEL CASTILLO: No. Actually, now everybody's up in Austin at this time. That's the other thing—my brother never met Alex in Brownsville. I never met Alex in Brownsville. Albert, the bass player from Del Castillo, is a fantastic guitar player. He and I used to play in high school in tenth grade in the band I was telling you about, Rage, back then. Albert was my roommate. I hope I'm not talking too fast.

HUDSON: No.

DEL CASTILLO: Is the coffee kicking in? So Albert and I knew each other from way back. But once again, Albert and I are the same age, but Alex and Mark are eight years younger. Mark had a rock band called Milhouse, and I recorded and produced their albums. So that's how I met Mike. And Mike is a very, very unique drummer. He's like those monkeys that can play—like all four of his limbs are doing different things. So while Mark is doing this whole thing with Milhouse, he did one song like a Del Castillo style, and it turns out that that was a lot of people's favorite song.

Meanwhile, I'm a recording artist and producing people's projects. I started writing with a couple of people with similar styles of songs. So my brother and I—the whole reason Del Castillo got together was my brother and me. A, we never played together; B, we thought, "Hey, why don't we record something? Yeah, I heard some of that stuff you did." "Yeah, I heard some of the stuff you did too. It's pretty cool." "Yeah. Why don't we put something together for a Christmas present for Mom and Dad and maybe cousins and stuff?" So we're like, "OK. Hey, that's a great idea. That way it's one project, but you can give it as multiple presents, right? Hey, good gift, gift of music."

So we started writing things and recording things. And then Alex started coming over with Mark, and they would play me stuff. I said, "You wrote that?" They're like, "Yeah, we wrote that." I was like, "That's really good." So we just started recording because I have a recording studio. I've been recording—that's what I do. Other than playing live, I record and produce music. So we recorded this batch of songs. One of my . . . oh, I forgot to mention that all this time, I'm giving guitar lessons. So one of my students, during the course of this time, his name is Paul Hurdlow—because, Paul, you need props. He was the head attorney at this firm. I would play him stuff over and over throughout the course of three or four months. He said, "I'm sick of hearing this music. It's not going anywhere." No, he didn't say, "I'm sick of hearing this music in here." He said, "This music needs to get out. It's not going to go anywhere if you just keep playing it for me. I'm hiring you guys to play at my company party." I was like, "OK."

So, literally, my brother and I got all the guys that we did the songs with together: "Hey, we've got to learn these songs. We have this gig we've got to play at. OK, why don't we make some CDs? Since we're going to be there, maybe they'll buy a CD or two." We ended up selling a whole bunch of CDs. I went up to Paul and I said, "Did you tell your attorneys to buy the music?" He's like, "No, I didn't." So we thought, "Well, we did all this rehearsing. Why don't we just do one more show?" So we played at Fat Tuesdays, and Danny Crooks was running that bar with a guy named Frank. I forget Frank's last name. But they were running Fat Tuesdays on Sixth Street. I had never seen Danny Crooks that excited ever. He came running up to us afterward and said, "Oh my God! You guys got us." He said, "You guys got to start playing here and do a residency here. I'm also opening up the Steamboat off of Congress on Riverside."

That's how Del Castillo started. It was a reluctant kind of "OK, sure."

The irony of life is, prior to that, I toured throughout the country, trying to do showcases in Memphis and this and that, went to LA, played the Whisky a Go Go, always trying to showcase, and nothing ever happened. And then when you just kind of say, "Let's do something for our friends and family"—fifteen years later, here we are.

HUDSON: Well, I know a lot of writers have talked about you all—the energy of two brothers onstage. I know in one of the videos I watched, your hands were moving at exactly the same time and in the rhythms. I mean it was two in one.

DEL CASTILLO: Yeah, that's pretty cool.

HUDSON: Yeah, it was very cool as far as watching it and, of course, hearing it. So you and the guitar, I mean, did that come out of classical background?

DEL CASTILLO: No, I cannot. . . . I'm a complete rocker. I'm self-taught for starters, my brother and I. He took a couple of lessons. I'm self-taught. I taught myself theory while traveling all through the ages.

HUDSON: Do the leads go to one of you specifically?

DEL CASTILLO: Well, we try it off where we harmonize. We both can play equally the same parts. What's really cool is we can harmonize and play some really cool things. I taught myself theory traveling because I wanted to learn to get out of just one box—you end up starting to play one way, and so I wanted to learn how to play in different ways. My brother taught himself for the most part as well. He took some lessons. He went to the University of Texas at Brownsville.

Anyway, so yeah, we're both pretty much self-taught. It's interesting to go back to the DVD that you're talking about. A friend of ours—a local, incredible musician/producer named Carl Thiel—met Robert Rodriguez, and Robert said, "Hey, do you know any bands? I'm kind of moving on from Los Lobos. I want to work with somebody here in Austin." He said, "Yeah, you got to go check out Del Castillo." We were together for six months just doing these residencies. By then we had moved to Momo's down on West Sixth Street. So Robert came out and saw the band. So we had the buzz of "Who's this band that Robert Rodriguez wants to see? You?" Next thing, he wanted to film us. So that DVD was filmed by Robert.

Funny side note about the DVD is we sent it to a fan, somebody bought it, and they sent it back, complaining, "The DVD, it's skipping." We're playing so fast they thought that the DVD was skipping. We looked at the video, watched it, and said, "There's nothing wrong with it." They said, "Well, it was messed up when I saw it."

HUDSON: What was the name of it?

DEL CASTILLO: It's just *Del Castillo Live.*

HUDSON: I believe I was there when you all sort of swept the Austin Music Awards. I think I was there interviewing other people and just hearing, "Del Castillo! Del Castillo!"

DEL CASTILLO: Like who is this band? It was us, and Kevin Fowler won a lot of awards that year as well.

HUDSON: Oh, man! Was it? The website says 2003.

DEL CASTILLO: Yes, it was 2003.

HUDSON: So that's when my consciousness got your name flying around. But I will have to admit—it's been just since we decided to talk and since I talked to Patricia Vonne that I paid attention to the music.

DEL CASTILLO: There are some wonderful songs.

HUDSON: Well, it satisfies all of the things I'm interested in. So I'm interested in songs, and I'm interested in rhythm—love rhythm. I've got three sets of castanets with me. I have a collection of various drums at home. I love rhythm, and I love when your body just has to move with the music. Those have been my responses to your music in the last couple of days. I'm just blown away by how much I love it. One thing I would be curious about is where are you going in the future? I did read a review that said that as a group, you all had disbanded for the time, and Alex was going out to do some other things and so were you.

DEL CASTILLO: Well, I've done quite a few things—we all have. We all continue to work with Robert Rodriguez. He has his own band called Chingon, which is a movie band. Basically, Chingon really is Del Castillo with Robert. That's what Chingon is—except for most of the stuff. I might record the drums here like on a computer recording of the drums, as opposed to getting Mike Zeoli to play drums. But when we play live, it's Del Castillo. It's Alex singing, my brother and I, and Jimmy Hartman is now playing bass with us, because Albert. . . . See, like I mentioned earlier, Albert was like a caged lion. He's a phenomenal guitar player. He's the guitarist on Joe King's album—the album that Joe gave you. Great guitar player.

HUDSON: What's his last name?

DEL CASTILLO: Besteiro. Albert Besteiro. Alex was wanting to do a lot more different style stuff, so that's kind of what led him to go on doing his thing. Albert was wanting to play a lot more guitar, so he started to play a lot down in Brownsville and then missing rehearsals and stuff because he was doing his thing. We ended up getting a different bass player. Jimmy Hartman and Danny Ortiz, another Brownsville native with an incredible voice. He was the one who came in and did a phenomenal job taking over Alex's slot.

More so than anything, is just after just grueling and grinding and doing it for so many years, we needed a break from each other, from the music, from everything. In 2015 . . . let me backtrack. In 2005, I don't know if you see those . . . you can't see them, but right there, that's sheet music from a conductor—sheet music. I did a score, the music for a short film called *Killing Snakes*. The producer of the movie wanted to record it at Abbey Road. So I was able to go to Abbey Road Studios to record with an orchestra. I also orchestrated it as well. While I was on tour with Del Castillo playing Latin flamenco rock stuff, I'd come home to the hotel and write classical stuff. It's really a hybrid. It's not truly classical. It's classical with flamenco guitar. I just call it beautiful music. That's what Del Castillo has always been. It's a hybrid of so many different. . . . As we said one time, it's a sonic landscape, an endless well of sonic landscapes.

HUDSON: Absolutely.

DEL CASTILLO: That's what's so cool about **DEL CASTILLO**. We're all from Brownsville, but Alex sings like he's straight out of Spain. He has such a beautiful, passionate voice. And then, of course, Albert is the one doing the *gritos*, like the Pancho Villa thing. That's Albert—what a character. And then my brother and I were self-taught doing our versions of flamenco rhythms, because flamenco guitar is played with your fingers. There's no pick, but we play more like Al Di Meola style, like a hybrid style.

HUDSON: Some people mentioned Gypsy Kings, Santana, and then some rock groups kept being mentioned. People write about the hybrid nature that you all were doing.

DEL CASTILLO: *Rolling Stone* said it's like Eddie Van Halen fronting an early Santana. It's like Eddie Van Halen. We don't sound anything like Van Halen.

HUDSON: I guess that was pointing to guitar work—to good guitar work.

DEL CASTILLO: That's the interesting thing and also the thing that can hurt your band as if. . . . Well, you have such a unique sound that really is unclassifiable. You can say we're world music. But to say we're flamenco, we're not true flamenco. We're definitely not Latin rock, because when you think of Latin rock, you think of Maná.

HUDSON: What about this term *nueva Americana*?

DEL CASTILLO: Nueva Americana—that's just something that we're trying.

HUDSON: Somebody made that up. It's a good one.

DEL CASTILLO: I think our manager came up with that because we're just trying to have a name for the music. It's like Robert Rodriguez says— it's like Latin music for the people that don't like Latin. I forgot how he worded it, but he said it so perfectly. It's like—it's not Latin rock, but it's not flamenco, and it's not traditional. It's just cool music—very, very passionate, spiritual music.

HUDSON: Right. Part of your definition applies to a lot of Texas music and this hybrid aspect. A lot of the people I've interviewed for various projects end up talking about how there's no box.

DEL CASTILLO: Too rock for country. Too country for rock.

HUDSON: Whatever all that is. There's a lot of discussion about Texas music as a genre. Of course, South by Southwest has brought that up, and just what is that? I have interviews with Flaco and Santiago Jiménez Jr., Linda Escobar from Corpus, Rosie Flores and Patricia Vonne, and Max Baca and Josh Baca. Wow, those men on that accordion, right? The more voices I get. . . . At first, people thought [this book] was just going to be all conjunto players, and I said absolutely not. I want the textures and voices of a culture that has roots with Mexico, Spain—Latin roots. So I started off with the label "Hispanic heritage," which doesn't work at all because I'm not interviewing any Puerto Rican artists. I'm not interviewing any Cuban artists.

DEL CASTILLO: Good luck with a title. [Laughter]

HUDSON: Mexican American, no hyphen.

DEL CASTILLO: I'll keep thinking for you as well. But it's interesting that I'm doing a lot of work with this gentleman from Milan, and they are so enamored. He manages three or four bands. I've mastered some of his bands' music. I've performed with them. Alex has performed with them. Patricia Vonne has performed with them. He got David Hidalgo from Los Lobos to perform on one of the tracks. They are so enamored with Texas and Mexico. It's amazing.

It's one of those things where the grass is always greener on the other side. . . . I totally love Europe. I love the UK. All Europeans love Texas. There is something to be said about Texas, and also the weight of saying you're from Austin. When you go tour Europe and you say you're from Austin, it's like, "Well, these guys must be pretty good. They're from Austin." So it carries a really cool weight—some kind of cachet of sorts. Yeah, it's interesting with this gentleman I'm working with. They're very interested in Texas. He's all about Robert Rodriguez and all his movies. That's one of the reasons he sought us out, because he's a huge fan of Del Castillo and knows what Del Castillo is doing with Robert Rodriguez, with the Chingon music and stuff.

HUDSON: Who came up with that name?

DEL CASTILLO: Chingon? Robert.

HUDSON: That's very good. When I walked into the studio, I was greeted with colors and textures—a lot of things that remind me of other cultures, and sort of a spiritual kind of grounding that you may be interested in talking about.

DEL CASTILLO: That's awesome to hear. Well, I am a seeker. I'm very much into spirituality. I've followed the teachings of Sathya Sai Baba. I grew up Christian. My parents are devout Christians—Catholics— but I always felt like there was so much more that was not being said. So I started studying the Eastern teachings—the Hindu teachings and the philosophies. Basically, in Buddha's teachings, Buddhism, those were . . . without getting too deep into it because once you start talking religions and stuff, it gets very sensitive. But Jesus's teachings were basically Buddha's teachings that were put in his words, and his followers created Christianity, which I think is a beautiful religion.

HUDSON: Do you know there's a book on the lost years of Jesus?

DEL CASTILLO: See, I told a friend of mine to get the book, and he bought it from Amazon, but it was a different book than the one that I got in India. I've gone to India twice on spiritual quests. I was fortunate to go see Sathya Sai Baba prior to his passing. Both times I was there in December, on Christmas Day. To hear Sai Baba speak of Jesus. . . . I grew up going to church my whole life, and nobody spoke about Jesus the way he did. It's like he knew Jesus. You know what I mean?

HUDSON: Yeah, I do.

DEL CASTILLO: It's like I had goose bumps. I couldn't believe the intensity that he spoke with and the beauty of how he spoke of Jesus. With what's going on right now, you turn on the TV, and there's all the stuff about Muslims and everything. Once again, there's a blanket statement that all Muslims are bad. I was talking with my dad, and I said, "Who's the last guy who blanket stated that a whole religion was bad? His name was Adolf Hitler." So we've got to be really careful about blanketing all people. There's two people in this world, good and bad—period. That's it. There's a shift, a major shift, going on right now, and it's happening right before our eyes. I was talking with my wife about that. There's definitely a shift going on and not a good one. It's negativity. It's just breeding hate, breeding negativity. That's what Hitler did for seven years. He just kept bombarding the media. They controlled the media, saying, "Jews are bad. Jews are bad." When you keep hearing something long enough, you're going to start believing it. That's what the climate of the news media is starting to say: "Muslims are bad. Muslims are bad. All Muslims are bad." Yes, I agree that if you want to come to this country, you need to do it legally. I agree with that. But as far as blanket stating that all the Muslims are bad—it's getting pretty hairy out there.

HUDSON: Well, in my mythology class, we look at the archetypes, and one of them is the Trickster. The Trickster is a very important archetype because sometimes it's very necessary to upset the status quo.

DEL CASTILLO: Absolutely. For the people that really run the show, chaos creates war, and war creates money. War is a great way to make money.

HUDSON: And destruction sometimes often is a part of creation. So another—maybe I'm being too optimistic—but another way to look at the chaos right now is that it's leading to the opening up of something else to be created and grow in a good way.

DEL CASTILLO: Yeah, but there will be a bad point in order to get to that good point. Have you heard of the Georgia Guidestones?

HUDSON: No.

DEL CASTILLO: Look that up. Some billionaire came and bought this land outside of Atlanta and basically set up a monument with a set of ten guidelines inscribed on the structure in eight modern languages. It's basically the new Ten Commandments. One of them is that we must live in harmony with nature, so there should only be 500 million people living on this planet, not 6.5 billion. Look up the Georgia Guidestones. It's really intense.

HUDSON: I want to keep being open as I lead groups of students in the classroom. I don't have any particular agenda to shove down their throat. The longer I teach, the more I realize that not only am I some sort of Trickster in the classroom, but I get to stir the pot, because I teach literature and writing, and two classes are going to be writing about Texas music and using songs that I love. "Corazón Loco"—I don't know. I'm going to have to fill the room with that one.

DEL CASTILLO: Awesome. There's another song off our fourth album called "Castles." That's just a beautiful song. On your drive back, call that one up.

HUDSON: OK. Yeah, I was going to ask you if you had some songs in terms of my classroom and teaching that I might want to give to the students, just to let them respond.

DEL CASTILLO: "Castles" is in English and contains some of Alex's greatest lyrics. It's a very spiritual song. He went with me the second time to India in 2005 to go see Sai Baba. George Harrison mentions Sai Baba in "My Sweet Lord." "Guru Sathya," and then he's doing the chants at the end: "Guru Krishna, *hare rama.*"

HUDSON: I know of him. My yoga teacher plays a lot of chants and mantras and so forth during yoga class.

DEL CASTILLO: Awesome.

HUDSON: I don't know. Here I am hearing about India again. Last year I had my very first experience going to a country I've never gone to by myself.

DEL CASTILLO: Which was?

HUDSON: Spain. I've been all over Europe. I've traveled eight countries in three weeks with students and guides. My mother died in May, and I was a bit rattled about that. She was ninety-one, and it was time. But I didn't realize that she was my anchor. I didn't realize my relationship with her worked like that with me. So all of a sudden, I just was really cast adrift and realizing, because I mean the last year of her life she was bedridden. I'd go up and get in bed with her. She would reach over because I couldn't touch her. She was in a lot of pain, so she'd reach over and put her hand on mine. She'd ask me if I was a little girl again. Her mind was fine till the end. So I got to have that, and then it was gone.

So I decided to go to Spain because of two Bob Dylan concerts there. I ended up in Granada at the foot of the Alhambra, with an Airbnb room in an old house for twenty dollars a night. The gypsies played and sang and danced. You may know this guy. There was this phenomenal dancer, Christo. I stumbled upon him with one of the leading flamenco dancers visiting Granada; he was hosting a class. I'm sitting there wandering in this building, and there's this primo teacher with this beautiful young man. So I wanted to get him some extra money. I watched him dance in the streets. Night after night he taught. He was from Brownsville.

Anyway, I can't take my eyes off your necklace. Tell me about that symbol.

DEL CASTILLO: I was in northern India in Delhi. A friend of mine, Scott Roddan, who just came in recently to record his album—he's now living in Spokane—he and I flew to India. When we got to India, to Delhi, he went up north to Tibet or to the north toward Tibet to see the Dalai Lama, and I would south to go see Sathya Sai Baba. Prior to us leaving, we both stayed in this hotel run by Tibetan monks. It was awesome. Five or six o'clock in the morning, you just hear "O-om." They're just like chanting. In one of the little gift shops—I knew exactly what Omar wanted to get. I had it visualized, and I found it in a little shop there. I've had this with me for—I've worn this every day since 2000.

Being that you said you're an educator, my great-uncle—maybe you know him? Américo Paredes. Have you heard of that name?

HUDSON: Yes, of course. And Tish Hinojosa—

DEL CASTILLO: Oh yeah, she was one of his students. He's interesting. I didn't know much about him growing up. What's funny is when I was in tenth grade in English class, my English teacher said, "OK, today we're going to talk about Américo Paredes." I said, "Hey, that's my uncle." My teacher said, "Yeah, right." I was like, "No, really, he's my uncle. He's my great-uncle."

HUDSON: Wow. So if you were putting together a collection of influences, was he an influence? Did you read or did you know him?

DEL CASTILLO: Well, the interesting thing is I just knew of him. My dad—being an educator—would always rave about "Oh, it's my uncle. It's my dad's mother's brother."

HUDSON: What did your dad teach?

DEL CASTILLO: He worked as a principal for more years than as a teacher. As far as I remember him, he was always the principal, the organizer. That's where I get that from. So he would always talk about "Oh, Américo, Américo Paredes, he's your great-uncle. He wrote *With a Pistol in His Hand*. He started all these programs at the University of Texas, and he did all this research for finding lost *corridos* and stuff." I was like, "Oh, cool." Well, when I moved from Seattle to Austin, I had not met his son Alan Paredes, and my dad said, "You need to call Alan and Vince, his two sons." I called Vince, and ironically, Vince is the musician in the family. It just didn't click. I mean he's a wonderful guy, but I just like . . . I don't know. Something just didn't really click in our initial conversations. We've since become much closer. So I called Alan, and he just said, "Oh yeah, come on down." It's like, "Oh, OK, I'm going to talk to him."

So I fly down to Austin, and I go to his house and I meet his dad. That's the first time I really got to sit and talk to his dad. . . . He was a researcher, and he told me more about the del Castillo side of my family than any del Castillo told me about. He was a Paredes, my grandmother's side. I learned a whole lot.

HUDSON: What did you learn about the del Castillo side of your family? You said that was Spain?

DEL CASTILLO: Yes. Well, actually, we were Jews from Spain, and during the Spanish Inquisition, we fled to France and stayed there for about twenty years and then came to America. What's interesting is my dad, being a devout Catholic, denies it. The first time I think he denied it. I said, "Well, Dad, that's what Uncle Américo said in his . . ." "Oh, no, he's a kidder." And I said, "Oh, now he's a kidder." It's interesting to hear the story and just get a whole different view. Also my aunt, prior to passing, told me that when Cortés came to Spain—if you it look up, you can find him—his name was Bernal Diaz del Castillo.

HUDSON: So from France to South Texas—not through Mexico.

DEL CASTILLO: Paredes and the del Castillos came from Spain. Bernal Diaz del Castillo came with Cortés from Spain to Mexico and documented everything. Another interesting story is when Alex left the band, we got an email from this gentleman. He lives in Las Vegas, and he was in a Journey tribute band. His name is Juan del Castillo. He says, "I want to audition for your band." We went, "Oh my God! Are you kidding? Your name is Juan del Castillo?" We had to be related. We started swapping stories and stuff. So small world.

HUDSON: That's great. Was Spanish your first tongue or a second language?

DEL CASTILLO: Unfortunately, with the climate—born in 1964, growing up in the late 1960s, early 1970s—and with my parents being educators, Spanish spoken in Brownsville in the 1970s was frowned upon. You were considered ignorant or less educated. So to my parents, it was a stigma, speaking in Spanish. I talk to Alex about this because he was raised by his grandmother, and she spoke Spanish to him. We were just talking about this yesterday. He used to get in trouble at school because he was speaking Spanish. Of course, the climate of America is completely different now, but back then we were not supposed to speak Spanish.

So, unfortunately, my Spanish was terrible. It was horrible because my parents would speak to each other in fluent Spanish. My aunts, uncles, everybody from my parents age upward spoke perfect Spanish. All the kids. It's like my sisters, my siblings learned to speak better, especially the ones that stayed in Brownsville, working in that environment. But I lived in Memphis and worked in a music shop; then this one Mexican family came in to buy some guitars. They never point at me, "Hey, go take care of them." I'm like, "*Hola.*" I was embarrassed. I was like, "Oh my God. This is terrible." My Spanish has improved tremendously, but starting from negative 80 percent. Maybe we're like at 20 percent now.

HUDSON: Well, the other thing I listened to coming in was the CD *20 Corridos.* I thought, "Why do I have this? Where did it come from?" It comes from Mexico, and I bought it at some flea market there.

DEL CASTILLO: Interesting.

HUDSON: Listening to those and the rhythm, quite often a waltz rhythm—that's telling that story, and I had no idea. It sort of fell out of the thousands of things I have. And I thought, "Well, I'm not going to end up talking to him about *corridos.* Why is this in my car?" And then, of course, you mentioned Américo.

DEL CASTILLO: Américo, yes. The interesting thing is the *corridos* and the Hispanic music was completely influenced by Czechoslovakian and German. The accordion comes from Europe. They brought it over here when the Germans had settled Schertz, Niederwald.

HUDSON: Santiago Jr. is committed to keeping his father's sound pure, whereas Flaco is Mr. Rock and Roll, and I was in Montreux, Switzerland, and Bob Dylan asked Flaco to get up on the stage and play with him, which is why I think I should be talking to Bob.

Let's talk about one of your songs.

DEL CASTILLO: Our first album was the truest collaboration between my brother and I as far as we wrote together, but he and I are very self-contained of sorts. So, generally, the entire Del Castillo catalog, for the most part, is made up of songs either my brother wrote with Alex or I wrote with Alex—one or the other. This is with the exception of the first album.

My brother and I wrote some instrumentals and some songs together. So the writing process would be, it's always—I being a producer, my brother also does a lot of production as well—we come to the band with a full song and say, "Hey, guys, here's a song." It's already pretty much arranged with maybe the exception of a little here and there that the drummer, Mike, or Albert would change

HUDSON: Collaborative, yeah.

DEL CASTILLO: Collaborative. But for the most part . . . we let Alex write all the lyrics for starters. He's the best one. He speaks the best Spanish out of us all. But also his lyrics are very—I love his lyrics. They're so cerebral and they're very eloquent.

HUDSON: Did he write "*Corazón Loco*"?

DEL CASTILLO: Yes. He and Mark wrote that song. So he has a very unique, very poetic lyrics. The sad thing is like in Mexico, they said, "Well, that's not proper Spanish." It's just like trying to correct Muddy Waters, saying, "You're not speaking proper English." You see what I'm saying? That's what Del Castillo's music is—breaking a lot of rules.

HUDSON: OK. Well, that will probably be a perfect conclusion to this conversation—that we are about breaking a lot of rules. All right, thank you.

RICK DEL CASTILLO toured with several bands before he founded the band Del Castillo with his brother. He has provided music for famed film director Robert Rodriguez.

Ernie Durawa

Tuesday, December 29, 2015, we talked at his regular gig at Strangebrew in Austin (now closed). He showcased many wonderful artists and friends each night for three or four years. They named the stage after him too. He was honored.

In 2017 Ernie started the same showcase at El Mercado on Tuesday night in Austin. Even as this man showcases other performers, he is an integral part of the history of Texas music. His stint with the Texas Tornados (both with Doug Sahm and his son Sean), as well as his time playing jazz, have put him at the center of the music scene. Ernie is as humble as he is talented and a joy to know.

HUDSON: The article about you on your website is fantastic! I loved the comment that if you cut Ernie open, you would find every kind of music. That speaks to the eclectic nature of Texas music. What terms do you use when you talk about your music?

DURAWA: Randy Garibay Sr. wrote, "I don't do Tejano music." He was a great blues singer. I am playing with the Texas Tornados now, and we really don't do Tejano. It is more Tex Mex conjunto with Flaco on accordion. Tejano seems to be synthesizers with electric drums and Mexican cowboys. I personally am not too crazy about the music!

HUDSON: Maybe Tex Mex is more accurate. Let's talk about your family roots.

DURAWA: I have these photos of my mom, dad, and stepdad. They are all riding burros. I am not sure when or where. But it does look like Mexico. I was Saldana, but my stepdad was Durawa. When I was a little kid, about eight, my mama had a bar on the west side of San Antonio. We lived in the back, and I couldn't help but hear those bands all the time.

HUDSON: So you had the music in you.

DURAWA: Down to my roots.

HUDSON: Are you fluent in Spanish?

DURAWA: Yes. I don't speak as fast as they do in Mexico, but I speak Tex Mex. We mix it up some. San Antonio is my hometown, but I have been in Austin for forty years. I just found some new cousins there I didn't even know existed. They gave me the cool photos of Mom riding a burro.

HUDSON: We are looking at Los Jazz Vatos, your latest project. And this project of showcasing music each month. Hello to Paul Oscher, your guest tonight. You get to play with so many different people each week. What fun.

DURAWA: Tonight we have no rehearsal, so we will wing it. It's a cool band tonight—sax player too.

HUDSON: Your choice of people? Do you ever invite a complete stranger?

DURAWA: I do, but before I do, I listen to their music on YouTube. I want to like their music, and many do ask to come in here. I try to find guests that have some sort of following too. I ask them to work at plugging the gig and get an audience. I have been building a following here.

HUDSON: So many songs and albums to count on your website. Unbelievable history.

DURAWA: I have more to add, so I called my webmaster this week. The first Los Jazz Vatos album was done two years ago. We only have two albums; *El Jefe* is the second one. Kerry Awn did the artwork (on the back of the album). I have one Tornados tune here—"Laredo Rose," by Rich Minus. With the horns, it is fun. I also have the original art here.

HUDSON: I was in the Fire Station Studio in San Marcos, and I interviewed Freddy Fender during that Texas Tornado project. I wrote a story for the *San Antonio Express-News*. Somehow I missed talking with you.

DURAWA: I am an original Tornado. I have been in the band thirty years, but it doesn't feel the same without Doug and Freddy. Of course.

HUDSON: I loved the rocking version I heard in Kerrville.

DURAWA: Yes. It was a shock to lose Freddy. He was only fifty-eight. I have no idea how much longer we will keep doing this. I was also teaching a lot, but it seems to have dried up now.

HUDSON: Your history is so rich and layered. You could represent what Texas music looks like!

DURAWA: I am getting a plaque from Texas State University for my contributions to Texas music. That feels good.

HUDSON: Are there stories you have that no one has heard? A challenge or moment of joy people don't know.

DURAWA: I spent those years with Delbert McClinton. I spent four years touring with him, 1977 to 1981. *Saturday Night Live, Austin City Limits, Solid Gold,* and more. And I had Delbert here as my guest a couple of weeks back.

HUDSON: Let's talk about a story that's new in 2015.

DURAWA: I am in love with a beautiful woman. I just turned seventy-three. I have never been a songwriter, and I might think about it some, but I have never really tried it. We just got back from Switzerland, where we played the Lucerne Blues Festival. And Muryali Coryell will be my guest in March. Luis Ortega flew in to play here. I had Los Texmaniacs here last week. I've had lots of people say I should write a book about what I am doing. I can talk about it, but I can't sit here and write it.

HUDSON: Let's talk about the music and songs you really like. I know that's hard with your rich history.

DURAWA: We grew up listening to all kinds of music in San Antonio. We were playing in black blues bands, and at a young age I discovered Buddy Rich, who was playing jazz. Growing up in Texas is being in a melting pot. I spent five years in Chicago. That was my formal training. I never regret those years! But the winters drove me out. My mom was getting old, so I came to Austin and was literally starving here in 1975. Delbert is the guy who saved me. Then I had a steady income.

HUDSON: I love drumming, and I have a collection of drums. And I play castanets at times, a gift from Patricia Vonne. I really love rhythm.

DURAWA: I played in nursing homes on New Year's Eve. It's perfect because it is early. Who wants to be out late with the drunks? I am playing with Corky Robinson, an eighty-six-year-old bandleader. He's a great sax player, and he comes around and likes to dance with the women. He lives in assisted living, but we really like this gig. I don't take New Year's Eve gigs. I did that enough.

HUDSON: Let's talk about a beautiful moment for you.

DURAWA: I am enjoying each moment—there are so many. It was great playing with Delbert a few weeks ago. I have studied rhythm so long, and when I play with people, I do the math. They don't really understand. Most people are playing a straight eight note. If it goes faster, it is rock and roll. Technically it is eight notes. Los Texmaniacs do play some straight eight notes, and some two-four. I laugh with Speedy Sparks, saying that after all this technical training, I ended up old, fat, and stuck in a polka band. The Tornados play some two-four. We play a lot of polkas because Flaco is a polka player on accordion. Los Texmaniacs brought Josh Baca—and man he can play. I thought it was Flaco. I asked him how, and he said he learned it from Flaco. He's amazing for sure at twenty-four. He has charisma that will take him far.

HUDSON: Do you have any tours that stick out?

DURAWA: I just got back from Switzerland, and I really had fun playing Lucerne. Murali Coryell grew up with Jimi and Miles coming to his house. His dad played with those guys. His dad is a famous jazz guitar monster who played with Miles.

HUDSON: It does look like jazz really calls to you.

DURAWA: I had to read music for this album, without losing the feel. It was more challenging to me. Let me give you the CD to listen to. I'd like to hear what you think about it. It will make you move. I love playing cool blues. I am glad I did not pigeonhole myself into one style of music. I get calls from jazz guys, blues guys, and country guys. Austin has everything, including Cuban and South American and punk bands. People from New York visit and say that this is not happening in New York City. I am from San Antonio, but they are a big city with a small mentality. Luna Vibe is a cool club in San Antonio, and I play there with Murali in March.

HUDSON: You played with the Westside Horns, I think?

DURAWA: Yes, and I toured with Johnny Nicholas and Stephen Bruton before he died. We toured all of Italy. It was a cruise ship tour, but we started in Monte Carlo and went to Venice. Johnny set that up. I saw Marcia Ball in Lucerne when I was there. She and Johnny played in Hawaii too.

HUDSON: Seems like you are really a jazz player at heart.

DURAWA: Yeah, but growing up in Texas, you play what the people want to hear. And when you are starting out, you heed the call. I can play country music. I have been very fortunate.

HUDSON: You started off saying you were very blessed. I did interview Kirk Whalum and Arnett Cobb back in the early days of the music foundation. Kirk said that what he loved about jazz is that you could be playing something and leave space for someone to go off [ad lib] and create while you were holding the space. Then it comes back together. I love the idea of listening to the rest of the band in a way that you are holding the space.

DURAWA: Yeah, the drummer and the bass player hold it together. An old saying—the band is only as good as its best drummer. Or what's it like to play with a bad drummer? Like a tennis shoe in a dryer.

HUDSON: What do you consider your challenges?

DURAWA: Right now, at my age, it's to get out of bed and do what I am doing. I am glad I am doing what I am doing. I had a long talk with my girlfriend today. She is younger. We had a nice conversation about that. We were talking about differences in age and race. She is white, and I am Hispanic.

HUDSON: What do you call yourself?

DURAWA: I guess Mexican American. I don't like that word *Hispanic*, really.

HUDSON: Do you have a song in Spanish you love?

DURAWA: *"Sabor a Mí"* is a good one. Flavor of me.

ERNIE (SALDAÑA) DURAWA is a Grammy Award–winning drummer who has toured with Delbert McClinton and Doug Sahm, playing with the Sir Douglas Quintet and the Texas Tornados.

Linda Escobar

A Woman of Family

My friend and videographer Chumbe Salinas insisted I listen to Linda Escobar at the Conjunto Festival in San Antonio. Chumbe and I had been in the process of videoing some of my interviews, as well as the Texas Heritage Day I produce in Kerrville each September. She knew Linda personally, so I trusted her judgment and was not disappointed. Connecting with Linda through Facebook, I have come to know even more now about her commitment to family. Throughout our friendship, she has shared the death of her mother and hospital stays with her kids, all while stating her great faith in the outcome of the circumstances of her life. For Linda, Facebook is a place of sharing love and faith, as well as her journeys in music. She has become an inspiration to me in my own life.

HUDSON: It's Saturday afternoon in October, and we just finished lunch at La Margarita in San Antonio. We're going to talk a little bit about Linda Escobar's life. I'm already amazed and impressed over this whole notion that you've been playing for fifty years. You said you started quite young. I thought it might be fun to just talk a little bit about your whole sense of family because I know that's important to you and in weaving your history. I know that there's a lot of stories about your father.

ESCOBAR: Yes, and I'm going to start by telling you about my music life. It began when I was about three years old and I was asking my mom to hurry up and finish combing my hair because I had a very important lunch date with my father, who was in the hospital. Imagine this little girl and her mom going up the stairs because we didn't have elevators in Alice, Texas, at the hospital. I think it was two or three stories. You see this little girl and her mom going up the stairs, and then you see this man sitting on his bed in the hospital. He knows that his daughter is coming because he can hear her—the clatter of her brace—because this little girl had polio.

He knew I was coming, and as soon as he opened the door, there I was. I would jump on his bed, and I would feed him because he didn't want to eat. My father was very depressed because he had experienced a head-on collision. He was one of two that survived, and I think there were three or four people that passed away in that crash. He was coming back home from work. He broke his leg in nine pieces, and the doctors wanted to cut his legs off, but he begged them to patch him up however they could. I get there, and I'm feeding my daddy. Of course, I get the Jell-O.

From that scene, we go to our little humble home in Alice, and all of a sudden, my mom has to start working. So she gets up at five in the morning to make the refried beans and *papitas fritas*, which are like French fries. You can smell the beans cooking, the tortillas cooking, and I knew that my mom, my sister, and my two older brothers were going to have to go and my dad and I would stay behind. They would leave in the pickup truck, and I would take care of my father while he was bedridden. He would grab his guitar, and he'd start singing and singing. That's when the love of music, the passion that I have for music, was instilled in my heart and in my soul, at a very, very young age.

Shortly after that, because my father couldn't return back to his previous occupation, he started singing for a living, and he started recording with Los Guadalupanos from San Antonio. I was a little girl, amazed at how my father's voice and singing was coming out of the radio every day, every morning, and I was just so proud of him. I wanted to be just like him. I guess I would memorize the songs at this early age. One night, at the age of six years old, I begged my father to let me go onstage because I wanted to sing a song.

He had no clue that I could sing well enough, that I could stay on key, that I could stay on beat and know when to come in and all that. I showed him, and he was just amazed and so were all the people there. It was called La Villita dance hall. People came up to the stage—and that's, right there, when I knew that I was going to love this, and that I was going to get into this, and this is going to be my life.

My daddy said, "Make sure you know what you're doing because you can't get into this career with one foot in, one foot out. You've got to get in with both feet." I said, "I will, Daddy. I will, Daddy. This is what I want." So I started recording, and it was a father-and-daughter team. We were just playing all over, all over the state of Texas—San Antonio, and we played Houston all the time, the Valley, McAllen, just everywhere.

We got signed up by Bernal Records, which is Paulino Bernal's label, who had the best artists. He had the original Los Dinos, he had Los Relámpagos, Ramón Ayala, Cornelio Reyna; he had Carlos Guzman, Los Fabulosos Cuatro, he had Conjunto Bernal, and he had Eligio Escobar, my father, and Linda Escobar as well. He would book these caravan tours, and we were gone for three months, which were the three months that I wasn't in school. It was the summer.

HUDSON: That was OK with your mom?

ESCOBAR: Oh, absolutely, yes, yes. I had my mother's blessing always. She would even make my costumes, my dresses, and all. I started touring at the age of eight. I cowrote a song and recorded *"Frijolitos Pintos,"* which means pinto beans, I guess from the fact that that's what I grew up smelling in the morning at 5:00 a.m.—my mom's refried beans. So I made this little song. My father helped, and it was a smash hit, an overnight hit. It was the song that was sung in all the households, in Hispanic households—mothers to their babies, grandmothers to their grandchildren. It was just the song that this little girl sang on the radio all over, nationwide.

Everybody, all the promoters, all the people, everybody wanted to see this little girl sing live, so I was in high demand, and this was in 1965. That's when the Beatles were on and Elvis—and Escobar, this childhood star who was just selling records like hotcakes. It sold over a million records, that song. So we continued touring with our record company, continued recording, and it just went on like that. It was just a beautiful life for a child, for a teenager, especially from the small town of Alice, Texas. We had nothing at all.

We moved to Corpus Christi, and I graduated from Incarnate Word Academy. As a matter of fact, I started flying from Corpus to Chicago and of course to Los Angeles and Miami, Florida, and all these at a very early age, eight years old, by myself because my father would travel with the band in the van, and he would fly me back and forth. It was just such a wonderful life for a child.

It has been my life to do this, to continue not only to sing, but to promote and preserve conjunto music, which is the roots of our culture. It's an accordion and a *bajo sexto*, bass, and drums, and we sing about real things in life. Some are happy, some are sad; some are drinking songs. It's just what we as Hispanics, the simple people, go through, day in and day out.

HUDSON: Well, I can hear the family woven all through that.

ESCOBAR: Yes.

HUDSON: And I know that the family has a very important role in the culture as well. You invited me to your award dinner tonight, and I said, "I don't want to just walk in on a dinner," and you so graciously said, "Well, they're going to be making more food because that's what we do."

ESCOBAR: Yes, that's what we do—we want to feed everybody. Yes, I hope you can make it. That's how my mother was too. She always made extra in case somebody came over. My grandmother was the same way. Family is just really, really close. I have two older brothers and a sister. We all live in Corpus. I take care of my mom. I have my two daughters and my son, and now I'm a grandma, and nothing makes me happier than being with my grandchildren and with my children, my brothers. We get together often. That's what familial love is all about.

I'm just so, how can I say, blessed that I had my father by my side for thirty-seven years. He passed away in 1994 of esophagus cancer, and that was a very, very hard time for me. I stopped singing for the world, but I sang in two church choirs because I didn't have the happiness that it takes to get onstage and sing conjunto music. I felt sad and lost, and I just wasn't the same without my father.

HUDSON: Thirty-seven years?

ESCOBAR: Yes, yes, so five years later, lo and behold, I meet a Japanese accordion player singing conjunto music. The funny thing is that my father had prophesied that to me when I was a little girl that someday I was going to meet a Japanese person playing conjunto music. Where he got that notion from, I'll never know, but I remembered it the minute or the second that I opened the newspaper and it said, "Japanese Conjunto to Perform at Mario's in Freemont, Texas." I'm like, "I have got to go to hear this man. I remembered what my father told me, and there's a reason why I need to go."

HUDSON: That's beyond magical.

ESCOBAR: Yes! That's why I know that my life has been destined to be what it has been, what it is: for me to get polio, so that God could give me an extra—a good singing voice.

HUDSON: And your dad's legs must have healed to some extent.

ESCOBAR: They did, but he was a little bow legged. He was always in pain. It used to hurt me a lot when his comrades, other musicians, were like, "Hey, Eligio, you just get off a horse?" and stuff like that. They didn't mean anything bad about it because they would ask my dad, "Did you ride a horse?" And yes, he did. He rode a lot when he was in the ranch where he grew up in Ben Bolt, Texas, but it would hurt me because I would say, "You all don't even know that my—" I wouldn't say anything, but I would think it—that my poor daddy broke his legs in nine pieces, and it's a miracle that he's walking right now.

HUDSON: You got through your polio OK?

ESCOBAR: No, even right now I'm in pain. My hip really, really hurts all the time. My leg is very weak—a very weak left leg. People can't tell by looking at me that I have a handicap, and I've always been ashamed to talk about it. For the longest time, I didn't want to talk about it, but now I'm a proud polio survivor. That just goes to show you how hard I've had it, and yet I have survived. Only the strong survive actually in this industry, in the music industry—for a female who has a handicap—and I just know that this is my life, to stick with conjunto music.

I've given more than fifty scholarships to children who possess a God-given talent that promotes conjunto music. There have been accordion players, there have been vocalists, there have been *bajo sexto* players, bass players, drummers, but I want to encourage them, and I want to help them like my father helped me. It makes me feel good.

HUDSON: Well, you're just providing a space for that energy to go right through you to someone else, and that's really beautiful.

ESCOBAR: Thank you. I'm their *madrina*, their godmother, now. I've always told them that they have an open line to me, 24/7—if ever they need advice, they're in trouble, anything—that they can call me. They're all over. I even have one in California. This little boy is just phenomenal. All over Texas, from the Valley, I have plenty of students here in San Antonio who have gotten a scholarship from the Conjunto Heritage Taller, and also in Houston.

HUDSON: Now how did you set this up? Because this was in your father's name, right?

ESCOBAR: Yes, because when my father passed away, he said, "*Mija*, always remember to honor your veterans. It's just so important that whenever you see a veteran, thank him." I said, "Of course, Daddy." He wrote the song, "*El Veterano*," which is a ballad about a Hispanic soldier who got called to serve and bravely went with honor to fight for his country. It's just a beautiful song.

So I started the Veterano Conjunto Festival honoring all veterans, in memory of Eligio Escobar, and my theme song is his song, "*El Veterano*." We've had fifteen festivals already, and the money that I raise, I don't keep it. I give it to the community. I give it to these children.

HUDSON: Is this every November?

ESCOBAR: Every November. It's always the Sunday before Veterans Day.

HUDSON: Wow. So, it sounds to me like how you're feeling about life is that you've really been blessed.

ESCOBAR: Yes, I have.

HUDSON: No matter what circumstances there are.

ESCOBAR: No matter what circumstances.

HUDSON: Because I share that too; I have that. I'm the oldest of five, and my parents were very, very close. I just lost my dad in May, and my mother is ninety; not many people my age get to have their parents, so I really resonate with what you said.

ESCOBAR: Absolutely.

HUDSON: How much it means to feel that, passing it on to the grandchildren, and now I have a great-grandson. So I really feel the passageway of nurturing.

ESCOBAR: Absolutely. I have two little grandsons right now who are very musically inclined, and I believe that they're going to follow our legacy.

HUDSON: That is great. So you've gotten this far, and you had a fiftieth anniversary. People are probably asking you, "OK, what's next? What are the next fifty?" Are there some new plans in the making?

ESCOBAR: Yes, I'm very adamant about putting out a gospel CD of Christian music where I want to write the songs. I want to write my life story in Christian music. I want some of them to be for children and then some for adults. I want to continue promoting conjunto, Tejano, and helping people and organizations—and just promote it, 100 percent.

HUDSON: One of the best ways to do that is to share your story. You just don't know what happens when people hear your story. For example, I interviewed young Terri Hendrix, who covered up her epilepsy for many years, and I was around when she revealed that that was one of her struggles. No one knew. No one knew when she walked out onstage in those lights what she might face. She has started her own foundation called Own Your Own Universe. It's another statement for women and all people to take ownership of your world. It's really inspiring. I can tell you've done that.

ESCOBAR: Yes, I've gotten onstage when I can barely walk, and people wouldn't even know. I just get that strength from God up above, and like I said, by the grace of God, I'm able to do my shows, travel, and just be where I have to be.

HUDSON: I like what you said about being selective. It's not about sitting around and hoping that somebody calls now. You get to look.

ESCOBAR: Yeah, pick and choose. It's just important. I want other conjuntos to follow the same way. Don't just take what you're offered because you work so much more. I see people pay sixty, eighty, one hundred dollars to go see country and western singers. But a singer from Mexico? Why can't they do the same for us, for conjunto singers? It's our bread and butter too. It's not about going and playing in a canteen and getting twenty-five bucks for each member. Look at how many people you made happy and things like that. This is God-given talent—it's just so beautiful, and to have to just give it away like that, people take advantage.

HUDSON: What about your notion of the history of music as you were coming along? Were you aware of other superstars, of people who were trying to cross over?

ESCOBAR: I was the first little girl in the industry ever, especially here in Texas. There might have been Joselito, who was a young little boy from Mexico who sang with mariachi, but really, aside from Shirley Temple, there was Linda Escobar. There was another little child who was performing professionally as a recording artist and coming out in TV shows and things like that. When I got a little older, I started seeing other female singers I got to meet, like Elsa Garcia and Laura Canales.

HUDSON: Did you know Eva Ybarra?

ESCOBAR: I didn't meet her until later on, in my later years. My dad always used to say this: "Competition is good for the pie, and there's enough pie for everybody." He said, "And always give credit where credit is due." I grew up with that in mind. I always give credit where credit is due, and the more, the merrier. I love it that there are so many female singers right now. It's wonderful. It's almost getting to be fifty-fifty, when before it was ninety-nine to one.

As I was growing up, I remember meeting all these movie stars from Mexico—Lucha Villa, Lola Beltrán, Flor Silvestre, Antonio Aguilar, José Alfredo Jiménez, Vicente Fernández, Cantinflas. We shared the same stage. We were in the same shows together, and it was awesome. Then I started noticing that we were starting to have bands that were bigger than just your four-piece band. We were now playing with La Sonora Santanera, which was a big orchestra from Mexico. We were playing with Little Joe and the Latinaires, Sunny and the Sunliners, and Freddie Martínez. It was more like six or eight guys up onstage versus just your four.

I thought that it was pretty cool to progress into this other style of music, but my father was like, "No, you are going to stay true to conjunto. You are not going to record with those guys." Little Joe asked my father if I could record a song with him, and my dad said, "Absolutely not." He says, "No, my daughter is conjunto, and she's going to stay conjunto forever." So I had to adhere to his rules.

It was just wonderful. One story in particular sticks out: We were on tour, and I think it was up in Oregon. We were going from California to Sunnyside, Washington, and I was asleep in the back seat of our 1968 Camaro. My brother was with us—my brother, Danny, and my dad. They stopped at this rest-stop park, and he nudged me and goes, "*Mija*, you want to get out and use the restroom?" I said, "No, no, no." I was still asleep.

They get out, they go in there, and I sit up. I look and there's a swing set. I'm looking at the swing set. It would be nice to go swing for a little bit. I said, "Yay!" So I got out of the car, and then I see the squirrel go into one of the pipes underneath the swing set. I said, "All right, I'm going to catch the squirrel. As it comes up from the back, I'm going to grab it from above its head and hold its jaws like this, and it won't bite me." Sure enough, the squirrel comes up, I grab it, and I had it there in my hand. I look over there, and I see our yellow Camaro going around the mountain already. My dad and my brother left me because they thought that I was still asleep in the back seat of the car.

I just threw that squirrel as far as I could, and I started running and running. I couldn't see the Camaro anymore, and I started crying. There was this family there in a station wagon—mom and pop and like a hundred kids. I'm like, "That was my daddy. He forgot me, and he left me." "It's OK." They calmed me down. "They'll come back for you. They're going to realize that you're not there, and they're going to come back."

Sure enough, about thirty minutes later, here they come. My brother said that he looked back and he goes, "Papa, *donde* Linda? Dad, where's Linda?" My dad goes, "What? She's right there." So they somehow made a turn and came back and got me. We always used to laugh about that.

LINDA ESCOBAR has been singing for six decades, performing Latin, Latin pop, Tejano, and traditional Mexican genres.

Rosie Flores

A Rockabilly Filly

On February 21, 2015, I drove over to an address east of Highway 35 to see Patricia Vonne and was surprised to meet up with Rosie. These women are roommates, and I had the chance to sit at a long table in the kitchen, drink water infused with cucumber, and share stories with both of them. I had included an interview with Rosie in my book *Women in Texas Music: Stories and Songs* (University of Texas Press, 2007), and I wanted to update our conversations with a renewed focus for this Mexican American collection. I had the chance to recommend her as an emcee for a radio series on the history of rockabilly music with producer Alex Gillespie. We were awarded a Peabody for this, and my music foundation was a sponsor of the project.

HUDSON: We had fun in New York. I was staying at the Chelsea Hotel. I had on my leather painted shirt; you had on your fancy clothes.

FLORES: I made my Manuel dress and my boots, and the announcer said, "Rosie, come back and show us your boots," and two unrelated people came up to me at the after-party and said, "We thought the announcer said, 'Come back and show us your boobs,'" because I had this embroidered, rhinestone Manual dress covering my breasts.

HUDSON: I took advantage of a moment in NYC to do my little Leonard Cohen moment and have a room at the Chelsea Hotel, although I was not hanging out with Janis Joplin like he was. So in my research, you have been described with the terms rockabilly, country, honky-tonk, jazz. Now we read about your Tex Mex heritage. Let's talk about your family and San Antonio, and we will see where it goes.

FLORES: I did grow up in San Antonio during a wonderful time; it was the fifties, and I believe that one of the main reasons I have such a big heart for rockabilly fifties music is because I was there. I am not a younger girl who's enamored with the fifties. Some of these rockabilly girls out there have taken on that persona. They weren't even alive in the 1950s, but I really was. I think that's why I love it so much, because when I was a little girl hanging out at my grandmother's house, there was a band that used to practice about a block away, and you could hear that music. I was around six or seven years old, and me and my brother, who is two years older than me, would follow the airwaves. You know those cartoons where they follow the airwaves? And our parents would say "We're going to go hear the band," and we would sit there in the garage and watch this 1950s rock-and-roll band, which is basically a rockabilly band playing these Buddy Holly songs and Elvis songs. I was just wide-eyed watching these drummers and guitar players. This was impactful on a little six- to seven-year-old kid.

HUDSON: And you could have been hearing accordions.

FLORES: But I wasn't. There were no conjunto bands in the neighborhood. It was more of a Jewish neighborhood. Actually, we lived on the Jewish side of town. There were a lot of Jews in my class because I remember Hanukkah was as important as Christmas was in my early schooling, which was cool. What I am trying to tell you is that it was the fifties and that's the music that was popular. My parents are really young. They were in their twenties when they had me. All of their high school friends were getting married, and we would go to their weddings.

I probably went to ten to fifteen weddings when I was growing up, because my parents had a lot of friends—they were very social. What kind of band was at each wedding? A fifties rockabilly rock-and-roll band, and they wanted to dance to music and dress up with ponytails and skirts, and I would get on the dance floor and a young kid would ask me to dance. But the odd thing about it was a lot of them were Hispanics—a lot of them were Mexican families. Mom wasn't Hispanic, but she married a Hispanic guy. So all the live music I was hearing was rockabilly

HUDSON: In what part of town?

FLORES: I lived on the north side of town near Woodlawn Lake. I didn't live on the west side of town like Tish Hinojosa did, and like probably the Rodriguez family did, and like a lot of people I know. I don't know why we ended up there, but we were there, and I think that area was very Jewish. I got to go see a famous cowboy band when I was a kid, and I was really into Roy Rogers and Dale Evans. We were into Buddy Holly, but we were also into Ritchie Valens. We were into this guy's voice, and we didn't know he was Hispanic. His name was Ritchie Valens, and he would sing rockabilly stuff. It's more like I yearned to know what that was because we would go to fiesta and my aunt, who is my dad's oldest sister, was a seamstress, and she had a daughter into flamenco dancing. She would have her dance at fiesta, and we went to see her a few times. I saw some of my heritage coming out, along with the music that went with it. Besides, of course, the chicken mole and all the Mexican food that was my heritage—the food my cousins and aunts and uncles would cook and the barbacoa and all the stuff we had in food. That's where my Tex Mex heritage came from.

My dad was into jazz, and he would play the Mills Brothers and Peggy Lee. Those were the records that he collected. He was into Rodgers and Hammerstein, all of the Jewish songwriters, so I grew up singing all the musicals. If you listen to "Rockabilly Filly," I'm singing when I'm like a little tiny girl. "Tammy Tammy Tammy is my love." I was singing them—I was younger, and my dad was recording me. My dad would buy the *Hit Parade*, and we would set up the two-track tape recorder, and we would read the lyrics and sing all the songs. None of them were Hispanic. So that's what I was cutting my teeth on.

HUDSON: Now you are eating an avocado . . .

FLORES: What's wrong with that? I thought you were going to make a reference to it being guacamole.

HUDSON: Healthy. I'll make a reference to healthy.

FLORES: I've had been into health food since I was in college a long time ago in San Diego. I started teaching guitar. I had about thirty-five students a week. I was in my early twenties, and I taught for about four or five years. I would take lunch breaks, and four doors down was a health food store, and so that's what turned me on to that. If it hadn't been for me teaching guitar and finding it, I would be eating French fries and junk food for the rest of my life.

HUDSON: Did you ever run into expectations because of your name? Because Patricia said if she used Rodriguez, then people looked at her and said, "You're not Mexican."

FLORES: It happened to me a lot. Yeah.

HUDSON: Did the name affect your booking? Because we talked before about Nashville and Las Vegas and Los Angeles and rockabilly and country . . . all the threads that are woven together to get this rockabilly center for you.

FLORES: When I first was starting to get in the press, when I got signed by Warner Bros., my first single was "Crying over You." As a matter of fact, I think this is kind of an interesting point to get out there and make note of. I was the first Hispanic woman to enter the country Billboard charts. Of course, it was after Johnny Rodriguez and after Freddy Fender, and it was actually before the Texas Tornados because they got signed after I did. I was really extremely thrilled about this because I was such a huge Doug Sahm fan. I'll have to credit the Texas Tornados with helping me fall in love with Tex Mex music. And of course Flaco! They are the ones that showed me where I came from. So talk about late in life.

You know who else took me? Michael Ramos, the piano player who is actually the head guy on the Doug Sahm tribute that's going to be previewed at SXSW. I am part of that, and Patricia is part of that. They are doing the tribute Saturday night at SXSW, and Michael Ramos took me to my first Tejano festival in San Antonio—the Accordion Festival. He took me to the festival with the drummer that I was playing with at the time, who was really into it, when I first moved back here in 1988 from the LA music scene. I said to myself, "I want to go and discover my Texas roots. I am leaving LA." And I came out of that LA scene.

I know I am jumping around because I keep thinking. Your question was, "Did you ever get anybody who says, 'Hey, your last name is Flores. What's up?'" So in 1986 I was signed to Warner Bros., and 1988 was when my first album came out, *Crying over You*, and *that* is when I entered the Billboard charts. In 1986 I had a single come out, and I was nominated as the best new female voice by the Academy of Country Music. I was up against Pam Tillis and Holly Dunn. I didn't win, but it was a song I had recorded with Vince Gill singing with me. I was performing around LA during my country/rock era—my Tammy Wynette–style vocals because she was my favorite girl at the time. I started every show dealing with these outraged Mexican-supporter Latino people who were very enraged at me for being too white. It was really kind of hard for me to take abuse. I was like, "Man I've been writing songs, and I've been onstage working on my craft and my career for a couple decades, and I am finally getting noticed for this. Why are you giving me a hard time?"

That's right—I haven't been playing Hispanic or Latino music. I don't have an accordion. There was an accordion player that had heard the David Hidalgo version on my first recording, which is why they labeled me Tex Mex. There is a song called "Midnight to Moonlight." Pete Anderson said, "Let's make this a Tex Mex song and put David Hidalgo on accordion so it's like really cool." Then I was like, "Yeah," and then I thought, "Maybe this could be the first track every time I do an album; I should do a Tex Mex song." You know, let me go ahead and find my voice, and on the second album, I wanted to do a song do with Freddy Fender. And I started thinking this could be really great. They are calling me Tex Mex, so why don't I go ahead and develop that into my sound? I had my whole album laid out, talked to my A&R person, and she threw the list back to me, saying, "I don't see any singles here," and got up and walked away. It hurt my feelings so bad.

HUDSON: Was she just looking at titles?

FLORES: Yeah, she was looking at titles. I wanted a duet with Steve Earle. This is going to be half English and half Spanish—a Tex Mex song that I want to write. We can bring in either Freddy Fender or Johnny Rodriguez because I knew both of them. I had some song ideas, and I just told her all about it. I was so excited talking about the whole thing, and so I said to her, "Don't ever get up and walk out on me like that when I am talking about my music. You are my A&R person, my go-to person; this is about us trying to make my next album. What's going to be my follow-up? You walked out on me and threw that thing and made a scene in front of people like Brenda Lee and Rodney Crowell and Rosanne Cash. These are my peers, and you made it look like we're having a fight or something; you really embarrassed me." I said something to her like, "Don't even come to the recording studio. Just keep the record company stuff out of it. Let me just do my part." I was so mad. It was the argument that got me dropped from Warner Bros. I didn't even get a chance to make another record. It was BOOM. I had put out a single, and it didn't do very well. I don't know why, because it was a great song.

Did you ever see the Buddy Holly story where he said, "You're not going to change my music. I'm going to produce it, and this is the way it goes." That's me. I am the female Buddy Holly. I write my own songs, and I want it to be my way. A lot of the time, women who are strong and independent get called something else that starts with a B. They get the "B word" thrown at them. I had to correct one of my musicians the other day because he was talking about somebody else, and I said, "Watch what you say with that word." The women you are talking about are highly strong, independent women, and if you use the B word on her, that is not right. The B word is for somebody who's actually kind of mean, and maybe they are on their period or something, and they're emotional and having a fit. There should be a word for guys who do that too. You'd never call a guy that.

HUDSON: I hear that you have had some situations where there are expectations that you were going to be more Tex Mex, and I love the fact that you actually thought of integrating your roots with one song per album as Tex Mex. Obviously, you had an awareness about something cultural that was in your blood.

FLORES: It was in my blood, and I still love listening to David Hidalgo and his accordion on my first record *Midnight to Moonlight*. When that got thrown back at me, I ended up getting signed by Hightone Records, and I was basically, "Screw country music," because they don't get me, and they were turning further away from traditional country. I was signed as the new traditionalist. Do you remember that phrase? I was there with Lyle Lovett, k. d. lang, Dwight Yoakam. I was trying to bring back country music in the traditional sense. It was turning to pop, and I wanted to put the twang back in it. I was like, "Let's get more Tammy Wynette and Kitty Wells and Loretta Lynn in this country."

HUDSON: I think that's still a heavy conversation today.

FLORES: Well that's where Ameripolitan comes in. These are music awards for outlaw country, rockabilly, honky-tonk, and western music.

HUDSON: How does that differ from Americana? I was at the first meeting to set up Americana Music in Nashville. And the conversation kept coming back to "How do we set ourselves apart?"

FLORES: At the beginning, they didn't know how to describe what Americana was. I had two number-one records on the Americana chart, but they do not recognize me and have never nominated me for anything, even though I was at the beginning of it. It developed around people who are not really country or rock and roll, but rather songwriters. I became more rockabilly soul and stayed with honky-tonk roots, and stayed with the jazz stuff, whereas Americana is described by Dale Watson this way: "It is more folk oriented." You have Alison Krauss and Emmylou Harris and Rodney Crowell. Everything is roots music. I think the difference is that Americana is more folk based. Robert Plant is now being a folk singer because he is working is Alison Krauss and Patty Griffin, whereas our stuff is hillbilly, Hank Williams, Johnny Cash, Jerry Lee Lewis. Early jazz and early western, forming into western swing. Honky-tonk is not Americana. Rockabilly's not Americana. So does that help clear it up a little?

HUDSON: It's interesting to discuss labels, because everywhere you go labels had a beginning, and then they evolved and none of them really do the job. Rockabilly is a good label for you, but even that is a little confining. I mean, you don't want everybody to come to your show this afternoon to expect rockabilly. You're playing with Jim Stringer and the AM Band, right? So we are going to hear jazz.

FLORES: You're going to hear some jazz because that's a really big part of who I am, going back to my roots.

At the time of this interview, Rosie is gearing up to perform at the Austin Music Awards in 2019, as well as the Outlaw Country Cruise, and putting out a new album, *Simple Case of the Blues*, which showcases her in a new light (again). The music is full of soul and yearning, bringing the listener through joy and heartbreak and back again. It was produced by Charlie Sexton and gives her a chance to follow another passion: the blues. This chameleon's career spans more than four decades.

ROSIE FLORES is a singer, songwriter, and guitarist who has performed everything from punk rock to country, rockabilly to the blues, for more than forty years.

David Garza

Talking Texas Music in Mexico

I met David Garza in San Miguel de Allende—a Texan living in Mexico. I had heard him solo at various places around town and heard his hot band play. Now, in 2017, David has moved back to Houston, Texas, and is recording an album. I knew when I met him in San Miguel that he had a distinct story to tell.

HUDSON: One time I saw you and said, "You are David Garza." And because I am from Kerrville, perhaps, you knew I had the wrong David Garza in mind. And you said, "Yes, I am David Garza but not *the* David Garza."

GARZA: I have seen him at Kerrville, and I almost met him once in Austin. My stage name now is Lynx Maples, because of the name. And David Lee Garza, the Tejano artist, and David Garza, the heavy-metal guitarist. Audiences would get us mixed up. Lynx Big Leaf Maples—after my trips to Lost Maples Park in Texas.

HUDSON: Can you give us an abbreviated version of your life story with some tracking of your connections to Texas?

GARZA: My dad was from Galveston. I just realized recently he had more freedom than most Mexicans in Texas. It was on the Chittlin' Circuit—a place for big bands, with lots of people passing through. He shined Robert Mitchum's shoes when he was five years old. He's a Galveston Mexicano who did not experience much racism. Then I had friends in the Central Texas area who experienced much more in the seventies than my dad did in the thirties. He met my mom in DC, got married, and I was born and raised there. I remember asking him to speak Spanish when I was four or five. I wanted to be bilingual. He would not do it. When I moved to Texas, I asked my aunt why no one spoke Spanish. She said we were discriminated against in the Texas school system, so we always spoke English in the house because we did not want our kids discriminated against. So here I was, this kid from Maryland, named David Garza, and my brother was blond with blue eyes. People would ask my mother if I was adopted from India or Hungary.

I realized over time that I had experienced some racism in Maryland, but it was more covert. People in Texas would ask me if I were Mexican and then tell me they hated Mexicans. Well, OK. In Texas City, there were a lot of workers there in the plants. I thought it was funny as a child. I remember my first day in school there. A big cowboy dude just looked at me and said, "Are you Mexican?" I said yes, and he said, "I hate Mexicans." It took me a while to figure out this wasn't OK. I was not Mexican enough for the Tex Mex dudes.

Most of my friends were outsiders. My dad bought an old fishing pier, so I spent a lot of time out there. Then my best friend was a kid from Indiana who had moved to Texas City. We fished all the time and shared our dreams and our hopes. All the stuff that got me in trouble as a youth, not understanding well enough, things that got me relegated to the corner—I had a difficult time compromising when I started music in my thirties. All those things that were weaknesses became my strengths. People started saying, "Oh, we love that you don't compromise." I had to learn to connect my internal desires with writing.

I had several jobs—one at a brain injury rehab, working horticultural therapy with Bonsai trees. I went to Abilene Christian University, and that's where I learned to sing. Everyone on my mom's side is a musician. This cool guy in our dorm asked me to ride the joy bus to church. People there might be very fundamental, but they were good people, and they introduced me to a cappella and four-part harmony. I realized later that the song leader was just taught by some guy in a church when he was a kid. He made it swing every time he led the singing. And I have a good sense of timing because of him.

HUDSON: I grew up in a Southern Baptist Church with a phenomenal choir director named Paul Paschal. You could count on great music in every program and at every church service. Music and churches seem to go together at times. Maybe more in the South? Willie and Bobbie started in their church in Abbott.

GARZA: You don't associate the singing with work, and you feel better afterward. It is associated with community and self-expression. Make a joyful noise. I started off in Maryland, then Church of Christ in Texas City. Then I started questioning everything. Do miracles happen now? What about synchronicity? I worked through *The Artist's Way* by Julie

Cameron. For the first time I said to the universe, "I need a job that gives me time off." Three days later, I got that job. I had time to work on my music then. And I worked through this book.

I played my music in San Marcos, and things got better. Then I had a big bad thing happen, and I decided to play my music on the East Coast with this songwriter named Burt Reynolds, who played at a venue in Austin. In 1999 or 2000 he said, "Go to San Miguel if you really want time alone." I thought about it and called my mom to tell her I was coming down there for a week. I didn't speak any Spanish, and these two Mexican widows became my friends on the bus down. They were bringing these grandkids for their friends to see. They bought me coffee and translated for me along the way. I got there, and I loved the hostel so much I asked the manager for a job. I made breakfast one morning, and the assistant manager said he wanted to hire me. I stayed there for ten months, and that is when I met you. I started writing for the newspaper. I played my own stuff in the theaters.

The second time I came down was magic too. A friend in Austin asked me to bring him down to buy some paintings. Before I came down, I asked the universe for a sign. I turned on the TV, and a *telenovela* was playing. Two people were in romantic conversation, and the waiter who brought them coffee was someone I knew in San Miguel! I said, "That's my sign!" I packed really heavy. I had several job offers and a band offer when I arrived. A guitar player asked me to play. We formed a band, and we were the most popular band in the area for about three years. Things kept falling into place, so I stayed with it.

I have gotten to sing every kind of music imaginable. The guys in the band grew up watching American music. They said they did not want to do any songs in Spanish. That was odd. They were from Mexico City and Celaya. Growing up in Mexico City is like New York in another country. You can grow up hearing only American music. I have been in that band since 2004, and we only do one song in Spanish, "*Oye Como Va*" by Santana.

DAVID GARZA, a classically trained guitarist, pursued a solo career, producing and promoting his self-produced recordings until signing with Lava/Atlantic. His songs have appeared in several television ads and shows.

Henry Gomez

Mariachi Voice

Henry arranged the music for the last album of Terri Sharp at the Blue Cat Studio, in July 2019, working with Joe Trevino. He has been playing professionally for forty years. Mariachi music was his first calling. Now he's moving in a new direction—three-part harmony.

HUDSON: Let's talk about the music you play and love.

GOMEZ: I have played mariachi music for forty years, and now I am moving into a new area with trios. The instruments are *guitarrón*, guitar, or *requinto* (a small guitar that plays the melody), and the three voices all harmonize. I play Wednesday through Sunday at Mi Tierra in San Antonio, and I work on projects with Joe Trevino at the Blue Cat Studio, my home base. I arranged the last album for Terri Sharp, and we used Bobby Flores on violin and Michael Guerra on accordion. When did you meet Terri?

HUDSON: I interviewed her for a newspaper column when I first moved to Kerrville. She had a reputation for her songwriting and a gold record with Hank Jr. We became fast friends, and I took her to Laredo to play music at the home of Ramon Luera. He had music every Friday night at his house. We both met him at the Conjunto Festival in San Antonio, and we spent several great weekends in Laredo as Terri sang with all the men gathered at his house on Scott Street. And Ramon documented everything, so we have some good video. I was sad at the loss of her life to a brain aneurism in 2016. I am still missing her, for sure. She played her style of Mexican music due to her great passion for the music in local restaurants, and then decided to create an album. I am sorry I never got her down to my place in San Miguel de Allende, but I did bring her some mariachi pants I bought off a guy in the square one night! Fit her perfectly, and we did a photo shoot in those pants.

GOMEZ: Yes, we loved working with her at the Blue Cat.

HUDSON: Tell me about your family.

GOMEZ: My dad's parents were from Guanajuato, and my mom's family were from Jalisco. I remember when I was about ten my dad would go down and swim the river to go home to see family. It was easier then, and the people knew where to cross. Dad would play Mexican music in the house all the time—rancheras and mariachi. We would go hear music at a theater [Almeda] on Sundays, and mariachi bands would open. I watched some kids in the neighborhood play guitar, and I wanted to do that, so I started. Then a priest at the Guadalupe Catholic Church asked us to create a mariachi group to play in church. We formed a group, practiced, and started there. I wanted to write music/?create arrangements, and my mother called to let me know the Guadalupe Cultural Center was offering a four-month course in music composition. There were eighty in that first class, and then the group disappeared, and I was the only one. I ended up in that class by myself. I guess the others were scared away by an assignment to bring in an arrangement early on.

HUDSON: Let's talk about the different styles of music you play.

GOMEZ: A mariachi band is usually twelve musicians, but due to economics (paying a group that large is difficult), we see the group at four or five. Now I am doing something new, playing with a trio . . . a *requinto*, *guitarrón*, and guitar. My favorite songs are the fast ones, *sones*—"La Negra," for example. The music comes from the thirties or forties in Mexican villages.

HUDSON: And where did your family live?

GOMEZ: Dad's family is from San Francisco del Rincon in Guanajuato, about thirty minutes from Leon. I have not been there, but I do want to go see my cousins now. Dad's last wish was for me to visit family. My mom's family is from Jalisco.

HUDSON: I took the bus from Nuevo Laredo last May—a first-class bus to Querétaro. I had an easy and pleasant experience. How do you self-identify?

GOMEZ: I think the main ingredient is Mexican American. My music is Mexican with the taste of San Antonio—a fusion of soft rock, jazz, conjunto, blues, and country.

HUDSON: Aha—a definition of Texas music, that fusion of styles?

GOMEZ: Well, San Antonio has a unique soul. Terri Sharp wanted the sound of Mexico, and I produced her last album with just that. We had Bobby Flores on violin, Michael Guerra on accordion, and Flaco on accordion. Blue Cat Studio with Joe Trevino is my home base; we think alike.

HENRY "KIKÉ" GOMEZ is a renowned arranger, composer, producer, and studio musician. He has recorded with Grammy-recognized artists from mariachi, Tejano, conjunto, country, rock, and Christian genres.

Michael Guerra

A Man with a Mission

Stephanie Urbina Jones called me up August 31, 2016, saying, "You need to come to the Blue Cat Studio today. Michael Guerra is coming by to put down some accordion on my new album, *Tularosa*. He's a great guy that you ought to meet." When I arrived at the studio, I noticed his positive attitude at once and knew he would be fun to talk to. He tours with the Mavericks and adds accordion on many recordings—he's a master.

HUDSON: I saw on Facebook that you were going to the Blue Cat, and people were wishing you good luck on your new project. And we know you tour with the Mavericks. We know you play with tons of people. You get called into a lot of projects I know, but let's talk about your album— your new project now.

GUERRA: Sure. Definitely. We are actually on our second album, and my first album, of course, came in 2012. That was my first, with original music and some covers. But this new project—totally as songwriters—is with my buddy, David Pedrazine. He's a writer and my business partner in writing; our writing has gotten a lot better and more experienced. And after two years on that record and then just writing for this new album, everything is just getting a lot better. But yeah, this new music totally has got some Tex Mex roots in it. Pretty much accordion driven, you know, but it's got all the sounds from Americana to conjunto to *cumbia*—and English. There are mostly English lyrics. I don't even think I have one that's in Spanish. I think I actually have that in my notes to write one in Spanish and to put it on here. I was like, "Write a Spanish song." I said, "I can't believe I didn't have one in here!"

HUDSON: Let's talk about your writing.

GUERRA: When David writes, he goes under the name of D. R. Pedraza. That's his writing name. But yeah, definitely, we've been writing a bunch of songs together, and we just narrowed down a few that just kind of seemed to work in this new album, but we're knee-deep in. I think we have about eight pretty good tunes that are pretty ready to go and that we've been mixing and editing. That's the kind of mood I'm in right now. I'm still recording, though. And I haven't decided whether we're going for a full album or an EP. And we're taking our time. We're in no rush. I'm with the Mavericks touring. And this stuff is usually just me recording this stuff and putting the basic tracks and then later bringing in. . . . And really, my bass, Junior Jasso, he's just coming to do the bass. I taught him how to play the bass, but then he went along and got better and better. And so, he's been my right-hand guy, like David. David's been my left-hand guy. Those two guys are very important to me. But yeah, we'll get the drummer in and get him to record all the stuff.

HUDSON: And this is gonna be the Michael Guerra trio or group?

GUERRA: That's yet to be decided. It's a new band name—we came up with Michael Guerra and the Nights Calling—the calling of the nights. And it just kind of came into this thing like, "Oh, you know what? Well, the night's calling these *cats* to play with us this time." It just kind of feels like that way, 'cause we don't really have a solid band yet. We've yet to decide what it's gonna be, or just Michael Guerra just for the fact that I have a very good opportunity with the Mavericks right now. They're on a record label called the Thirty Tigers. And so now, they have so much freedom, and they just released their record label, Mono Mundo Recordings—the Mavericks did. So, with that, just being in the studio and then hearing all this news, Raul and Eddie, you just kind of say, "Hey, now that means we can release whatever we want. That means we can release your record if we want."

A big old light bulb just [. . .] turned on in my head. And so, that's what I'm kind of doing right now when I go back to on tour—is to show some songs to Raul because he knows I have been in the studio writing and stuff, and he's been just asking left and right like, "Can I hear some stuff?" I'm like, "Well, I don't have anything, because all this time I'm at Blue Cat—I'm recording, recording, working, and then I'll get a copy or do a little rough mix."

HUDSON: I met you when Stephanie Urbina Jones called you to come into her project. So, do a lot of other people do that now with your particular reputation with the accordion? Do you get called to play on lots of other albums?

GUERRA: I actually had been getting calls before—just being in this city, just kind of knowing musicians and knowing how I play and what songs I do. They just kept on calling me for quite a bit to come and do sessions. And then some people send me their tracks and I'll come and cut it over here at Blue Cat and throw some accordion on it or something. But yeah, my name gets out there a little more—more out of the city. There's more people—some overseas—and they'll send their stuff and I'll record on it or put some stuff for them. So, yeah.

HUDSON: What was the biggest surprise and pleasure for you? Invitation wise. I mean when Flaco was invited to record with the Rolling Stones or when Dylan him called up to New York City—Flaco and I have talked for this project by the way—and he talked a little bit about phone calls he got along the way.

GUERRA: Right. And I don't think he even knew who the Rolling Stones were at the time. When I first moved to San Antonio after high school, I was eighteen. When I moved over here, I got a call from Cesar Rosas from Los Lobos, and I had just jammed with the Super 7. And so, those guys were like, "Who's this cat? He's playing the accordion and stuff." I had just moved and then Cesar called. He calls my house in LA. My mom's like, "I recognize the voice. It's Cesar Rosas from Lobos." And so, it was probably him calling me just because he wanted me to join his band. I believe it's Soul Disguise or something like that—his other band that he had aside from Los Lobos. But that was pretty big for me just because they were heroes. They are heroes of mine especially because I'm from East LA as well. I think that was pretty big. I was already moved over here. So, there was no chance of really hooking up with him 'cause I already had my stuff lined up for me. But I think it was probably that. I think that was one of the bigger moments that I realized, "Wow, I think this is heavy now that this guy's calling."

HUDSON: And you didn't join his band because you were doing your thing in Texas. So, what called you here?

GUERRA: It was the music, the Tex Mex music, the style of music that came out of Texas. My dad was from Brownsville originally and moved to Los Angeles in the fifties. So, he brought lots of music from here. Valerio Longoria, Flaco Jiménez, Esteban Jordan, Nick Villareal. All these cats like vinyl, and cassettes, and all this stuff that he had that I was just turned on to. When I was eleven years old, I started digging his music 'cause I didn't understand Spanish when I was young. They didn't teach us, but my dad plays *bajo saxo*. And so, he had several bands in LA that were from Texas and from Mexico. And there were different conjuntos. So, they were just garage bands that played at weddings and *quinceañeras*. That's how I was pulled into that sound of music, and just like really understanding what my dad was doing. So, that's what threw me in. It was just that music, and it's hard to find the musicians that you wanna do the right type of music with in LA.

I was struggling to find the right cats. I knew out here that I was just seen as a youngster by the older cats. So, that inspired me to come and move out here—to just find the right kind of cat and see where it would take me. I joined up with Rick Carino right away. I had played with Ruben Ramos first for a month when I moved here, and they were like, "Man, you could play." Then he told Rick Carino, "Hey, this guy can play. You should get him in your band." So, that's what happened. I started with Rick from 2000 when I moved here, 2000 to 2004/2005. Texas is its own country, and the sound called me out here.

HUDSON: Texas is sitting on top of Mexico, and this was Mexico. So, we are Tejano. And I just love all the layers of the cultures and the way the language reaches down like a root into the ground. And, of course, San Antonio is kind of the hub of all that, but you could go to Brownsville. You can go on the border. You can go to South Texas. Right? Just a lot of different sounds. It sounds like you have been part of the richness of it, rather than just in one niche. What is it like to tour with the Mavericks? They're not labeled Tex Mex, right?

GUERRA: No. It's always been a hard thing to narrow into a genre for them, and myself too. But when they do write reviews about the Mavericks, they always have that Tex Mex or Tejano included in what they think it sounds like—mariachi. You know, ska, because there's a lot of influence of ska in there. It's all that.

HUDSON: I don't know the ska feel. Please, explain that to me?

GUERRA: Ska is like a reggae-based sound. It's got this upbeat. Yeah. You gotta listen to it. You gotta hear it. You can listen to the Skatalites—something like that. But it's a whole other thing. It's more of a reggae thing. It's almost like that conjunto beat, but it's more on the up. It's a whole other feel, but that what's they get associated with a lot because that is a big influence with Raul and the band. And so, definitely, it's a lot of ska influence and the Tejano, Tex Mex, mariachi feel/?influence with the twangy guitars, but that does get in there a lot. In the reviews, you always see Tex Mex or Tejano. You always see that.

HUDSON: Tell me about a favorite song that you've written.

GUERRA: Well, one is kind of special. And it was one of the first songs I wrote. It's on my first album, *Voodoo Lady*. I kind of lost my ability to play. And I didn't know what the hell it was. All of a sudden, my body got numb, and my hands got tight, and I could not play. I couldn't play any instrument anymore, and it was like for two weeks that happened and then the vibrating had gone away, but then I was left with my hand just tight, and I couldn't play. I had to relearn my instrument. And it was a hard time for me. I went to the ER. They checked all my blood, and nothing was wrong. And so, I started thinking: "Shit, man, I got a spell on me or something. Wow, it's some voodoo stuff. And the girl I was with at that time believed in that stuff, and her uncle was like a *curandero* up here. He was a Catholic man. And he did the cure with the egg and stuff like that. And so, at that point, I was just like, "Yeah. Well, I'm a Catholic too, and we're not supposed to really do that. I don't think. But at this point, I am freaking out, and I need something to help me." I was doing whatever I could to free myself from whatever was going on. But I ended up writing a song.

I don't know if you have the first record if I gave it to you, but the lyrics kinda say it. I don't know if that girl was part of the voodoo-ness that put a spell on me.

HUDSON: Did it go away?

GUERRA: It gradually came on like every few days; then it would go down more and more into my body and I felt this tingling, and then I had like no sensation. After two weeks, it gradually went away. But then as it went away, like my fingers and my hands were tight, and I couldn't play. I couldn't hit the right button and stuff. And so, I had to sit down and kind of relearn. Like I know how to play, but I had to kind of relearn. And like I said, I went to the doctors. I went to the ER. They did not find a thing.

HUDSON: How old were you?

GUERRA: Well, I'm thirty-four now, but this was when I was twenty-three or twenty-four. And so, it lasted for a bit, and then I would have tightness in my stomach. I was playing with Rick Carino at that time. I missed gigs. I missed a bunch of shows. It was a weird time for me. There was no outcome. Nothing to say, "Oh, it was this." So, that's why I was just thinking like, "You know what? I had a spell on me." And I wrote the song.

I went to Floore's, saw the Mavericks, and watched Michael tour the world. He tours with Michael Guerra and the Nights Calling and with the Mavericks. December 2018 marked the debut of a new film with music by Michael, written by David Pedrazine: *A Chance to Say Good-bye*.

MICHAEL GUERRA began playing accordion with his father's band. He has performed with the Texas Tornados, the Sir Douglas Quintet, Los Texmaniacs, Raul Malo, the Mavericks, and his own group. He has written and produced for film scores and soundtracks.

Ruben Gutierrez

Talking on a Border

Schreiner University student John Zamora recommended Ruben Gutierrez to me, who was his band director at Ysleta High School. We met at a bowling alley with a bar attached. He was playing with his band, and our conversation was accompanied by the sounds of a bowling tournament. I had just talked with a class at the University of Texas at El Paso (UTEP) about my research, and I went to a local club with a student to hear a new young band. My research in El Paso was exciting for me as a woman who loves Mexico. Yes, I went to Rosa's Cantina, had a beer and some enchiladas, and bought a T-shirt and bumper sticker that adorns the wall in my kitchen. I live in a wooden cabin out west of Kerrville, and the walls cry for adornment. The bumper sticker reminds me of my dad singing "El Paso" as he walked down the hall of our family home in Richland Hills—a sweet reminder. Driving around El Paso brought me up to a wall—an offensive divider for me to see. I love the energy of the Frontera, and this wall said, "Let us stay divided." I am not about walls. Ever.

GUTIERREZ: I was born and raised in El Paso and got my degrees at UTEP. I have been all over the world, but I have never lived anywhere else but El Paso. I have always felt all the resources were here. Things always get better; the city is growing but has a small-town feel to it. We are over one million people and the border is opening up again. I was at UTEP for eighteen years, teaching commercial music and piano, the jazz band and some choirs.

Then I went to El Paso Community College as a full-time professor, and I was there for six years. In 2003 I had a jazz trio at UTEP. We were going to play this festival called Festival Chihuahua, and we were going on this tour the government was sponsoring. It included Zacatecos. It was going to include Mexican artists as well. It was the same year that Vicente Fox declared war on the drug cartels. People did not realize at that point how violent things were going to get. That affected the music exchange and collegiality across the border. And because of NAFTA, we could cross the border for clinics.

That all came to a complete halt. I do not remember the last time I was in Juarez, but it was probably about fifteen years ago. It has affected the music scene here. I do feel El Paso is home, and my wife is from San Antonio. We have lots of family here. We are raising our daughter here, and we are going to retire here.

HUDSON: I love it out here; the sky and mountains are so beautiful. You are involved in so many things. What is the source of all that?

GUTIERREZ: I never really thought I would be teaching college. When I got my undergraduate degree, it was in performance. I considered getting my doctorate at Arizona State, but the position at UTEP opened up. Back in 1993—that's where I got involved in music. As far as getting involved in all the different styles I play, my dad was interested in jazz. Both of my parents are second-generation Hispanic; my grandparents are both from Mexico. There were a couple of villages my maternal grandparents came from, but I can't remember. I was very small when they passed away. I think somewhere near Chihuahua.

HUDSON: Are you aware of the impact the culture of Mexico has had on you?

GUTIERREZ: Most definitely. It is kind of interesting. For the first five years of my life, I did not speak English. Both parents are bilingual, and they spoke Spanish only with their parents. My mom grew up in Marfa, Texas. I have an older brother and a younger brother. I do believe that when my older brother went into kindergarten, he did not speak English at all, and it was kind of an awakening for my parents. They shifted and started speaking to us in English. I had to learn English that year in kindergarten. Then we kind of forgot our Spanish.

I had a chance to play with a lot of Tejano groups in the 1980s. In fact, I had a chance to play with Selena before she became a legend. It was around the time she was climbing up the charts. I got acquainted with the Mexican culture and began speaking Spanish. But I do speak with an American accent. My dad listened to rock and jazz. He would have all sorts of music going on. I sort of played piano when I was very young and became interested in Ray Charles. I was two years old when I started playing. They would tell me the TV would be on, and I would play the melodies on this toy organ. I don't know how to account for that. That is the beauty of music. I am teaching high school students right now. I have two online classes that are American music history, from jazz to rock—early blues and ragtime.

HUDSON: I produce a tribute to Jimmie Rodgers in Kerrville each September on my university campus, and he played with Louis Armstrong. Many people don't know that. You know John Zamora and Madison Livingston, both Schreiner students from El Paso, recommended that I talk with you. Let's talk about your music now. You are playing here tonight.

GUTIERREZ: My group now is Souled Out. The name comes from the Tower of Power group who put out an album called *Souled Out*. The bass player lived in Austin and San Antonio, and Erica, his wife, grew up here. They came back here about fifteen years ago. The kind of music we are playing tonight is a variety from the 1970s and 1980s, but we give it our own twist—like Michael Jackson in Latin jazz.

I play piano now all the time. I used to play trombone, and I picked up guitar because I teach it. I also sing in Spanish, and my wife sings also. She's a choir director. We play parties and for private groups. One group wants us to play Puerto Rican songs. One thing about El Paso is the diversity. We play a jazz thing on Tuesday nights, and we get people from the army bands to come and sit in. I also teach the jazz band at El Paso Community College.

HUDSON: Someone told me there was a vibrant mariachi scene here. In fact, Stephanie Urbina Jones discovered a group that she wanted to record mariachi music with her on an album of country standards.

GUTIERREZ: What is their name? There is an all-female group here. If you would like, right down the street is a Mexican restaurant called Ay Cocula. And one of the violin players is a professor at ECC. It's right on the corner. Los Arrieros at Ay Cocula. They are the most well-known group in El Paso.

HUDSON: I have had discussions about the word *Hispanic*, and many people have different opinions. In fact, a teacher at UTEP came up to me at an oral history conference and suggested not using the term *Hispanic* for my oral history. I was giving a talk when she walked into the room, and I walked over and removed the title on the poster. Red letters that read Hispanic [laughter], Tejano, Tex Mex. She suggested Mexican American without a hyphen!

GUTIERREZ: It does depend on who you talk to. Chicano is more of a political term to me. It is almost derogatory—more like talking about the beatnik things going on. That was a protest group. I remember Chicano studies at UTEP, and I played for a movie screening of *The Alamo*, pre–World War II. I am Hispanic more than anything else. I do have lighter skin and more Hispanic blood in me. To me, *Mexican American* is like are we *black* or *African American*? Tejano is now a style of music.

HUDSON: It used to be the name for people who lived on the land in what is now Texas and was once Mexico.

GUTIERREZ: I would go with the word *Hispanic*. Even without the hyphen, *Mexican American* is offensive. It's like calling blacks *African American*. I think they would be offended because they are not African; they are just American. To me, that's the same thing with Mexican Americans. I consider myself an American citizen, and my homage is to the United States. I am proud of my roots, and I am proud of the fact I am Hispanic. I work in the Ysleta district, and it is 97 percent Hispanic.

HUDSON: Thank you for your distinct perspective.

GUTIERREZ: When I have visited other cities, the musicians do have a real tight bond. You go to New York or Los Angeles, you have friends, but so many are also just making a living doing that. There seems to be more dividers. Maybe competition. I feel a family here in El Paso. We help each other out.

HUDSON: Adrian from UTEP wants to introduce me to the indie rock scene in El Paso.

GUTIERREZ: I wouldn't know too much about that, but we were just talking about this with a bass player who was working with us named Greg Gonzalez. The band name is Cigarettes After Sex. They put up a YouTube page, and they got signed by a promoter and are doing tours in Europe. He's from El Paso, but he moved to New York.

RUBEN GUTIERREZ is a pianist who performs jazz, jazz fusion, classic rock, classic, Latin, and world music. He is a full-time professor of keyboard and commercial music at the University of Texas at El Paso.

Tish Hinojosa

Dreaming in the Labyrinth

I have known Tish for many years, and we previously did an interview for my 2001 oral history on Texas songwriters. Her journey has been faithful to her culture, her vision, her writing. One fond memory I have of her is from a Mexican restaurant called Rocky Joe's (now Acapulco) on Sidney Baker Street in Kerville. She performed a song by James McMurtry, "Crazy Winds and Flashing Yellow Lights." I loved her version about a woman who was not going to just sit by anymore. Now, in 2017, Tish is still striking out on her own path. I had the opportunity to book her for a special house concert series called 290 Texas, created by Paul Sumrall in Johnson City. My foundation was the sponsor at the time. We sat down to talk before a show in an art gallery in Johnson City. We also shared years with the Kerrville Folk Festival and Rod Kennedy, who also adored her. This interview was on February 5, 2015.

HUDSON: I just finished talking with Santiago Jr. and with Flaco, who is heading to LA to pick up his Grammy Lifetime Achievement Award. Flaco said with a smile on his face that you all had just talked, and he was honored that you had asked him to record with you. That's Flaco!

HINOJOSA: Actually, I am interested in working with both brothers.

HUDSON: Yes. They have an album coming out. And Santiago plays every Sunday from eleven to one at Carnitas Uruapan on Ruiz and Twenty-Fourth. Last week, Kimmie Rhodes and Deb Fleming showed up and asked Santiago to sign a *bajo sexto* that was Joe Gracy's, and then they played it. All this Texas music history in one place. Kimmie sang "*Volver, Volver*" with him.

HINOJOSA: I wish I had been there! In January 1985 San Antonio had this record snowfall, and we met at Tycoon Flats, where I was playing. And James was this young guy standing around. I walked up and talked to him. And we became friends. And I recorded that song "Crazy Winds" because I loved it.

HUDSON: You are not only known for talking about your family onstage, but you have a place on your bio for humanitarian work. I am interested in the kind of causes you're working on.

HINOJOSA: At first, I was just passing out bumper stickers, but I did get involved in United Farm Workers and used some footage of Cesar Chavez in my video for "Something in the Rain," a song about migrant workers getting poisoned by pesticides being sprayed by airplanes. It was an honor for me to get to meet him.

HUDSON: That song gives me chills just hearing the title. It points to something in a subtle, beautiful way.

HINOJOSA: I did not want a preachy song. It is a little boy telling a story of what happens to his sister. I think it's innocence.

HUDSON: I know you have spent time in Germany, and I would like to talk about your experience being outside the culture looking back in.

HINOJOSA: I'm not going to leave anymore! Nine years in Germany. Life is what happens to us, so I am not going to say it was a bad decision. I had always thought I might live in Mexico, but that never happened. Then, when I met the man who became my German husband, that opened up all kinds of cultural interests for me—and an opportunity to live in Europe. I was excited. I never dreamed I would be inside such a different culture. I toured there in the 1990s and wanted to visit a German house.

It is interesting how people live in other cultures. I learned a lot from hanging out there. They are not into ownership. It is urban living. I did a lot of walking and rode a bike and trains. Nothing wrong with the American dream of owning something; that is security, and my mother bought her own house a few years before she died. My parents were both from Mexico, and they were poor in Mexico. My dad came from an agricultural background, and he left Mexico when he was twelve and came to San Antonio to live with an uncle, who was named Santiago. He apprenticed as a mechanic. My mother came from a harsher situation, and she had trouble with her eyes at a young age. And she was the oldest of four siblings. She left her mom's house as an adolescent to live in another house as a housekeeper. That's the background my parents brought to San Antonio. And now we have the songs I wrote—seeing my parent's struggles and seeing how important security was.

HUDSON: In Germany, you got to see different cultural values. Did that cause you to look at your life any differently?

HINOJOSA: Yes, it did. One reason Germans think the way they do is because they have security. They have great social programs. The criminal system is different, as they are recovery oriented.

HUDSON: Were you aware you were carrying the Hispanic culture?

HINOJOSA: Actually, over there, people saw me as Latina or Chicana.

HUDSON: My interviews with many accordion players reveal a German connection through the instrument, and then the rhythms.

HINOJOSA: That's because of southern Germany—Bavaria. It's like the Texas of Germany. They have their own identity. And it seems obvious to me they would get together with that instrument and the polkas . . . and also the Czech culture and the accordion. And we have both in Texas.

HUDSON: I was surprised the first time I realized the accordion came from Germany to Texas and then to Mexico.

HINOJOSA: That's why the accordion is most popular in northern Mexico. In southern Mexico, they have the big harps and the mariachi groups. And when you get to the Yucatan, you find the big harps. And Mexico considers the hillbillies to be in the north. They are ranchers and country people.

HUDSON: I met a man, Armando, at a Santiago show, and he described his music as *norteño*. I asked for that distinction, and he said, "I am more Mexican. I am from Durango, Mexico."

HINOJOSA: And we grew up listening to KCOR radio, the Mexican station; and we watched bullfights with our fathers and telenovelas with mother and Mexican TV. And after the bullfights, we watched the music shows that featured *norteño* music. And then there's Tex Mex. For me, that is Doug Sahm and Augie Meyers . . . soul brothers with the Mexican culture.

My brother graduated from high school in 1962. That was a special time in San Antonio. There was discrimination. So the Mexicans and the African Americans would form social clubs. Everyone would dress up in suits and beautiful dresses. And that's when all these great bands would come play. That's a lot of the beginnings of Tejano music—Sunny and the Sunliners, Al Gomez, and more. They took the discrimination and made something beautiful out of it. I was only five or six, so I did not realize what was happening, but now that I look back at it, I see the marriage of music there of soul and Tejano.

I feel really lucky to have been born and raised in San Antonio with this rich cultural history. And the 1960s . . . what a fascinating time to be listening to the radio. Brown power happened in California. I think Texas Mexicans were more into assimilating. I was a teenager in the seventies. We benefited from everything that happened in the 1960s. I was going to a Catholic girls school, and they let me pass out Cesar Chavez bumper stickers. Music was so reflective of the culture. I do feel my social awareness brought me to that music where everybody had a message. Dylan and Paul Simon, and Dylan's teacher was Woody Guthrie. I wanted to learn all these songs with social implications. Joan Baez.

HUDSON: I was in college in Fort Worth from 1963 to 1967. I discovered Dylan, Willie, and Leonard Cohen. And I have interviewed two of them.

I often think I must have lived in Mexico in a past life. The first time I went to Mexico, I felt I belonged there. And I grew up in a middle-class neighborhood in Richland Hills, Texas—a suburb of Fort Worth. My resonance with this culture makes no sense. I have an apartment in San Miguel de Allende

HINOJOSA: I love Mexico, and I have been there a lot. I have heard so much about San Miguel, and I was invited to play a private party there last summer. The American culture is integrated into the Mexican culture there. It is beautiful. I also played some orphanages there, which was very special to me. I love what the Americans are doing there. I took an entire suitcase of clothing for the kids there. The girls ranged from tots to teens, and it was really nice to see how they took care of each other. I also saw how the Americans there are supporting humanitarian causes.

HUDSON: Let's talk about your family in San Antonio.

HINOJOSA: My mother is very dark skinned. And my father's name is easily traced back to Spain: Hinojosa. Mom had a Spanish name with a lot more of American Indian in her.

HUDSON: Right now, in 2015, you have many albums with Rounder Records and one with Warner Bros. in both Spanish and English. I love that album—*Dreaming in the Labyrinth.*

HINOJOSA: Américo Paredes introduced himself to me on the radio. My mother passed away in '85, and somewhere in that time period—around 1992 or so—I went to Mexico to visit. It's a complicated story, but in this little town was a family my mother worked for. The dad had studied medicine in Puebla. Mom was his nanny. He adored her, so they stayed in touch. As they grew older, he always saw her like a sister. So we would go there to visit. He was so loving and sentimental. We would go visit, and I bought my first guitar in Puebla. Joan Baez's father is from Puebla. I loved this twenty-dollar guitar. On subsequent trips, he would always ask me to sing. My mother would always sing when she was young, so he would cry and say it reminded him of my mom. Then I went down there in '92; I was married with children. I also felt a connection to that family. Again, we started talking about music and songs. I used to sing some songs my mother would play for us. Then he asked me to do a song called "*Collar de Perles*." She never sang that one for us, so that became a quest.

I searched for the song. I was on a KUT radio show, and on one show I told the host about this song. Then the phone rang, and Dr. Paredes called in. He said, "I know the song you are talking about. Lydia Mendoza recorded it." From that moment on, Pat Jasper and the Texas Folk Life organization got their creative minds together and created an apprentice program, pairing me with an elder. Dr. Paredes was retired at that time, but he went into his office at UT. He was a radio DJ, songwriter, and poet from Brownsville, Texas. He served as a journalist and was in WWII. He became a student at UT in the late 1950s. His was a wealth of information. This man has a wonderful sense of telling the story of Mexicans living on the border.

HUDSON: So the term *Mexican American* is still appropriate.

HINOJOSA: Yes, and my mother did not like the word *Chicano*; she said it did not sound pretty. I grew up in the sixties, and both are OK with me. *Chicano* may be a bit more militant. I like *Latino*. It flows. *Hispanic* sounds Anglo. I am the youngest of thirteen, and we toss all the words around. *Tejano* is an interesting word and story. I was signed on a tour in 1994 for *Destiny's Gate*, a sweet country recording. My producer was also the president of the label, Jim Ed Norman, and he was a very brave man. He wanted us to go out on a limb. We decided to create a record that was bilingual and that touched on spiritual issues of both cultures.

It was not a Tejano record. It was more of a cultural blending. We recorded it live in a convent in San Antonio, now an art center. It's on the river downtown, across from WOAI. It has a beautiful chapel. We took a recording truck and moved into the chapel for two weeks. We did this for the sound as well as for the history. My record was about being inspired by Sor Juana Inés de la Cruz, the sixteenth-century Mexican nun—a woman who chose her life path to read and write.

HUDSON: I love handing over the twenty-peso note with her picture on it in Mexico. Here's Sor Juana.

HINOJOSA: Her poem is called "The First Dream," and that's why I titled the record what I titled it. And the "Labyrinth" came from Octavio Paz.

HUDSON: *Laberinto de Soledad, Labyrinth of Solitude*—a way of saying that the culture has a mask that no one else gets through.

HINOJOSA: Those were my two inspirations, and the way I wrote the record . . . well, I'm not really into weird stuff, but in one night of dreaming, I wrote eight songs, and they are the core songs on that record. The way they reflected off each other in Spanish was an amazing journey. It kind of took us all by surprise. I had the bilingual version in a few days.

The truck came in from LA, and I was honored they would do that. And Jim Ed came to San Antonio to produce the record and listed me as co-producer. We had some mariachis on the album, and Flaco. Accordion and mariachi blended in with keyboard and Spanish guitars. It has this kind of churchiness to it. Ethereal really. It has a lot of layers.

HUDSON: And the cover art was ethereal.

HINOJOSA: Butch Hancock did the photography, and I really liked the picture he took. It looked like an angel running through the convent. That was an amazing process, and everything went so smoothly. The record was set to come out in March 1996. What else happened that year? Selena died. Here I had a record in English and Spanish and made in Texas, but when I was interviewed then I had to explain what the record was not. It was not Tejano music. No one knew what Tejano was on the national platform, so everybody was making assumptions that everything Tejano was what Selena was doing. It was terrible timing, and what happened to her was horrible. I kept having to explain what it was not. The record unfortunately just died. It got great reviews. And it got me the concert at the White House, which was wonderful. But it caused me to be dropped from the record label. They wanted to release the Spanish version in Mexico on Warner Bros.

You mentioned coming back to Kerrville. For a lot of people who have a long history there, there is a sense of family, open arms, and acceptance. That crazy hippy-loving environment. It is so wonderful to see my son and daughter being adults there.

HUDSON: And the lovely spirit Dalis Allen brings. She is so inclusive.

HINOJOSA: Rod Kennedy was a great person with so many visions, and he was a very complicated man.

HUDSON: He loved you!

HINOJOSA: Someone told him I was playing at San Antonio College. I could not believe he was sitting there listening to me. I knew who he was and the reputation of that festival. We talked about music afterward. I told him I would love to play the festival, and he said, "Well, it's a songwriter's festival." And then he said, "Why don't you try your hand at songwriting?"

HUDSON: That's interesting. You're right in the middle of the Texas songwriting genre.

HINOJOSA: I have him to thank for that. Something about me starting to write. As soon as I opened that door, I realized I had a lot to write.

HUDSON: I love your new album, and I love the song "After the Fair." I am wondering why that pulls at me so. I wonder what you are saying that I am feeling!

HINOJOSA: I think the whole idea of "After the Fair" is complicated. It ties in that culture thing I was feeling in Germany—fitting in and not fitting in. A fair can represent a lot of things. It was a wild ride going to Germany, like a ride at the fair. I was in love, and everything was beautiful. Then the reality hit when two different people from two different cultures start breaking against each other. My American ideals were different; my expectations of what I was hoping for in the relationship were different. I thought we could go on loving within the commitment we made. I never had really considered the idea that men are from Mars and women are from Venus—apples and oranges. All these years, I was thinking apples, and he was looking at me thinking oranges.

I was fifty something, and he was in his late forties. I wanted a life mate, and he wanted more freedom. That became a problem for us, and I was feeling uncomfortable in Germany. I found myself alone a lot. I wrote the song earlier in Germany when a fair came to the area where I was living . . . where the Beatles did their music. It was the funkiest, highest-crime neighborhood in Germany, but I loved the multicultural flavor. There were a lot of Turkish people . . . and a big immigrant population.

I took German classes with immigrants from all over the world. I could be Mexican or American. I could hang out with the Latinos. Because I married a German, the law required one hundred hours in German [class]. I think that is a great idea. I loved it. I interacted with people from Pakistan, China, India, Afghanistan. I found a wide range of why people were taking classes. I was not there as a hardship case, but I wanted to do this as a courtesy to the country. These were the wonderful things that happened. The song is about fantasy and love—all those wonderful things. And there is a dark alley of the things I realized as well. The compromising. I never thought I would be coming back to Texas with my tail between my legs, but I did. I stayed on the ride too long at the fair! The last couple of years were tough.

HUDSON: And let's talk about your project now.

HINOJOSA: I am excited to work with Flaco. Coming back to Texas after a long time was hard. I lost a lot of momentum. But I know 2015 is going to be a good year with new creative work. I am making up for lost time. Chaos and upheaval were part of my return, but now I feel rooted in Austin. The new project is a Spanish record, about me interpreting beautiful songs from the past—songs that embrace Mexico's history as well as my parents' history . . . a lot of songs from the 1930s and 1940s. Songs from Lydia Mendoza. Everything from the border stuff: conjunto and *norteño*. And between the lines of all that, the beautiful timeless boleros—and *corridos*. I still have my cassette tapes from all my meetings with Dr. Paredes. I would go to his house with my guitar. He would play songs for me and tell me stories. Sing the *corridos*. All these pieces of culture from the border. The songs are the magic pieces. I did a bilingual children's record after working with him.

HUDSON: I love the fact that you've chosen to do this in Spanish.

HINOJOSA: Yes, getting out of myself as a songwriter. [She was a New

Folk winner at Kerrville after being inspired to write by Rod Kennedy.] I think it's glorious and beautiful to reinterpret songs I heard my mom sing when I was young. I knew about Santiago Jr. and Flaco from childhood on. That is who we heard in San Antonio. I am excited to work with them. Santiago is one of the kindest people to work with. We toured the borders and cultural museums together. And Flaco played on my album in 1989 with A&M, on the song "The Westside of Town." I told my Westside story. Since then, Flaco has played on many of my albums. He is such a creative man and such fun to work with. I am glad we are all older, seasoned, and I am ready to do this. People have been asking me for years and years to record more Spanish songs.

HUDSON: The statistics are that the Hispanic population in Texas and in this country is growing. The white culture has been the dominant voice, and that is changing. I think it is exciting for you to bring the language to more people with your music.

HINOJOSA: You know, Europeans start learning their second language when they are five. I don't know why we can't do that.

HUDSON: I love the language and how it feels in my mouth. I speak it when I visit Mexico, but I am not practicing enough to be fluent. Someday!

The party is starting at the Taste Wine and Art (at the Kirchman Gallery in Johnson City). So thank you for your time!

LETICIA "TISH" HINOJOSA performs both traditional folk songs and original works in both English and Spanish. The award-winning artist has released albums on several labels. She has lived and performed in Europe but calls Texas home.

Flaco Jiménez

A Lifetime of Achievement

We are here in the home of Flaco Jiménez in San Antonio, and in front of me is a giant seven-foot-long snakeskin. My father skinned snakes, and I teach mythology, so snakes have a lot of meaning for me. After taking a moment to admire and reflect, I was invited to sit down and start this lovely conversation. Flaco and I had met up many times, including one time at the Jimmie Rodgers Tribute in Kerrville years ago. Now this man was packing up to head to LA to accept a national heritage award, but he took time out to talk with me.

My colleague Chumbe Salinas set up her video to document the conversation. Flaco's open loving eyes are always inclusive when he is surrounded by fans after or before a show. I have witnessed this. And this intimate conversation at his house did not change anything; he was still warm and inclusive. He does not seem to be aware he is *the man* for so many musicians, friends, and family. He just does what he does.

HUDSON: So, tell me about the snakeskin.

JIMÉNEZ: Yeah, that's a rattlesnake—about seven feet long. I didn't kill it myself. It was a present from a friend.

HUDSON: In mythology, the snake can represent wisdom and transformation because it sheds its skin. A friend of mine, Hans Bauer, wrote the story "Anaconda," and he did a lot of research on snakes that I find fascinating.

JIMÉNEZ: Well, in Texas, we say a rattlesnake's just a snake.

HUDSON: We don't want to talk about all the Flaco material that is covered so well and about our experiences together. One of them was Montreux, Switzerland. I was there working on my first book and received a press pass, and you gave me a backstage pass. Oscar Tellez (RIP) was hanging out, along with Lou Ann Barton. We were sitting backstage with Tony Garnier (bass player for Bob Dylan), and next to us was a closed door. Dylan was behind that door. They tapped you on a shoulder and said, "Dylan wants to talk with you." So you and Oscar went behind that closed door, and Oscar returned with a signed Swiss note for me. I still have it

JIMÉNEZ: Yeah, I thought I was going to be rejected. So many people did not know that I knew Dylan. But then they talked to Dylan, and he wanted to see me. Someone was in there with him, ironing his stage clothes. He invited me to get up onstage with him.

HUDSON: I was on the front row, and you joined him, playing "On the Borderline."

JIMÉNEZ: Yes, that is one of his favorites, which I recorded with Ry Cooder. And we did a movie, *The Border*, with Jack Nicholson. It's a real good, nice song.

HUDSON: All the stories about you comment on how you have crossed over with the accordion into rock and other genres. I was in college at TCU in 1963, and I discovered Bob Dylan; Willie Nelson; Peter, Paul, and Mary; and Leonard Cohen. They moved my heart. I would love to hear your Dylan experience. I know you recorded with him.

JIMÉNEZ: When I first met Dylan, it was [doing] a record that Doug Sahm was recording. Not the Quintet, but Doug Sahm and Band. Doug decided to get Dr. John and Augie and Dylan and Fathead Newman to play. At that time, I was here in San Antonio, but I did not know about the project he was doing. Doug called me from New York, and he invited me to come sit in with them. I said, "Man. . . . What am I going to record?" I just said, "OK, I'll just chance it and see what I can blend in with the project. Actually, it *was* the Sir Douglas Band, and Dylan was sitting in.

HUDSON: A kind of Texas gumbo there!

JIMÉNEZ: It was a big enchilada with different flavors. It was at Atlantic Records; recorded in New York. There were a couple of songs for the accordion. They chose the songs, so I just tried to sneak in there and add some trills or something. It made the accordion blend real nice on what they did. Oh man.

HUDSON: Were you aware of who Dylan was?

JIMÉNEZ: Of course, I knew the name. Everybody knows Dylan. I wanted to meet Bob Dylan—everybody does. So I said I would go.

HUDSON: You are known as the ambassador for the accordion, the one who took the accordion into new worlds. One of the articles I read called you Tex Mex, conjunto, *norteño*, rock and roll. The only genre not there was psychedelic. [Laughter]

JIMÉNEZ: OR rap.

HUDSON: We know the German connection and the history. I would love to talk with you about going into those other worlds. Was that deliberate or just the way the universe handed it to you?

JIMÉNEZ: Well, I started listening to different kinds of radio stations when I was a teenager. I tuned in to different stations, and one was KNBT in New Braunfels, and it was polka music. I was acquainted since I learned this from my dad. I turned to country music. Hank Williams was singing "Your Cheatin' Heart," and the Cowboy Jamboree was on KONO. There were three stations I used to tune in to. I was just zig-zagging on those three stations. My dream was to be a part of those kinds of music with the accordion—to blend in with the accordion. And then rock and roll came, and I got into that. I did some stuff with different guys. I tried to get bits and pieces from different music.

HUDSON: Some of that was intentional.

JIMÉNEZ: Yes, I wanted to reach out.

HUDSON: Let's talk about challenges and surprises. If you look at Dylan or Leonard now, the pathway looks smooth, but we know better. Was there a time you struggled?

JIMÉNEZ: In some ways, I thought they would not accept me. Maybe they don't like what I want to do. But, it worked out pretty good. [Laughter] I was challenged in some ways by not being sure I could do it. But I was not stopped. I kept touring and just trying to do the best. Blend in with some ways that would fit. There's different things you can do with different artists. You can't do the same riffs. You have to create riffs for each style and each artist.

HUDSON: I think that's about listening.

JIMÉNEZ: And feeling. The soul of what you want to do.

HUDSON: I just heard about our energy field in a yoga class—how we feel each other. And a horse has an energy field that goes out a mile and a half. Interesting, as I have always had horses and have one now at my house. His name is Spirit. And I know musicians on the stage feel it too.

JIMÉNEZ: Yes, when you are on the stage playing, you automatically get into it. You improvise whatever comes to your mind. But you have to be careful to play something that fits. What helps a lot is the audience—an audience that is responding. That gives you more energy to let it all out. People screaming.

HUDSON: I tell my students they can make me a better teacher by responding like an audience.

JIMÉNEZ: Yes, that's the same thing. They can help you out. And vice versa. When I am playing, I feel like one of the audience. That's how I feel. I picture myself in the audience and look at myself playing.

HUDSON: It has always moved my heart to watch you play. I was in Austin and saw young Sahm, the Texas Tornados. I would love to talk about surprises along the way. Things that really pleased you.

JIMÉNEZ: Dylan inviting me to sit in at Montreux was not planned at all. The same thing with Willie Nelson not too long ago. That was surprising. Actually, we were in a hangout where I used to go, having a few beers, four guys. I knew that Willie was playing there, but we didn't have no passes or a plan to go. We had our little party at Ruben's Place, my hangout on Highway 35. One of my friends said, "Why don't we go see if we can get into the Willie show?" We didn't have tickets, but this guy went to the gate and told someone to send a message to Willie that Flaco was there. Then we got the passes to go straight to the bus. He started the show, but there was no plan made to sit in with Willie. I stayed on the bus.

All of a sudden, some guy comes running, saying, "Willie wants you onstage." Luckily, I had my accordion with me. I didn't know what song. He started with "Blue Eyes Crying in the Rain," so I set in with that. That was a surprise.

HUDSON: When I saw you at the Backyard in August, you were with the Texas Tornados. It was quite a wonderful Hispanic Heritage event. Ruben V was there, and Los Lonely Boys. I enjoyed seeing you play there. I want to give you the chance to talk about the heritage and what matters. Of course, Texas was Mexico at one time.

JIMÉNEZ: I was born here, and my dad was born here . . . and my granddad. Three generations. I dropped out of school, as there was no law to keep you in school—but with dad's permission because when I was going to school instead of doing the work, I was writing the songs. I was learning. I was not making good grades in school. He said, "Son, if you don't want to go to school, I'm not going to torture you at all. Do you have some idea about being a professional musician? I am going to let you do what you want." Of course, he wanted me to stay in school. He knew that I had something that I could survive with: music.

HUDSON: We can look back on that and say that was great. A good dad story.

JIMÉNEZ: But education is really, really important. I wanted the music.

HUDSON: What about with your own family?

JIMÉNEZ: I always tell them to go to school. That is the main thing for my family.

HUDSON: Do you consider yourself an ambassador for the music?

JIMÉNEZ: If they say I am an ambassador, I'll take it. I am talking about my education. At home, we always spoke Spanish. My mother used to speak a little English. I speak broken English and broken Spanish. Spanglish, perhaps. But I get around just fine. And I can communicate with both cultures.

HUDSON: Asking people to talk about their culture is like asking a fish to talk about water. I am outside the culture, and I love it so much. Of course, I love many cultures.

JIMÉNEZ: If you diversify life, you can get along well with people. I love Cajun music, blues, country, and respect all kinds of music. Different styles and cultures try their best to do the best they can.

HUDSON: Are there any specific descriptions you want to give me for the Hispanic culture? Specifically, stories of Texas and Mexico—this Tex Mex connection.

JIMÉNEZ: Well, I would say that I don't really zero in and describe the cultures. I put them all together. Life is like a rainbow in music. Any color you want—it's right there. You can choose whatever you want. When I recorded with Santana, I did some other rhythms.

HUDSON: I do see myself as a global citizen.

JIMÉNEZ: So do I.

HUDSON: I have my students write about Texas music. I used your Smithsonian recording with Max Baca, and the students wrote some wonderful responses on how they felt listening. What about you and songwriting?

JIMÉNEZ: Actually, the majority of songs on that album are my dad's songs. Traditional roots. A simple way of playing like my dad used to do. I'm just an accordion player, and I don't do much writing. Oh, I have written a few, but I don't see myself that way. The songs make sense, but still, if you ain't got it, you ain't got it—as far as writing.

HUDSON: Ray Price once said to me that all his original songs sounded alike and lived in a box at home. He sang the songs written by others.

JIMÉNEZ: In my accordion sets, I don't phrase the same thing twice the same way. If you hear a record, there's a different phrase of accordion in every song. I listen to others, and if they have the same pattern of phrasing, I change mine. And I respect them too.

HUDSON: It's like jazz, perhaps.

JIMÉNEZ: Improvisations. You satisfy the audience too.

HUDSON: I am reminded of an early Conjunto Festival I attended where I met Chris Strachowitz, a man from California here documenting our music. He introduced me to Narciso Martínez and Valerio Longoria. And last year I was there when you and Santiago Jr. played. You have a project right now, but you and Santiago Jr. are going to record together. I was at Carnitas Uruapan, and I heard about a tribute to your dad.

JIMÉNEZ: It's almost finished right now. We got together and decided to record my dad's songs. The style of my brother is exactly like my dad. It is like playing with my dad. I remember from way back when I recorded with my dad. I sang with him too.

HUDSON: Beautiful full circle here. That moves me. Let's end the conversation with a story about what's ahead. . . .

JIMÉNEZ: Well, I'm not going to retire, but I have slowed down for a while. I would say I would start with my first dream from when I was young. I had the dream to play accordion up to now. There's my dream. Keep on squeezing that box.

FLACO (LEONARDO) JIMÉNEZ began playing the two-button accordion with his father's band as a child and made his first recording in 1955. The Grammy Award winner has toured and recorded with multiple artists.

Gill Jiménez

His Father's Son

I attend the Conjunto Festival in San Antonio, with the encouragement from Chumbe Salinas and her video camera. She points to Gill, saying, "That is someone you should know. Flaco's son." Yes, Chumbe is a big Flaco fan and accompanied me on my early interview with him to document it. Gill had a stand at the festival, and after our conversation, I purchased a yellow-and-black T-shirt advertising his music. He was heading out for a tour, and I could see how very proud he was of his dad. Flaco played this festival too. Gill's enthusiasm for the music was evident as he took over the stage. And the crowd loved him.

G. JIMÉNEZ: Well, actually, Kathleen, first of all, I want to thank you all for sharing your time with me, interviewing me for this beautiful project that you're working on. Yes, I am the son of the legend Flaco Jiménez. There are a lot of people who are used to hearing Flaco with his type of style of music. When I came out, of course, my style is a little bit different. People don't know me yet; they didn't know yet who I really was. They would say, "Well, how come you didn't follow your dad's codes?" I said, "You know what? I got too much respect for my dad to even try and copy him or even to be a Flaco Jiménez, because I'll never be a Flaco Jiménez." I adore that man to the fullest, and I have respect for him as a son and as an artist. I just did my own thing, being a songwriter in full. I had to tackle it on my own. I didn't have no choice.

HUDSON: I love what you're saying about following your own path and honoring the tradition that supports you at the same time, and I know you told me yesterday that you even got a call from your dad telling you that he was proud of you.

G. JIMÉNEZ: Yes, he was. I get nervous when he calls. He calls me early in the morning. I was like, "OK, Dad. Yeah. OK." He just said, "*Mijo*, I have been getting called. You got so awesome, and I'm proud of you." I'm opening up the Conjunto Festival for the time here in San Antonio,

Texas. It was a beautiful feeling, hearing it from him. He knows. What's more than him telling me that? I said, "Oh yes."

HUDSON: So your journey, is there a certain point when you picked up the music, or was it just part of your life forever?

G. JIMÉNEZ: Well, yes. As a matter of fact, I started when I was eight years old, actually playing drums. My dad had me onstage playing with him, sitting with us, me and my brother, David. He would put us onstage with him already at that age. I remember one time, I would see the other people going up to him, and I said, "I like this." I remember telling him, "Dad, you know what, when I grow up, I want to be just like you." And then he goes, "Well, you know what, the same way I busted my behind to be where I'm at right now, you're going to bust your behind too." I always kept that in my mind. I never had the courage to even ask him how to teach me how to write music, play music, and stuff. So I had to learn it on my own.

HUDSON: Very interesting. What are some special moments for you in this journey? This festival, you opened it. You opened it on a very special night: sons of the legends. What I gather just from being at this event is how important family is.

G. JIMÉNEZ: Exactly. To me, for the first time, I was like, "Wow, I don't want to. So you're putting me up first to open up the festival?" And I go, "That's a big thing. That's a huge thing."

HUDSON: It's a huge thing.

G. JIMÉNEZ: And then, I'm like, "Well, OK, why not just do it, man? Why not?" I even get the chills right now by just saying it because it was my first time. People from all over the world are here, from California. You name it. They're all here.

HUDSON: Tokyo.

G. JIMÉNEZ: Yeah, Tokyo, they're here. They're going to see something for the first time opening up the big Conjunto Festival. So I did it; I gave it my best.

HUDSON: How did you pick the music?

G. JIMÉNEZ: I'm like my dad. He does a versatile kind of thing. I didn't want to go a nostalgic kind of way, like I play like my father, but I'm not Flaco. Flaco has got his own style. Today, I'm just looking forward to his performance. He's ready. You will see the difference. You've heard about him already.

HUDSON: Right. Well, you're definitely original.

G. JIMÉNEZ: Yeah, exactly. Thank you.

HUDSON: So family—you talked a little about family. I know people talk about the importance of family in this culture. You've already alluded to that, but is there anything else you want to say about the power of family?

G. JIMÉNEZ: Well, being there's five generations on the JIMÉNEZ tree, there's my great-great-grandfather Patricio, and I could imagine how he was. He was famous . . .

HUDSON: Yes, in history.

G. JIMÉNEZ: Yes. And then from there, my grandfather, of course. I did meet him. Beautiful. I got all his memory—beautiful memories that are unforgettable memories and I got to experience with my dad. He used to take us as little kids to his house, my dad, playing with him and everything. Then my uncle, Santiago, who was here yesterday as well. And then me. Actually, five generations and continuing.

And then, as far as my current project is concerned, it was all Tejano. It was an experience that I really had with this one because my dad had asked me if I was working on my project already for this year and I go, "Yeah, Dad. I've got it closed off. I'm not going to the studio." He looks at me, but for some reason or another, I kind of felt like he wanted to tell me something. I remember we're having breakfast, and he goes, "Do you know what? Come here, son." So we went to a studio, and that's when he told me—he opened up a golden vault of music that he had, songs that he recorded with my grandfather when he was a kid. That never came out. So he goes, "You know what, here is material that I want you to choose from. But that's called *conjunto*, *mijo*." And then I go, "Wow. OK, Dad." Like I said, I can't believe it to this day. It was a beautiful feeling. I said, "You know what, Dad? I'm going to do it."

As I sat there with him, he played them, and I could hear them—that raw voice with my grandfather's voice and his while recording. And then I could actually hear it in my kind of style. I go, "You know what . . . ?" And I started choosing this one, this one, this one. OK, I'm going to work on this one, this one, this one, this one. The next day, when I had the copy ready, I was even nervous to take it to him because he was going to hear the real deal. And I go, "Oh man, I don't know. OK, well, you know, constructive criticism or whatever, Dad. . . . If you hear something, let me know because that's the way I'm going to learn more." And I knew. . . .

As soon as he put it on, he was listening to it, and that day, his eyes got watery because those were his dad's songs that I recorded now; they never came out. And then he goes, "You know what, *mijo*?" He looks at me, right? I go, "OK, Dad. Let me have it, let me have it." He goes, "*Mijo*, that's a beautiful project . . . ," which means, "You did it." So he's real proud.

HUDSON: This is the beginning of a tour for you with that project?

G. JIMÉNEZ: Yes. This project before I started here in Rosedale, San Antonio. Well, right now, we're planning to take it to the California area. My manager is working on Phoenix.

HUDSON: So, it'll be Southwest.

G. JIMÉNEZ: Southwest, yes. But if it was up to me, Kathleen, I'd take the music to Africa. I want the whole world to hear that music.

HUDSON: Well, there is a global frame for what you're doing. I don't see this as a limit to the audience, don't you think? I mean, this music transcends. A friend of mine, Etain Scott, was here from Ireland. She looked at the crowd, and she listened to music, and she said, "This reminds me of dances in Ireland." She felt it sounded like Irish music.

G. JIMÉNEZ: That's what my dad tells me, because my dad has been touring Europe and all that. He told me the same thing. It's something that . . . it's really that they're all united and they just love that music.

HUDSON: Let's talk about the writing you do.

G. JIMÉNEZ: Well, the writing—my songwriting, it's so fun because I don't make things up. I'm like, I could write anything. I base it on experiences through my walk of life like I can hear a conversation that they're telling me. I might be in that conversation. I really feel it in my heart. I'm just listening, and if I feel it, I just can't wait to go home and just start writing what I experienced. I might be driving, thinking of something beautiful or thinking of something that I really feel. I go, "Yes, that's what I feel." So I go back home, and I just want to write it out. All my original.

HUDSON: Some of the writers that I've spoken with talk about the power of language. They just hear a phrase. For example, when I hear "past and present," my imagination goes to some point in my life. But I don't write songs. Do you ever get hooked by language or a phrase, or is it more the story of the idea?

G. JIMÉNEZ: It's the story and the idea.

HUDSON: Yeah. It's different for different people. Do you have any kind of ritual or discipline? Do you write at a particular time?

G. JIMÉNEZ: At night.

HUDSON: At night. See, I'm early morning.

G. JIMÉNEZ: Before I go to sleep, if I have something in my mind, I just want to. . . . Sometimes, I'm even asleep, and this has happened to me so many times in a dream, in a dream where I'm really having a beautiful dream.

HUDSON: Go ahead. A dream about what?

G. JIMÉNEZ: One time, I had a dream about this beautiful lady who I haven't seen, and I don't even know who she was. But our dream was so beautiful that I just—I put it on the title. I titled it "*Mi Almohada.*" Because when I woke up, I was squeezing the pillow and I thought it was her.

HUDSON: Well, definitely, dreams are a source for a lot of literature, for sure. Are there any ideas you have about the world or about life or about feelings that you really want to express? Are there some of your own personal ideas you carry around with you that come out in the songs?

G. JIMÉNEZ: Well, yes, all the time. If I were to ever fall in love again, that would be . . .

HUDSON: It's a good thing. We do that from time to time.

G. JIMÉNEZ: There are many things that run through my mind. As soon as I feel ideas, but real [ones], where I'm not making anything up—they're a real deal. That's what I like to write.

HUDSON: And you've written some love songs?

G. JIMÉNEZ: Yes, I have. "*Rosa tan Hermosa*"—that's the title of one song.

HUDSON: Let's talk just a little bit about this language and words.

G. JIMÉNEZ: Tex Mex. That is funny, the word *Tex Mex*. Flaco was a founder of that word—the main one. He's the one that created the word *Tex Mex*. I'm under my own record label. I said, "What, if we were trying to look for a title, it's Tex Mex that you created. My regular label is going to be named Flex Mex. It's like a flexible Mexican."

HUDSON: Flexible. So, do you have any particular way you deal with disappointments or challenges?

G. JIMÉNEZ: Well, to be honest, it's like Dad says: "Son, the one thing we cannot do is please the whole world. We cannot please the whole world. As long as you know and you're doing what you love the most—you do it well." If not, he would have told me already, "*Mijo*, you got to stay instead." My dad is like that. I have really experienced some like that. Criticism is going to be everywhere.

HUDSON: So you have a really naturally positive, optimistic outlook, right?

G. JIMÉNEZ: Yes, I do.

HUDSON: Are you born with that?

G. JIMÉNEZ: Yeah, I was born with that.

HUDSON: Because I was too. It's just a story in my family about me.

G. JIMÉNEZ: The word *negative* doesn't apply in my book.

HUDSON: I carry that too, and I didn't have to learn it.

G. JIMÉNEZ: My dad says, "*Mijo*, there's always a solution for everything."

GILL JIMÉNEZ is the son of Flaco Jiménez, who began playing music as a child and dedicated his debut CD, *Amor y Dolor*, "to my papa." His songwriting reflects his personal experiences and culture. His band tours and performs at major festivals.

Santiago Jiménez Jr.

He Carries His Father

It is January 13, 2015, in San Antonio, Texas. I am talking to Santiago Jiménez Jr., and we are in his studio surrounded by his music, his many awards, and a letter from the president. I have just been to Carnitas Uruapan to hear his regular Sunday morning show there. What a step back in time to people sharing food and music. Then again, maybe this is not a step back in time in a place like San Antonio.

HUDSON: Let's talk about some things that really matter to you in your career. Maybe things that inspired you? And something maybe people don't know about you?

S. JIMÉNEZ: Well, you know my grandfather Don Patricio; he was a musician in the 1800s. And when my father was young, he used to take my dad to New Braunfels to hear the German music—the oom-pah-pah polkas. We are talking about the twenties. My grandfather played at houses in the neighborhood. They would get all the furniture out and play inside in the living room. They would play from 7:00 p.m. till morning. I never saw it, but my father would tell me all these stories. He learned how to play the accordion from hearing these polkas. My dad started playing accordion late in the 1930s. Then he started composing, and he had about 150 songs. I was six years old when I would hear my father play the accordion. I would sit down by him on the sofa. I was always addicted to his music.

Well, Flaco was five years older, and he started before me. And he started playing like my dad, but as he progressed—he played more and more modern. He did not keep my father's style. He played more, heavier. Flaco got very famous. He is still famous! I remember one time, Flaco was playing in my house, and he would tell me to go into another room because he was practicing. I told him once I was going to be better than him.

Flaco started doing his conjunto and getting a big name, but I picked up the accordion from my father's closet. I never had one that was mine.

My mother would say that my father would get mad. By the time I put it back, I had untuned his accordion. He would get mad. He would play Friday, Saturday, Sunday. He would check it and see it was untuned. He would blame Flaco, but Flaco knew how to tune an accordion at that time, so he would tune it. But one afternoon I took the accordion from the closet, and [my father] was behind my back. I started crying because I thought he would get mad. He told me to play it right or don't play it at all! I started crying and just put it away. The following times, I knew he would not get mad.

I always wanted to be like him—to play like my father. It was in the blood. When I was fifteen, I started playing more. And by sixteen I knew how to play. I was forming my little band. I would play at birthday parties. But Flaco was already a big name, and Dad was professional. By seventeen, I was already professional. I played like my dad. My first album I did in 1960 was with Flaco. He played *bajo* with me. We recorded some of my father's songs. We did old style traditional—a three piece. Toby Torres played bass.

HUDSON: How does three piece fit into the history of traditional?

S. JIMÉNEZ: It's original conjunto. No drums. And sometimes my father just played with accordion and guitar only. They didn't have no bass. Then my father found this man who played upright bass, Ismael Gonzalez.

HUDSON: So your father was creating a certain sound. He was the first *acordeonista* who brought conjunto to San Antonio. There were other musicians who played accordion: Valerio Longoria, Pedro Ayala, and Narciso Martínez. They started in the 1940s and 1950s.

S. JIMÉNEZ: I told my dad his music would always be alive because I would be doing it for him. I have never changed my style in fifty-one years of playing his music.

HUDSON: That is a beautiful purpose. I just lost my dad in May, and I realize what I keep alive for him. We both love teaching. And I got to tell him before he died. Very special.

S. JIMÉNEZ: My father heard some of my recordings. Me and Flaco recorded for Disco Corona. We did two forty-fives. We recorded one of my father's songs and a polka. Flaco and I were both singing. Corona

Records put me and Flaco Jiménez on one song. Dad [listened to our recordings and] said, "That is not you; that is me." He insisted. He got mad when I told him it wasn't him. Two weeks later, he came to me and said, "You play like me."

HUDSON: I was reading Hector Saldana's story on you and Flaco recording here and doing your dad's songs.

S. JIMÉNEZ: Well, I went to Flaco's house, drinking some beer. I told my son to take me there. I wanted to go see my brother. We went over there, and my son-in-law went with me. They took pictures. He said, "Make a CD together." Then Flaco called me and asked me to make a CD with him doing Dad's songs. It is almost finished. No artwork yet. We want to finish the recording first.

HUDSON: Let's talk about some songs. I do love Spanish. *"Me Gusta," "Paloma Negra,"* and *"Volver, Volver."*

S. JIMÉNEZ: Those songs fit with me because I play them on my accordion. *"Volver, Volver"* got very famous with the Anglos. Flaco recorded it with Ry Cooder. Vicente Jiménez made it famous. Everybody sings it. It is international.

HUDSON: You have that lead on the accordion.

S. JIMÉNEZ: It is something I have created.

HUDSON: When I saw you Sunday at North Frio Cantina and Grill, you took that lead and held that note.

S. JIMÉNEZ: I was letting my accordion cry with that melody. All my music has to be my father's style. If I play *"Paloma Negra,"* I am going to do it my way.

HUDSON: That is what creative artists do! You take reality, it goes through you, and it becomes original.

S. JIMÉNEZ: I might do a little extra arrangement, but I do my father's style. I did some recordings, and everybody said it was Flaco's style. But it is me. His style is not for me. I would rather people say, "He plays like his dad."

HUDSON: Let's talk about songs.

S. JIMÉNEZ: I don't have any special songs. If I had one, I would include all eight hundred songs I have recorded. There might be a song that

Flaco and my dad recorded. It's a very beautiful song: "*Viva Felice.*" It makes me cry; I love it. It would hit me right in my heart. So I recorded it. I don't play it all the time; I let it rest. It is a sentimental song for me. I play it with power. The audience is asking for what they want. "*Viva Seguin*" is fun to play.

HUDSON: I know there is a lot of dancing when you play. What about the listening audience? Do you prefer to play for a dance?

S. JIMÉNEZ: No, I like to do concerts. I like people to sit down with no interruptions. That's where I get nervous. They are hearing you. A lot of people want to hear your story as well as the music. They are paying attention. I tell them a little bit of my story. I have to work with that. When you hear people clapping, you got them. And when you see a lot of people dancing, you want to play more. When they are sitting down listening, you can find yourself thinking, "Are they enjoying this?" When I see those reactions of people when they feel good, I feel good. There are a lot of good musicians who do not play by the heart. There's a lot of jealousy around Flaco and me. Lots of gossip. It's not our fault. We have been working all our lives to do this. Our heart is the music we pass to you. We play because it is our job, and it makes people happy.

HUDSON: How do you describe your music?

S. JIMÉNEZ: I consider myself Tex Mex conjunto. I don't really feel a connection with Mexico. I was born here in Texas, and my grandfather, Don Patricio, was from Eagle Pass, and my grandmother was from Montclova, Mexico. I call myself Latino American. But I do consider myself Tex Mex because we are near the border. *Conjunto* is a Spanish word for group.

HUDSON: Let's talk about an experience that really lit you up.

S. JIMÉNEZ: I was just local here in San Antonio, and I used to work for the school district many years ago when I was young. I used to play Friday through Sunday, but I wanted to be a full-time musician. One time they called me at lunchtime when I was at school. "Somebody called you from St. Louis." They wanted to hire me, but I said, "You are looking for Flaco." I could not believe it. I had never flown in a plane. From there, Carlos Chavez in El Paso called me. He started hiring me; then the Kerrville Folk Music Festival hired me.

HUDSON: I remember talking to Rod Kennedy about you, and he loved you.

S. JIMÉNEZ: Yes, yes. It was great to play there. And the audiences were so good. Flaco did a show at Kerrville once, but Rod Kennedy knew about me, and he got in touch with me. I played there seven years in a row. And he would hire Butch Hancock and many others I met there. Allen Damron too. Rod became a very close friend of mine. He loved my show, and people were responding. He would give me good hospitality.

HUDSON: Were you able to integrate your family with your work? Was that ever a challenge?

S. JIMÉNEZ: I have been married eight times. And I have been married to my wife for sixteen years. I have two girls and two boys. The reason I was not staying with my wives was they did not want me to keep playing. I would rather have a divorce than give that up. Nobody's going to take my music. My wife right now supports me. I'm going to be seventy-one, and she is going to be seventy-four. We don't have time to be saying, "I don't want you to go." She knows that, and I do.

HUDSON: What is something you want to do now. You have played festivals in Europe—I know that.

S. JIMÉNEZ: My dream is to keep playing for twenty more years. I am going to go day by day. I don't know what is going to happen in the future. As long as I can play, I can play here in the states, but I don't want to travel overseas anymore.

HUDSON: As we come to the end of this conversation, is there something you would like people to know that is not covered in all these stories you've shared?

S. JIMÉNEZ: I want people everywhere to know that I am still alive and still kicking. Promoters and businessmen. I want to do the shows people would like to have. I'm not going to disappoint nobody.

SANTIAGO JIMÉNEZ JR. is the son of Santiago Jiménez Sr. and the grandson of Patricio Jiménez, who taught him the accordion. He is a Grammy nominee, a National Heritage Fellowship award recipient, and a National Medal of Arts recipient.

Stephanie Urbina Jones

Mariachis Make Me Cry

I have been talking to Stephanie Urbina Jones for years. She has played the Schreiner University coffeehouse, visited my class, and performed at the tribute to Hispanic Heritage at the Texas Heritage Music Festival each September. In 2017 she was the featured guest following years of Max Baca playing the showcase. She was also interviewed for my second book on the women of Texas music. The following conversation took place during one of her visits to Schreiner—Cinco de Mayo, 2015. I had heard her song "Manuel's Destiny" at a house concert in Fredericksburg, and I knew I wanted to include the lyrics in this book (which appear at the end of part 2). I knew we needed another conversation.

Then I had the opportunity to recommend her for the Magic Town Music Festival in San Miguel de Allende, with my foundation as a sponsor. Maia Williamson heard her, became a fan, and invited her to the San Miguel de Allende Literary Conference in February. Stephanie and I were both faculty in 2016. I heard her workshop on songwriting, and the response from the audience was overwhelming as she told her story. I was invited into Joe Trevino's Blue Cat Studio when she added Michael Guerra's accordion to her mariachi country album. She played a cut from that same album with a mariachi band from El Paso. She is now also conducting shamanic workshops and presenting her music to new audiences in the international arena.

HUDSON: How do you label yourself and your music? You cross so many boundaries. After reading Dagoberto Gilb and Sandra Cisneros, after talking with Tish Hinojosa about language, I became aware that the specific language of talking about this music varied from person to person.

URBINA JONES: I call myself a Hispanic American country rock artist, but I am always trying to find words to describe what I do. Sometimes it is Latina country rock. I am always celebrating Hispanic heritage, since that is the core of my career and my calling. Latina and Hispanic resonate the most with me.

HUDSON: I want you to respond to a quote by Dagoberto Gilb in his collection of essays: He reminds us that Texas was Mexico at one time. So the word *Tejano* was a word that defined a person living here.

URBINA JONES: I resonate with that word, but I don't call myself that because my own style of writing is hybrid; it is not Tejano. I am finding a new way to express this culture in music. Many times, I say proudly I am Mexican American. In the beginning of my career, I was in San Antonio recording with a thirteen-piece mariachi band. You can't *not* be aware that that is a very important aspect of my career.

HUDSON: I realized at a presentation I was giving at a high school in Lubbock that as I talked about the word *Latina* . . . I was actually describing you.

URBINA JONES: I was born in Texas and didn't know my father growing up, and my last name was Jones. I didn't look Hispanic. When I started waking up to my heritage, I started creating myself as that look as well—the long, dark hair and red lips I saw on the posters. They carried a passion that I felt. I was born on the west side of San Antonio. My mom moved to Fredericksburg, and I didn't know my biological father until I was eighteen. I was told to not tell anyone I was Mexican American. It was small-town Texas. I felt it was a secret I carried around. I felt shame around it as a kid. I was seeing the other kids who did not have the opportunities [I did]. When I hooked up with my dad at eighteen, he took me to Mexico. I fell in love with this culture, these people, and their values. I knew I had to rewrite this story to help others appreciate what I was feeling about this culture.

HUDSON: We just shared a music festival in the rain in San Miguel de Allende. I was so inspired by your performance. Seeing you sing there, after we had talked about the culture we both love . . . I want to hear you talk about San Miguel.

URBINA JONES: Back about the same time I was playing with the mariachis, my grandmother, Manuel's daughter, took my hands as she was walking between the worlds. And she said, "*M'ija*, you will be a *mensaje* for our people." At the time I was writing songs, and I did not think I could do this. But when my grandmother spoke, I listened. After she died, I wanted to know more about her culture. My father sent me to

San Miguel de Allende. I was supposed to go for three weeks, and I end-ed up staying for three months. I was staying in a cinder-block home with a family while I was going to school, and when I walked in I said, "I can't stay here." But when I left, I realized I never wanted to leave. I felt so much love from the people. It was there I met these musicians who did not speak English, and I barely spoke Spanish, but we spoke music. We wrote *"Revolucion en mi Corazón"* there. I had the vision then of what was mine to do as an artist. Then that was it. I started writing with that in mind, and I haven't stopped. And I love it. I love that being from Texas, we cover such rich musician grounds. I started out in jazz and blues. I am a country artist. But when I sing something with a Latin music, something happens inside me.

HUDSON: You just had a country song go to the top in the finals of *The Voice*.

URBINA JONES: Yes, I am in Texas every year doing the Spirit of Christ-mas Tour, thanks to THMF [Texas Heritage Music Foundation], play-ing the nursing homes in the area to bring the spirit of Christmas. It is holy and exhausting and wonderful. I had just come home, and I got a Facebook message asking if that was my song with Blake and Craig. I asked, "Who?" And they said Blake Shelton on *The Voice* gave a song that I wrote to a guy he was coaching named Craig Wayne Boyd. Boyd had 2,500 other songs, and he chose my song. I had pitched that song to Blake sixteen years ago, and he never cut it. Then Craig won *The Voice*, and on December 17 he was on *The Today Show*, *The Tonight Show*, and *Ellen*. On Christmas Eve they released it, and it went number one on the Country Billboard charts. That was a gift—a dream come true.

HUDSON: That's a real presence in country music for you. My description of Texas music is often the metaphor of a tapestry where the music is woven from many diverse threads. I think while you make a statement about one culture, you definitely cross many boundaries, which makes you pure Texas music. Los Lonely Boys use the term "Texican," and Wil-lie plays on the song with them. Let's talk about challenges, now.

URBINA JONES: I see the way audiences react to what I am carrying, and not having a label partner or business partner to help me carry my vi-sion is a challenge. Finding the right people to take this to market—

that has been a challenge, and it gives me the freedom to create. I do the booking, flights, management, publishing, songs, and all! It is challenging to feel like, "I can't do this anymore." But I move forward and keep taking the next step.

HUDSON: I face the same thing. When I started the Texas Heritage Music Foundation in 1987, I kept looking for partnership, had different boards, and asked for help. For some reason, thirty years later, I am still the volunteer director with no salary. Curious. But I had freedom to create according to my vision. We celebrate the birthday of Jimmie Rodgers September 8 in Kerrville with Jimmie Dale Gilmore, and that is our thirtieth celebration. I retire as director in December with the programs I have created—coffeehouse, Texas Heritage Music Day—living on in the arms of Schreiner University where I teach. Exciting times for me. Let's talk about a song you really love, the history behind it, but also honoring you as a writer . . . as performer and messenger for the culture.

URBINA JONES: Songs lead me; they know where I am going before I do. I am learning to trust that. As I personally struggle with things in my life, I begin writing. The songs amaze me. I can't even believe sometimes they come through me, and I am so lucky to have them come through me. I had a conversation with Dad at lunch about our family being associated with Pancho Villa, and I feel sometimes like I'm downloading experiences from generations in a very compact way. Do you ever feel that way? That it is just coming through, and you just catch it?

HUDSON: Absolutely. That just happened today when I was writing about beauty at a story circle group of women. I was surprised at what I wrote with that prompt.

URBINA JONES: I always discover things about myself in the writing.

HUDSON: I want the words to "Manuel's Destiny" to appear in this book. Thank you for sharing your beautiful spirit. I use your songs and your story in my college classroom, writing about Texas music. Now onward to celebrating Cinco de Mayo.

October 2, 2018 (my birthday), Stephanie performed at the Grand Ole Opry, a childhood dream of hers. She performed with a mariachi group . . . another dream. She is a dreamer, and she leads shamanic journeys in a dreaming house in Mexico. She's also playing Gstaad, a big country music festival in Switzerland. Her new CD, *Tularosa*, received lots of press for her innovative interpretation of classic country songs using mariachi players. This woman *is* a dream.

STEPHANIE URBINA JONES has always been influenced by mariachi music, but she has embraced country, folk, and traditional Mexican styles too. She has performed at the Grand Ole Opry and at festivals all over the world as a solo artist and with members of the Nelson family and Vince Gill and the Time Jumpers.

Josh Baca (Photo courtesy of Hans Bauer)

Max Baca of Los Texmaniacs (Photo courtesy of Hans Bauer)

Rick del Castillo (Photo courtesy of the artist)

Ernie Durawa on drums
(Photo courtesy of the artist)

Ernie Durawa and Kathleen Hudson (Photo by author)

Linda Escobar (Photo courtesy Jorge Flores)

Rosie Flores (R.) and Patricia Vonne (Photo courtesy of Rosie Flores)

David Garza
(Photo courtesy of the artist)

Henry Gomez (L.) and Michael Guerra (Photo courtesy of Michael Guerra)

Michael Guerra in studio (Photo courtesy of the artist)

Ruben Gutierrez (Photo courtesy of the artist)

Tish Hinojosa (Photo courtesy of the artist)

Flaco Jiménez (Photo courtesy of the artist)

Gill Jiménez with Flaco Jiménez (Photos courtesy of artist)

Santiago Jiménez Jr.
(Photo courtesy of the
artist)

Stephanie Urbina Jones (Photo courtesy of the artist)

Stephanie Urbina Jones, Tish Hinojosa, and Patricia Vonne
(Photo courtesy of Stephanie Urbina Jones)

Esteban Jordan III (Photo courtesy of the artist)

Billy Mata at the Ameripolitan Music Awards (Photo courtesy of the artist)

Marisa Rose Mejia
(Photo by author)

Fritz Morquecho and Kathleen Hudson
(Photo by author)

Junior Pruneda with Bobbi Pruneda
(Photo courtesy of the artist)

Tomás Ramirez
(Photo courtesy of the
artist)

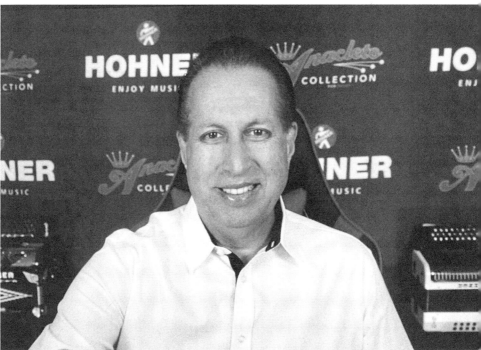

Gilbert Reyes (Photo courtesy of the artist)

Lesly Reynaga (Photo by Mark Guerra)

Florin Sanchez (Photo courtesy of Hans Bauer)

Poncho Sanchez (Photo courtesy Estevan Oriol)

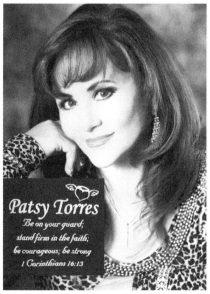

Patsy Torres (Photo courtesy of the artist)

Ruben V (Photo courtesy of the artist)

Patricia Vonne and Kathleen
Hudson (with *corazón abierto*
necklace) (Photo by author)

Esteban Jordan III

The Family River of Jordan

Many years ago, I went to a dance at the now defunct Longbranch Dance Hall on Harper Road in Kerrville, Texas. It was probably in the late 1980s or early 1990s. The headliner was Esteban Steve Jordan. I had heard him described as the "Jimi Hendrix" of accordion. And the black patch over his eye intrigued me. I had not done any research, so I had no idea who I was really seeing. That came later. The evening was exciting. The music filled me, made me want to move and dance, and added to my sack of experiences at the time. I was not researching or writing then. Just loving the music. In 1997 I used that dance hall to showcase Kinky Friedman, Little Joe y La Familia, and Willie Nelson at a hundred-year tribute to Jimmie Rodgers, who lived in Kerrville from 1928 to 1931.

HUDSON: Last night at the Conjunto Festival, I heard Rio Jordan, the children of Steve Jordan. I had no idea what I was in for. Today, I get to talk to Esteban Jordan III at Rosedale Park today in San Antonio. First, let's just talk a little bit about the event. I mean you were showcased last night as the son of a legend, but you've been involved with this event a long time.

JORDAN: Oh yeah. Well, the Tejano Conjunto Festival has been going on for years. It's our annual conjunto festival. My father actually performed here for the first twelve years straight every year. So he participated since the first festival. My dad had always been the musician that he was, had a great big following and lots of friends and family. We're natives to Texas, so this is our hometown.

HUDSON: It looked like you were having a lot of fun last night.

JORDAN: Oh yes. Oh yeah, every time, every time we perform.

HUDSON: Why do you think this festival is important?

JORDAN: Well, it grasps the roots of who we are and where we come from. Tejano music, conjunto music are American—from Texas to California. It's a thing here that just grew from back in the days of picking cotton and working out in the fields. That's where this music comes from. One person playing a *bajo sexto*, and then one just picking up an accordion and singing. That's kind of how it all started. Later on, they introduced drums and bass. The years came along, and that's what it is today.

HUDSON: What I love is the direction your family took, starting with your father, but then you're keeping that alive in your own way. That's very distinct.

JORDAN: Well, the thing is that I come from a family of nothing but musicians, both sides of my family, which is my mother's side and my father's side. In my father's family, everybody, one way or another, learned music. In my mother's side, everybody either plays an accordion or some type of instrument.

HUDSON: DNA.

JORDAN: Oh yeah. I mean back in the day, I was talking to a friend of mine. I was like, this was like things my father would tell me and teach us. We're with him 24/7 learning. Back in the day, music was a pastime. Families would sit down on a Monday night, and everybody would pick up some kind of instrument. That was the thing. You got to play along with the vinyl record or the TV, you name it, or they would play their own music. But that was just a tradition; that is fading. Sad to say, it is fading. I think it's something that helps people in general—sound, music . . . just . . . it stimulates creativity. It's a healthy thing, I believe.

That's one thing that my father believed in. He believed in the harmony and happiness of what he did and expressing it through his music. He had a chance to learn from everybody, living through the eras of the forties, fifties, sixties. During the sixties, he toured with the late Willie Bobo. He was a very famous timbales player and bandleader, jazz influence back in the sixties. And then after that, he did his own, and he had the Jordan Brothers who were really my father's brothers. They would get together and make their own band. They performed out of California, San José, the West Coast. They performed many years in Phoenix. They would come back to Texas, to their hometown, Del Valle.

HUDSON: So last night, I saw you pick up a flute. It was a really beautiful image. And you'd already had Juanito Castillo just going nuts on the piano and accordion. And then you picked up that flute. So you're definitely continuing with the tradition of not just repeating what someone else has done.

JORDAN: Well, one thing that I guess helped me was that I learned saxophone through school, middle school, high school. I didn't really take it up seriously during that time until I moved with my father, and then things became real, and I had to start learning what real music is about. Learning from my father, that's pretty much what gave me that edge. And not only that—one thing that my father, like I told you, he would mention, "Oh, man, I can play over thirty something different instruments, but I never could ever play saxophone or anything to do with wind." That was one thing that my father would say. Anything else he could play.

So that was one thing that he thought was pretty special, and he loved that I would pick up the saxophone and then try to learn what I'm applying to guitar and then singing and playing along with him as he's teaching the accordion and so on. It's interesting incorporating different instruments into Tejano and conjunto and being able to stay with the same roots and trend or what my father used to do as far as performing. That's the challenge for us.

HUDSON: Right, that is a big challenge.

JORDAN: Oh, well, my hope is that this is something that my father kind of laid on me as far as like a discipline, which is being able to influence other musicians in the right way because that's really what my father— that's really one of his biggest impacts—being able to, through his style of music and through hard determination, really going outside of yourself and dream. You know what I mean? That's one thing that I have to give my father tons of credit for. He would actually go beyond and outside of his normal comfortable zone to find or rent somewhere and then come back to his roots.

I started realizing that a lot of master musicians—or anybody learning a craft or trade—needs to be a tourist. It's like you grow up; and as you're growing up, you go out and explore. But eventually, with age and time, you come back to you—what's real. So it's just a constant circle coming back to the roots.

HUDSON: I love hearing you say that. I've been teaching since 1968, so that's a lot of exploring. I like to consider that I'm still exploring. I do the circular thing, and I use what works. But then I'm always willing, even after all these years, fifty something years, always willing to look out and see what I can change in the classroom.

JORDAN: Oh yeah, of course. Not only that, one always keeps in mind what you want as far as teaching, not just really playing into doing it just because I have benefits here, or doing it because you think somebody else would be like, "Oh, he's doing something." Really have true intentions as far as yourself to bring something different. That's really the thing that my father would do for lots of people. Throughout the years, he had tons of different musicians. One way to know that he would influence people, whether it be through music or not, was because he was the type of person who was able to talk to the highest down to the down-to-earth. He was just a natural spiritual guy. I am thirty-four and I've gone through a lot and been through a lot as far as hanging around the business and my father. But like I said, it's taught me a lot of things.

HUDSON: What do you do to take care of yourself? Do you have any practices or hobbies? Music, I guess.

JORDAN: Music, that's constant. That's always around. Any chance that I get as far as music, I mean that's natural. But I stay active. I love to do different things. I love to go fishing. I love to exercise, just stay fit, just like any normal person. Like I said, my whole goal I guess as far as all this is really to influence more musicians, and so they can also get more educated in their business so they can bring up the industry and everybody.

At one time, conjunto and Tejano was at an all-time high. This was during the 1990s. It was huge. It was a time that it was very, very popular. People would come from all over the world. It just settled down over the years. A lot of it has to do with the music that the people are influenced by. It has to do with the ideas—the creativity behind what you do.

So the whole thing really to me is not really repeating too much of what's happened—only if you were to do like, say, I bring out a song that my father did back in the day, and I'm just pretty much recording something that was done to the best. The only way I would put something out like that is if I'll do as best as I can to make it sound maybe better or have something more, but to also respect the work that the artist created and put into it. That's pretty much like the idea that I have behind the music.

And what's exciting is that all this new music that would be coming out and what my father has done, that he did before he passed away, is going to influence a lot of people. It's going to influence the industry. I'm positive that it's going to bring in ideas. And it's all for the people. That's really what ultimately why my father did it. He developed what he did, and he put himself fully into his craft. He just loved that people love it.

HUDSON: That was your family I saw onstage last night?

JORDAN: Yeah.

HUDSON: Did all of you play with your father?

JORDAN: Yes. We literally were my father's band for roughly about twelve years up until he passed. We were the band Juanito at first. He wasn't playing accordion with us; he was playing the drums when we first performed, when we first were being introduced with Juanito back in the early 2000s. And then a few years later, Alex Alejandro, he got into the scene. That's just how it came about.

HUDSON: It was just a big discovery for me. I just suddenly looked up at the stage. I hadn't even planned on being there that late. But when I saw you on the bill, I thought, you know what? I have heard Steve Jordan. So I'll have a connection. I'd better stay. All of a sudden, there was some element of discovery for me. I'm going to try to articulate that. What was it that caused me to see something that was so brand new?

JORDAN: Well, I guess we've been so low on our key, especially since performing with my father. He's always been the man, by far the greatest influence that we've ever had and we've ever known. Really working with him, it's a little different. It only became a reality that we had to perform on our own when the complications started coming around with my father's illness, which is cancer and all that. So that's when we had to kind of take over as far as performing. We were playing at Salute, which was very famous but unfortunately closed down not too long ago. We literally played there for years. Every Friday, that was my father's home spot really for years. My father had been performing there for years, even before we were performing there.

HUDSON: That father-son dynamic can go in a lot of different directions. Some sons feel like they can't fill their father's shoes. Some sons feel like they are challenged. I mean, there's so much of that in the music business. It looks to me like you transformed what you had and kept moving.

JORDAN: I guess to me the thing is the only way you can outgrow or, I guess, I would say, *realize* what you are takes time. Time is key. Nothing is learned in a day. Things take time to craft, like anything else.

HUDSON: Things happen in the right time.

JORDAN: Oh yeah. There are tons of coincidences that will be just at the spur of the moment. For one thing or another, it may or may not happen.

HUDSON: A lot of people consider that it is all timing. I'm allowing this project to sort of grow. So I started off talking to Max Baca, and I've worked with Flaco and Santiago. And then I deliberately went to Austin and talked to Patricia Vonne. And then I just sort of let things evolve to see, rather than having a list to track down. So you were part of an organic awareness that I've had.

JORDAN: We played here many years. I think the last time we performed here was about three years ago. So it's been awhile since we've taken the stage. But as the years come around, we would grow and grow more and more with just time.

HUDSON: So, do you have some specific plans for the future? Do you have something now in terms of recording?

JORDAN: Oh, we just got done with a project. We recently signed with the VMB Music label, and they're based here in San Antonio with Gilbert Velasquez. He's a well-known producer and engineer in San Antonio. He was good friends with my father. We just recently signed with him. He's going to be helping us put out an album of my father's, which is exciting stuff because this is all unreleased material that we didn't get a chance to put out before his passing. So this is just something that's one of his wishes for us to continue to put out all the work that he did.

HUDSON: Do you describe yourself as a particular genre of music?

JORDAN: Well, I've never really thought or believed in putting certain genres because I know and I see how genres kind of isolate music or anything. It just keeps it in its section, which has a lot more to do with these people and music in general. But as far as that, to me Tejano means Texas. So when I hear Tejano, I think of Texas music that was made here in Texas—music that people grew up with. That's my idea. I don't classify it as a certain type of style. I think any music from Texas—if you're born in Texas and you write songs—oh, your music is Tejano.

HUDSON: And Texas was Mexico. I mean, Texas was Mexico first.

JORDAN: Yeah, it's its roots. The roots come a long way, and they just keep growing.

HUDSON: Well, I've been reading some essays by a writer named Dagoberto Gilb. He was working construction, and he got his master's degree. He's just kind of a writer for the people. He does essays on the culture and his experience with the culture and relationship to Mexico and the language. He was in El Paso. There's something distinct about the culture. I mean, we're capturing it here.

JORDAN: It's the harmony. That is universal. Anybody can feel that. You don't have to like a certain type of music or like a certain type of style. If you hear something and it sounds good, you're going to naturally like it. That's just a natural thing. Anything that sounds good, you're just going to be attracted to it naturally. So that's the idea behind creating, making music, performing. You just want that people will love it and like it. Unless you're trying to say something—then it's a little different. Then there's a lot of people that they want to express themselves in different ways. Then there's thought behind what they're doing. So then, that's when different things come into play as far as "Oh, I like this style." But it's a little different. You might not like it. That's the only difference.

HUDSON: OK. Last but not least, let's talk about the music and the songs, just some favorite songs and songs that make you want to pull up that flute.

JORDAN: I have tons of favorites. How can you not? But playing with my flute or the saxophone, the soprano, any instrument that you pick up, you can apply it to anything. That's the beauty of it. I love picking up the flute for any type of music, whether it be something that is known for it being like Latino or jazz or whatever, or I can play a rock song or blues—you name it. As long as it has all those notes that are on every other instrument, you can play anything. I picked up the soprano, which is a saxophone, but it's just a smaller saxophone. It's an upper-scale saxophone, which is in the higher register. They have four different types, but I just play one of the four. It's fun. It's fun. There are different sounds and stuff you can get out of playing the woodwinds. I love it.

HUDSON: The whole sound I heard last night—I don't have anything to compare it to.

JORDAN: You can't. My father was a very unique sound. It was something that he crafted himself. It's something that has to do a lot with family and blood, yes. It's not something that can be duplicated that easily, not unless you really force yourself to really discipline and learn the music just the way it was laid out, which is the biggest challenge to a lot of musicians. So, it is just something that I believe just came naturally as far as in our bloodline. It's just a Jordan flavor. It's something that I can't explain it.

HUDSON: What do you know about the history of your family?

JORDAN: I know certain things. My father's uncle, who was Lupe Moran, was actually a music maker. He would make some craft guitars. He was a big influence on my dad growing up. I guess he was maybe the reason why my dad kind of picked up a guitar and picked up a two-row accordion in 1945 at the age of six or seven.

HUDSON: Thirty-five other instruments, we hear.

JORDAN: Oh yeah, over the years, of course. Really his first instrument was guitar. But coming and going back to Lupe, he was a crafter. He would make guitars. I believe he made four *bajo sexto*s that are still out and about in the States and stuff. Like I said, he had a big influence on my father growing up. Of course, growing up in that era also had a big influence for his situations in that time—the segregation and all that stuff. That's what it was, unlike nowadays.

HUDSON: Did you hear stories from him about his past and childhood?

JORDAN: He would constantly reminisce, us being together or being around my uncles, you name it, family, friends. Something would always come up. It's also a big thing that we would do as far as our part. Nowadays, there's a lot of distractions. There's internet and all these gadgets that we actually put a lot of time in, but we would listen to a lot of the stories because we knew that he was wanting to express something significant about himself. It was interesting to us. It was interesting how he lived.

Like I said, time is a big factor when it comes to anything. One lesson grows, and then you take it upon yourself to learn because you're interested. It's your own interest. I feel that one should go after what you feel that you can do, and go with what you love. I guess that's what everybody seeks. Well, I'm a quick thinker. I catch on real quick. So I caught on quick to avoid wasting time . . . and going through things that they've already given me, like the heads-up: if you touch the stove, you're going to get burned. And then you're like, OK, well, maybe I should touch it because maybe I don't believe them. And until you touch it, you'll learn. I kind of took the opposite by believing what they say because they have age and they have time, and there has to be some truth to what they're saying. So I kind of took that direction. I kind of realized pretty quick to avoid wasting time and to continue to do what you love. I mean, it's just that.

HUDSON: That's great. That's two things: avoid wasting time and continue to do what you love.

JORDAN: Well, I mean, because I guess eventually one might say, "Oh, well, I wish I could have done this. I wish I could have done that." The thing is to do it. If you really want to do it and love it, don't be afraid to take a chance on something that you feel is right. But only do it, I guess, if you're on the right side. You know what I mean? It's something that my father would tell me. If you're in the bad street, something bad will happen. Bad things can happen to you. If you're doing good, good things are naturally going to happen. It's just words from the wise. My dad would do that a lot with us. We call them "*consejos.*" Everybody else calls them just words of wisdom. There's just tons of names for it. But it's just somebody that knows—telling you [things] for a reason, so you don't have to go through it. They're just giving you the heads-up. Whether you want to go through it or not is your own choice.

ESTEBAN (STEVE) JORDAN III is the son of Steve Jordan. The bilingual artist is proficient on accordion, guitar, percussion, woodwinds, and vocal. He performs Latin jazz, Tejano, conjunto, rock, folk, and zydeco. He founded Boderland Bellows, an accordion repair and tuning shop, and has launched the podcast Squeeze-Box Stories.

Billy Mata

Time to Dance

It's a rainy Friday in May 2015, and I'm sitting down with Billy Mata. We have known each other for a long time. My first experience with Billy was just listening to his really great band play dance music at the Inn of the Hills in Kerrville. I was hooked and had to learn more about him.

HUDSON: Let's talk about your music. I find your choices in music interesting. I've heard your music. I've danced to your music. I've watched you with a crowd and know that you also entertain at festivals.

MATA: I have to start from the beginning, as my love for music started as a child. You got to remember I was child of the sixties. Before there was the Beatles, it was Johnny Cash's "Ring of Fire" and then the Four Seasons, and the television shows that used to interest me where you'd see Nat King Cole, or Bobby Darin, or Frank Sinatra, Tony Bennett.

HUDSON: And you were a kid in South Texas?

MATA: Yes. There were only three channels on the TV back then, and that's what you got—the *Hollywood Palace* or the *Ed Sullivan Show*. So I love music. It was in me to like the singer. I could hear melodic things, although I didn't pick up a guitar until I was eighteen. My guitar-playing skills are lacking because of that. When I got a little older, into the sixth grade, I got with this group of fellas, and you got to remember, I'm the only Hispanic—one of the very few Hispanic people—that went to this school. This is a public school. I've been going to Catholic school six years, and then I flunked sixth grade, so I had to repeat sixth grade at a public school.

HUDSON: Did you have a sense that you were in a minority? At that age, you didn't realize it, right?

MATA: No. I thought I was one of the fellas, but what was neat was that generation of kids didn't look at in a negative way. They knew there was something different about me, but they didn't care. They thought I was cool because I happened to like their music too. So I became friends with these kinds known as the kickers [*laugh*] and that's how I got to learn how to pretty much live with the country life.

HUDSON: Did your family have any musical roots?

MATA: Yeah. My dad could sing. He just never did it professionally. He did it amateur. My brother sings in church. All my family can carry a tune. At one time, my oldest brother, David, when he was in ninth grade, he took up the bass guitar and was playing that for a while.

HUDSON: So it sounds like you knew you'd like to perform?

MATA: Yes. I was very shy back when I was a kid, and I was just thinking that the only way I was going to get a girl to look at me was to be able to do something like that. I wanted that to happen.

HUDSON: You're actually not the first musician who said that. It's quite interesting the number of guitar players who say this.

MATA: Well, guitar players need it. You're not going to edit that, are you?

HUDSON: That's hilarious. No, let's not. So you were young and you were one of the few Hispanic performers, yes?

MATA: Yeah and then I'll never forget that year in sixth grade. We had an assembly in the cafeteria. I think we were supposed to go outside and it rained. One of the teachers said, "We need to have somebody sing a song," and everybody looked straight at me: "Let him sing." It was my first time I ever had to sing in front of people, and I stood up and I'll never forget that after I got ... I don't know how bad or good it sounded, but I'll never forget the applause that I got from these fellow students, fifth and sixth graders, and I thought, "Wow. This is awesome."

HUDSON: Do you remember what you sang?

MATA: All I know is it was a Johnny Cash tune. It was probably "Ring of Fire" because that was the very first song I ever learned how to sing as a five-year-old kid . . . learned it by who was on the radio all the time. And that's what started it, and then, as I got into seventh grade and eighth grade, I started learning more about Johnny Bush and Mel Tillis, Ray Price. And so I followed my early part of my career doing a lot of that material, knowing full well in the back of my head that I like other things too. But you got to understand the segregation of music back then: "You're either country or you're not."

As I got older, in my late thirties, I learned more and more about

Bob Wills. He wasn't just a fiddler that had a couple of hits like "San Antonio Rose." He was an innovator about music, about taking different cultures of music from Mexican, to German polkas, Mexican polkas, which is the same thing, except with Mexican polkas, you play it on stolen equipment. [*Laughs*] That's a joke I like to tell in South Texas. But anyway, he would play all, but he liked the blues and jazz, the big band. And he learned how to take a hoedown fiddle song, play it like so, and then whenever it was time for improvisation on the solos, that old bass and drum would just start swinging away, and man, if you can't tap your toes and feel good about that, then you're dead. I knew that I had to start expanding my musical horizons, and I'm doing western pretty much because I still love the honky-tonk step.

HUDSON: It feels more authentic to me, and I don't know what authentic is.

MATA: A lot of people in Nashville don't either.

HUDSON: I don't know where you were with your own cultural roots.

MATA: I was lost. Back when I met you, back in the mid- to late 1980s, I was still chasing that Nashville dream. So I was having to do a lot of cover material. I was very unhappy with that because I was strict in choosing what I like. I didn't like what everybody else liked. Everybody: Alabama, Restless Heart, that was the deal. There're a lot of people that had very soulful voices back then. Earl Thomas Conley was very rich in his voice, but he's a good songwriter. He wrote "Smokey Mountain Memories," "This Time I've Hurt Her More than She Loves Me," and all Conway Twitty songs. So I know he had some real deep country roots. So I would do those; I would sell that.

Then I'd have guys that come into the bar for free and they say, "Play some Restless Heart." And then I started to talking to Bill Green. He was booking me at that time, but he was also my producer, and I said, "I want to play the dance halls again." In all honesty, I was making the same amount of money on a Saturday night that I would make a whole week at a hotel. Think about it. I'm singing six nights a week by Sunday.

HUDSON: You almost get treated like jukebox sometimes at a hotel.

MATA: I wanted to get to the point where people would come to see me because of what I'm like—what's in my heart.

HUDSON: Did Bill move you back in that direction and help you? Most musicians need somebody to help them move the pieces.

MATA: I was almost a Ray Price, Johnny Bush cover band. But whenever they came to town, nobody came to see me. They came to see the real deal. So that's when I knew I had to do something different. I had to set my own pace. It was bad enough already that back then—a lot of people had told me through the years, "I didn't start following you because I thought you only played Spanish music." And I said, "Why did you think that if you see me playing at a honky-tonk? "Well, 'cause your name's Mata." I said, "Well, OK," but point is I'm not playing at the Royal Palace. I'm playing the Golden Stallion, Randy's Rodeo, or Farmer's Daughter. Does that tell you?

HUDSON: So you really heard that?

MATA: There's people, and they're mad at themselves because they said, "Yeah, I could have been listening to you all these years thinking that you know," and it wasn't 'cause they were prejudiced. They just didn't like that music. They wanted something else, I guess. And so I've had to fight through that, fight through the stereotype of my name. The stereotype of the name and then . . . so the stereotype of the name carries on in the national too. I could have signed on with any numerous labels, and thank God Bill Green was around to watch over for me because they all said the same damn thing: "Can you sing in Spanish?"

HUDSON: Just because of your name?

MATA: Yeah. I said, "Why can't I just do what I do?"

HUDSON: What about Johnny Rodriguez . . . a country singer who's going to sing Spanish, and be some kind of crossover, and pull all that together?

MATA: I understand all that. It's all about money. They may be about money, but I'm about fans, giving them what they deserve to hear.

HUDSON: You have a loyal following.

MATA: I do. I'm very blessed and thankful for that.

HUDSON: You have certain places you play that you're known for, certain festivals where you can always count on that Billy Mata's going to be there.

MATA: A lot of the Western Swing Festivals I'm a part of. Dance halls. In San Antonio, I'm known for Leon Springs Dance Hall and Martínez Social Club. And then in Austin at the Broken Spoke. Fort Worth is the Stagecoach Ballroom or Pearl's Dance Hall. And then I travel all over the country, but those are the spots around here where people can catch me.

HUDSON: One of the people I've talked to for this project is Junior Pruneda, and he plays every Sunday afternoon in Hunt, Texas. There may be ten people there.

MATA: I tease him. I said, "You know, you were almost my father-in-law."

HUDSON: Oh really?

MATA: I used to date his daughter, yeah. That was a long time ago. Didn't work.

HUDSON: Junior had some really interesting things to say about his choices. I guess you know Junior because he plays western swing, wins awards, and has played with the best?

MATA: Oh yeah. And he was the trailblazer for me. He was around before Johnny Rodriguez. I was fifteen years old when Johnny Rodriguez became well-known. All that time, I was thinking that I was going to be the first Hispanic country artist because I thought it was my idea.

HUDSON: [Laugh] I totally get that.

MATA: But someone else had the idea before me. But you know what? There's always a reason.

HUDSON: I have learned to live in accordance with the acceptance principle, just like as I go through these interviews and travel around, and doors open and doors close. I was giving you space to not show up today and I said, "Well, I can come back." And I just kept telling myself, "I'm here. It's raining. If it's not a good time, if one of us is going to be in trouble on the road, this won't happen."

MATA: I work from one to seven, and then after that, I go check on my daddy. I have to get his blood pressure checked every night. My mom's got dementia. So I do that and, of course, all in all, I'm juggling my career and taking care of that. I don't have to work, but I promised the guy I would help him 'cause I like to work, like working with my hands, doing the hats at Paris Hatters in San Antonio. I worked there from 1981 to 1986. Left to go to work for George Harris. I was going to retire after George sold it, and then Morales Feed and Supplies bought it out and I stayed there for three years. And then I was going to retire from that and just concentrate on my music, and then this guy gets wind of me being free, "Come on man. Help me out here." I said, "OK, OK." I enjoy it, though. It is a lot of fun to meet a lot people.

HUDSON: And hearing stories.

MATA: And a lot of famous people come in and stuff. Now, they have an honor of saying that they made a hat for a saint—Pope John Paul II. They made a hat for him or presented him a hat.

HUDSON: I did not know that.

MATA: Yeah and they just canonized him. I'm Catholic, so I know all this stuff. They just canonized John Paul II as a saint. So yeah, that's pretty awesome.

HUDSON: I did not know that. In all these interviews, I've talked to people about terms and labels. You easily said, "I was the only Hispanic in school." Some people don't like the word *Hispanic*.

MATA: I don't give a damn. I want people to know I come from Texas. I was born and raised in San Antonio, Texas. I'm proud of that, home of the Alamo, home of the republic, home of the battle of independence.

HUDSON: And this was once Mexico.

MATA: Yes, it was. And my father was born in Mexico, but he came over here with his mother. I always thought there was a good song in that.

HUDSON: But do you have a sense of your heritage culturally?

MATA: Of course I do, or I would have never kept my name. I would've changed it if I hadn't. Because I want people to know, "Yeah, this where I came from," and then if people want to know my story, about my family, then I'll tell them. My mother is one-fourth Irish, and her mother died when she was eight weeks old or something like that, and the father was just one of those hit-and-run deals. That's something that happened back then. So my grandma had a little American Indian in her too. Don't ask me which tribe because I don't know. So I have a little bit of everything in me. My father was raised by a stepfather and was treated like a stepchild. The guy that my grandmother married was Mata, OK.

There's the double-edged sword about my decision to be who I was.

It didn't go over well with my Hispanics—not necessarily my family, but people. They come up to me, and they see me in my hat and boots, and they see me singing and ask me why I don't play no Mexican music. And I said, "I like what I'm doing." Just like I didn't come here. I wasn't born to be like everybody else. I was born to be Billy Mata—whatever that's supposed to be.

I was going to tell you about my father. He wanted to learn English, and he wanted to be American. He signed up. He lied about his age to go to World War II, fight in the Pacific. He became an army medic assistant. I asked him, I said, "How can you lie about getting in so early at seventeen?" He said, "Well, I know I'm going to get killed by Japs or I'm going to be killed by my stepfather." That's when I knew that my poor father had a tough life. So anything that I'm having to deal with today is a walk in the park compared to what he had been through. He's eighty-eight, yeah. I'm fifty-eight because he's thirty years older than me.

HUDSON: I still think of you as that thirty-year-old kid, but of course . . .

MATA: Keep going thinking that way. Sometimes my brain thinks that, but a lot of times, my body doesn't behave that way. I've got a bad back. I've got arthritis in this elbow. I got sciatica. I'm wearing a brace right now that keeps me walking. It's a tough deal, but I think what motivates me to do it is just my pride in what I do and my kids, my daughters. I have three of them—two from one marriage and one from another marriage.

HUDSON: Marriage and musicians. I don't know a whole lot of those that go through smoothly, except Junior. Oh my gosh, that woman he's married. Bobbie is amazing. And she has some stories.

MATA: George Strait. God bless him. George Strait had the same woman, and a matter of fact, George Strait's old bass player is working for me now, and it's such an honor to have a guy like him. I learned so much about George's wife. But yeah, marriage—you got to have that really, really special person, whether you're a female, an artist, or a husband. That guy has got to be very special too. Most cases, it's usually the husband that's a musician too, and you work together. I think part of the problem is me. My situation was that I'm a loner. I don't like to be around people, except for when I'm in front of my people—the crowd, I love it. But I'm like Dave Letterman. I get to the house, and that's it.

HUDSON: I've decided to accept that about myself as well.

MATA: I've learned that being alone is really cool. It really is because I recharge myself, and now that I'm helping my parents with their situation, and I'm traveling a lot more than I have, I find I need that recharging ability.

HUDSON: Last night I talked to Chris Strachwitz. He's eighty years old—came over here from Germany and just loved the music. So he's documented conjunto, Appalachian, little gospel singers screaming their lungs out. He just found American music so authentic. And he commented last night that he's never been married and never had kids, and he's eighty years old with this body of work and that's been his passion. It's really beautiful.

MATA: I don't regret having my kids because I've always thought I would be a fairly good dad. I'm never going to be like my father. My father was the best, but I wanted to try to be a small sample of him and I think I have. A lot of people will say, "Well, you didn't stick it out with your wife, so how could you be a good father?" I say, "Well, you don't have to be in the same house to be a good father. You could be a great father by showing up to their deals, their little events at school, and that's important." And I even altered my booking schedule around my daughters' things sometimes when they were in high school. The two older ones—they're out of high school, and one's married and one's living out of town in Fort Worth. The other one's fourteen, and she's pretty smart. I'm going to have some DNA testing on that because that couldn't have come from me.

HUDSON: [*Laughs*] Right. Even though you've chosen an area of music, you still do not want to be put in a small box. You can play what you want onstage.

MATA: I do, and I'll start off my show with "Goodbye Liza Jane," which is an old Bob Wills classic, fiddle tune, and then I'll go right into "Corina," and then one of my favorite shuffle tunes is "Stardust Cowboy" or "Wishful Thinking." Then I feel out the crowd and see what they're dancing to. You got to know when to put those in, and then next thing, there are people looking at you like, "Wow, they know that song," and then, "Hey, honey, let's go dance. Might get lucky tonight." I'm helping Americans all over the country.

HUDSON: Very sweet. I like that. I need to come to one of your dances—that's what I need to do.

MATA: I want to do "Minnie the Moocher" one day. [*Laughs*]

HUDSON: You can be all over the map. Willie and Bob Dylan just get to be who they are, and it sounds to me like you kind of moved into that place of just being who you are. Are you still working with Bill?

MATA: That's where I do all my recording—at his studio. When you're associated with somebody good like Bill, you just stick with it. There's all kinds of people that come up and say, "I'd give you a better deal," but you can't find a better friendship.

HUDSON: And you can't replace the history.

MATA: No, no. History and friendship is the most important thing, and Bill Green has never screwed me over, and he will never. He's about as honest as a line is straight.

HUDSON: Right. I teach a class now at Schreiner on Texas music. And I asked Bill to send me some samples, and send me some of the stuff he's done to use in the classroom. And he did that for about a year. It's a freshman writing class, but I have them write about the music, and now with you too, I can even show them a performance and let them practice their descriptive writing on that.

Now, what's a challenge for you?

MATA: When someone in the crowd calls out, "Play 'Free Bird,' man."

HUDSON: That's the example so many entertainers use. There's always somebody in the back, calling to play that song.

MATA: No, I was just going to tell you if you look up BillyMataEntertainer.com, that's my online bio web.

HUDSON: Let's talk about a song.

MATA: Tommy Duncan is a hero of mine. The vocalist for Bob Wills. A lot of people thought for years Bob did all his singing, Bob did all the hollering, and he did you know, not to take anything away from Bob. But I'm just saying Bob was smart; he knew who to hire—Tommy Duncan, after Milton Brown left the Light Crust Doughboys. They needed a singer that could sing all kinds of stuff. They went through seventy-nine auditions or something like that. I don't have the number in front of me. And they found Tommy Duncan singing at a root beer stand. And you know what song they hired him for? "I Ain't Got Nobody." [*Singing*] "I ain't got nobody, nobody cares for me." Yeah. That was the song that won Bob over. Tommy died in '67. Leon Rouse is still alive.

HUDSON: So you got the Tommy Duncan hat?

MATA: Yes. And I'm trying to finish the Tommy Duncan trilogy. I started it in 2008, and of course I got volume one and two done, but three is money, you know. It takes a lot of money.

HUDSON: So you're doing a collection of his songs as a tribute to him?

MATA: Yes. I've done volume one and two. One is the original—I mean the early years. Volume two is the stuff that Tommy did on his own. And volume three will be when they got back together.

HUDSON: Are you doing any writing?

MATA: No, I'm not a writer. But I have a friend of mine that wrote "A Private Party" for me, which happened to be a good hit for me. I always send my ideas to him. If I have a title idea, I'll send it to him, and either we come up something or we don't, you know.

HUDSON: There are a lot of great performers who are not writers; they bring who they are to the song, and it becomes theirs. What's a favorite song, quickly, that just lights you up and just expands your heart and makes you want to do it?

MATA: I have a lot on my list of five or six, so could I do those. "Stardust" by Nat King Cole. "My Cup Runneth Over" by Ed Ames. "Danny Boy" by Ray Price. "El Paso" by Marty Robbins. "I Found a Dream" by Tommy Duncan. [*Singing*] "I found a dream, a dream." "Ring of Fire" by Johnny Cash.

HUDSON: Thanks for meeting me on this rainy day. Congratulations on your awards and your music. Inspiring.

BILLY MATA has been performing for more than four decades, from top-forty country music to western swing. Mata has won numerous awards and has shared the stage with several bands, including his own.

Marisa Rose Mejia

The Joy of Youth

I heard this young woman outside of Mi Tierra on a stage one hot afternoon. I was with Jesse Trevino; we had met to talk over our favorite food, after he had photographed Michael Martin during a Bob Dylan birthday celebration in San Antonio. We walked up close to the stage with our eyes wide open. This was real talent, and her voice did not match the very young person we saw dancing with poise on the stage. Then I invited Marisa to the Schreiner coffeehouse in March to celebrate Women's History Month. She knocked us all dead. I invited her back in September 2018 for the Texas Heritage Days event. Each time we met, I told her I wanted to talk. So on Sunday, October 22, 2018, we talked over the phone. During all this time, Marisa was winning prizes, playing festivals, traveling to sing, and playing with a band.

HUDSON: I saw on Facebook you were interviewed recently for the *San Antonio Express-News*. As you think about that interview, what question was not asked that you might like to talk about?

MEJIA: Maybe other things I do besides singing. Other things I do with extra time I have on my hands. I really enjoy reading and writing. Those are my favorite things to do. I am in karate, and I go to church every Wednesday. I am in a Bible class then. I'm part of different clubs at school too. I am in the seventh grade.

HUDSON: I just watched my granddaughter, Maya, play volleyball, and she is in the eighth grade and thirteen. Interesting to compare. Are you able to integrate school and these other activities with your singing life?

MEJIA: Yes, my family is very supportive.

HUDSON: I remember that at the coffeehouse at Schreiner, your dad came with the music and your mom was so great. All on a school night. You really inspired the students.

MEJIA: It was exciting to me. Thank you for giving me the opportunity to play there.

HUDSON: How would you talk about your journey into music?

MEJIA: I think it started when I was very young. I was about two years old, and my parents would play this tropical music. I knew from the first note what song was playing, I was told. I was listening to Shakira, Juanes, Selena. That was my favorite music to listen to. *Musica tropical* from the Caribbean. Latin music.

HUDSON: I heard Juanes in a store in Mexico once, and I couldn't quit moving. I came home and discovered he was a superstar.

MEJIA: That was my favorite music when I was little. I would just jump up when his music came on and get all excited. When I was five or six, I enjoyed singing in the car. Then perhaps the summer of the first grade, I told my parents I wanted to learn the guitar. During that time, I was singing at school in the elementary choir. My music teacher told my parents, "She has a gift. She can sing." My parents replied that "She has a good voice," and the teacher said, "No, this is special. Put her in voice lessons."

I was very shy, singing in my room and practicing the guitar. Then, at eight or nine, I began with the violin. I found it very interesting—another instrument with strings. After that, I turned ten and told my parents that I wanted to get over being shy and learn how to sing publicly. So, they put me in performance classes to gain confidence, and they put me in vocal lessons. People kept telling us, "She's pretty special." We were very humble about it. We still are. It's just something I love to do now.

HUDSON: But you are getting recognition from others now. I saw the *Brownsville Magazine* Music Award. How does that affect your plans?

MEJIA: When I was little, I never really thought about music as a life plan, but I am making plans for the future now. I love to write. I will sing in the future, make my own music, and be well-known. I write in English and in Spanish now. I do a variety of music, Latin, hip-hop, and different types of songs and music. If it comes into my head, I write it down. I find it very easy to write. It's just writing what I feel when it comes to my mind.

MARISA ROSE MEJIA plays guitar and violin. Her musical influences span from Selena Quintanilla to Adele. She has made her mark on the festival stage and released her debut single *"Vueltas y Vueltas,"* which is gaining a solid following on social media.

Fritz Morquecho

You Can Call Me "Boxcar Fritz"

I have known Fritz in Kerrville for years. He shows up at many local events, parties, funerals, *quinceañeras, y mas*. Now, on October 5, 2018, at eighty-three, he travels with a portable oxygen tank and jams at the Dietert Center every Thursday at noon. We meet at the Donut Hole on Sidney Baker Street for another talk. He tells me about his family in Kerrville, his love of the accordion, and his desire to keep on playing. He often plays the Jimmie Rodgers Tribute I produce each September, taking the stage to pay tribute to Mexican American heritage in Texas music. In 2018 he was our honored guest at Schreiner University, and he watched the young Marisa Rose Mejia perform a 10:00 a.m. slot. The oxygen tank only slows him down a little.

HUDSON: Fritz, Let's begin by talking about your new challenge in life —that oxygen tank.

MORQUECHO: I was out in my yard one day, and a man came by to pay me for a gig. He asked me who did the yard, and I answered that I was that man. "*Viva* Morquecho," he replied. Then a week later, I started a tiller and began working on the yard again. I was getting tired, but I was stubborn and kept on. We needed fodder for the yard. I went to the store to pick up a bouquet of flowers for a friend and had to put it down. It was too heavy for me. I noticed these things, and one day at a Wednesday gig, I also carried a change of clothing so I could go to the hospital to check. They told me to go back home. By Friday, I was having a hard time breathing, so I went back. "Whoops, you are not going home," the nurse said. I ended up on 24/7 oxygen with a diagnosis of idiopathic pulmonary fibrosis.

The lungs got messed up. Nothing really "happened." I was told to go home and do nothing. I carry a gauge, and they told me to stay above the nineties. That was not possible, so I tried things. Dr. De Los Santos, who also played guitar, did tell me to try playing the accordion and see how I felt. I found by sitting down on a stool a little bit higher that I could still do this. And I could keep the gauge measuring my oxygen. Everybody keeps saying, "You are looking good." I feel pretty good.

HUDSON: Yes, and I saw you play a few weeks ago at the Dietert Center jam session.

MORQUECHO: Yes, the leader of that group is also playing trumpet now in my mariachi group. We still play in the area. We have worked for big families like the Garza, Hernandez, and Beall families. I was at a funeral recently, and a family asked me if I had a video, thinking that his father might outlive me, and he wanted my mariachi group at his father's funeral. [*Laughter*]

HUDSON: Let's talk about that award you received.

MORQUECHO: I received the letter in December 2015 to be inducted into the Tejano ROOTS Hall of Fame Museum in Alice, Texas.* It was quite a drive, but my family drove over, and Stewart Crawford and his family came from Comfort. There were seventy-two inductees, and I was chosen for playing the accordion. I saw pictures of Flaco and Little Joe when they were much younger.

HUDSON: Let's talk about our dear friend, Junior Pruneda. I know you both grew up here.

MORQUECHO: I moved here with my family from Waring, Texas, when dad was working for the railroads. They had boxcars in town down by Buzzie's Bar-B-Q for the workers, and we lived in one. Call me "Boxcar Fritz." Bobby Puig, who played drums with me in the sixties, has written a book on this local scene. There was a train down at the depot (now Rails Restaurant), and on Schreiner Street there was a turntable for the train to turn around. We kids loved to help turn the train by grabbing onto a pole.

I had been playing guitar since I was about five, but the accordion hit me at twelve. I had an uncle who came to town from Lubbock to get workers for the cotton fields, and he had an accordion. Now my other

---

*ROOTS stands for "Remembering Our Own Tejano Stars." It was established in Alice because Ideal Records was established there in the 1940s. Sunny Ozuna, Laura Canales, and Narciso Martínez recorded for Ideal Records. On May 3, 2001, Texas governor Rick Perry signed House Bill 1019, which designated the city of Alice as the "official birthplace" of the Tejano musical tradition (see TSHAonline.org).

uncle had an accordion, but I never paid attention. This time, as we were unloading the car, the accordion captured me; I played on it all night, and by morning, I was playing "Margarita." Junior's family, his mom and dad, were always sitting out on the porch, so we stopped and talked to them. José María Pruneda told my dad to bring me over to play. Every Wednesday they had a gig in Bandera, and they took me with them. I am looking for a photo of Junior, Adam Ayala on bass, and me.

My dad played guitar and violin, and there is also a photo of me in his lap, playing the notes while he strummed the strings. I know that photo is somewhere in the family. I would sit on his lap on the left side, and I would pick the songs and dad would do rhythm.

I left Kerrville for Abilene. I had worked in the state hospital here doing some nursing and in the kitchen here and the barbershop. I moved to Abilene and started working in a laundry. I met someone at the state hospital there and told him I wanted to work in the barbershop. It happened quickly. He showed me the straight razors for shaving, and I told him I had never done that. I learned pretty quickly! I went out to hear some music, and the band was just breaking up that night. There was *no* accordion in Abilene, so they invited me to join them. I also heard of a new school, Garland's of Texas Beauty and Barber School. I left the hospital, went to school, and got a license. I always had three jobs going: music, barber, and mowing lawns.

We moved back to Kerrville, and I retired at age fifty-two from the state hospital. Then I worked in a barbershop in the Schreiner Department Store for thirteen years. Then I opened up my own shop. The Historical Society here has all the biographical information, dates, and places!

I am the only Morquecho left here; my two brothers have passed away. My daughter-in-law Rebecca is doing research on the family name.

ALFRED "FRITZ" MORQUECHO has been playing Texas and Tejano music since he was a child. He continues to perform with the band he founded in the 1970s. His accordion work has been featured in the Smithsonian Institution's Folkways Recording, and he was inducted into the Tejano Roots Hall of Fame.

Junior Pruneda

Grace on the Bass

Junior Pruneda has been part of my musical journey since I moved to Kerrville in 1984. He's a gracious, kind man with a beautiful wife (Bobbie). He always has a smile and a story. When he started a residency on Sunday afternoons at Roddy Tree Cantina, a crowd of music lovers gathered. They appreciate the history and heritage, and they want to dance.

HUDSON: Let's talk about a beautiful moment in music for you—a time that comes to your mind when everything was flowing.

PRUNEDA: I've been in so much and had such great experiences. I idolized Bob Wills. In fact, we thought when we died we were going to Bob Wills's house. [*Laughter*] Bob hired me and moved me to Tulsa, and I was going to be a steel guitar player with Bob Wills. We were at the Fremont in 1960 with the Newton Brothers on a revolving stage, and across the street at the Nugget was Bob Wills and the Texas Playboys, my heroes. Bob was eating, so Bobbie, my wife, and Bob started talking. Next thing I know, Bobbie brought Bob over to the Fremont to listen to me. We were Rudy Gazelle and the Jury, and we were a show group. They heard me sing and play bass, and Bob asked to talk to me at the hotel tomorrow. We just had Joey then, a baby. We were at the Ferguson Hotel in Vegas, and that's when he told me and Bobbie, "If you can play steel, I can hire you." I wanted to play steel anyway, so this was great. He said, "I want you all to move to Tulsa—and I will put you in the John Wills Band." Remember Roland Davis who lived here in Kerrville?

HUDSON: Yes, I met him my first month in town in 1984.

PRUNEDA: Roland Davis was a vocalist with my dad's band, and he idolized John Lee Wills. I lay in bed and listened to John Lee Wills music at night. So when Bob put me in the John Wills Band as a bass player, I was on a B team for his band. My dad was in hog heaven when he found out I was in the John Wills Band. Back to the hotel—Joey was a little baby while we were talking. Bob sat little Joey in his lap, feeding him saltine crackers, while we were talking. I can truthfully say that my son, Dr. Joey Pruneda, sat in the lap of Bob Wills. Bob said to him, "Son, I ain't got much, but here are some crackers."

When I was in John Lee's band, I remember unloading off the bus in front of John Lee's house, and Irene, John Lee's wife, asked us to come over and have supper (it used to be called "supper"), with their mother at the house that night. She wanted us to meet "Mama." We went that night, and Bob Wills's mama was there, the mother of the Wills, Bob, John Lee, Luke, and Billy Jack. There are four of them. And some sisters. So, Irene was in the kitchen cooking. Mama got her scrapbook, showing us Bob's photos when he was a little kid.

HUDSON: And you had a voice in your head saying, "Is this happening to me?"

PRUNEDA: I had a voice in my head saying, "Is this happening to this *mesquin* kid?" I mean, *wow*! And she went on and on with the scrapbook. Bob Wills wrote this book called *Hubinet*. And Bob's mom says, "Junior, I would love for you to have this book that Bob endorsed for me. I will leave it here with John Lee and Irene for you to pick up." I never did go get it. Can you imagine what that would be worth to a collector? Now I kick my butt for not getting that book. Of course, no amount of money would buy that from me!

HUDSON: Did you ever get asked about your heritage when you were playing with them?

PRUNEDA: No. I've had rednecks say, "Hey, Meskin!"

HUDSON: I love Mexico and the culture.

PRUNEDA: James Avery does too. We'd run around together and go bar hopping. And he adored the Mexican people. I've got to tell you a funny one. I was here with Ernest Tubb, and—do you know Cal Smith? We were traveling with Loretta Lynn and doing shows together. Sometimes, the Coal Miners would ride on our bus, and sometimes I would ride on their bus. Anyway, Cal came up with this idea. "Let's pull this joke on Loretta Lynn." Cal and I were brothers, partners. I was on the Coal Miners' bus, and Cal was in the stateroom with Loretta. She comes out there and says, "Junior, I am so glad you are here with us." I think she had a little crush on me.

Back then, I was about half-assed handsome. Then Cal said, "Damn Meskins—we don't need them." And he kept on and on. Loretta kept saying, "Honey, I love you. Don't listen to Cal." She is all shook up. Cal takes her off the bus, all shook up. He comes back saying, "Loretta is really hurt about this." Meanwhile, I am drinking with the Coal Miners. So Cal says, "Let's go tell her it was a joke." We were in a Howard Johnson's with glass doors. We opened the door. Then I let it backfire on Cal by saying, "So you think it's funny? The way you treated me on the bus! It was not funny." And Cal shoves me, and I caught my foot on the channel of the door. On my way down, I said, "You are a big man, Cal." We told her the next day it was all put on. We had it all set up. Loretta kept saying, "I love Mexican people."

HUDSON: I love the whole culture, and I am not sure why. I was raised in Fort Worth, Texas, in the suburbs. One Saturday as a teenager I was shopping with my mother, and I discovered the Mexican Inn. I just devoured the food and the culture in that moment. We did not have that food at home. White bread, American for me. But for some reason, this moment clicked, and life changed forever. I like to think that maybe in a past life that is where I lived!

Bobbie is with us and chimes in: "You know Junior is a different breed of cat when it comes to Mexican music. He always liked the fiddle and western swing."

JUNIOR PRUNEDA is known for country music, but his first love is jazz, and he had the opportunity to play with Maynard Ferguson and Woody Herman. He had a stint on Broadway playing in the orchestra for *The Best Little Whorehouse in Texas*.

Tomás Ramirez

Jazzmanian Devil

Tomás played sax with Kirpal Gordon at a jazz festival in San Miguel de Allende once, and the Texas Music Heritage Foundation sponsored the trip there on a chartered bus. I was a bit crazy then about showcasing the music and poetry I love! Well, I still am. I also heard him many times with the Texana Dames, a family close to my heart and included in my second book on the women of Texas music. Tomás has major jazz credentials, and we met up in 2015 on one of his trips to play at the Elephant Room in Austin. We both enjoyed the Vietnamese food at a restaurant on Oltorf next to Oat Willie's.

HUDSON: Let's begin with John Lomax.

RAMIREZ: I was in the fourth grade when I saw those songbooks in music class in Premont, Texas. I always thought that was an odd name: Lomax. I had never seen one end in an X. In Spanish that is unheard of. When I got older, someone gave me some old songbooks, and there was one by Lomax, *The History of Western Music*, and it was really western music—the cowboy songs, "Get along, Little Dogies." That was part of my musician heritage, along with Ravel and also Carl King (a marching band). I live in Austin, but I am back in Premont taking care of my mother now. We have a nurse that comes by every two weeks, and I am around.

I left Premont in 1967 as soon as I graduated, went to Corpus Christi, then moved to Austin and did a year and a half at UT. I was studying music education. When I started my student teaching, I saw a lifestyle I did not like. Many were total jerks. It was a rough life dealing with ninety teenagers. They were horrible, and I just quit. And I was doing a lot of LSD. I looked into a degree in applied saxophone, but that required a lot of classical music. I was interested in jazz. In the meantime, I was getting offers since I was in the UT jazz band. I decided, "What the hell; instead of studying to be a musician, I might as well be one—be a funk band," but it was a little eclectic.

HUDSON: My experience of you with music was jazz, saxophone, hearing you with Kirpal Gordon (poetry and sax), hearing you with the Dames, and I knew you were not trapped in any box.

RAMIREZ: Jazz is a philosophy that you can apply to any aspect of life. It happens at the moment. You have your form. After you state the obvious, you go for the subtle. [*Laughter*]

HUDSON: I had a chance to talk with Kirk Whalum one time, and he said at one point you go off and explore from a given point in the music, and then you come back.

RAMIREZ: I've never really been lost in it. I've always been very aware of what's going on at all times. I do not get "lost" in it. It's a process, and it takes a lot of concentration to do it.

HUDSON: What was the lure of jazz for you?

RAMIREZ: Like I said, you escaped the obvious, and you made it up. There's the asides. That caught me early on in life. I applied it to every band I was with. Sometimes it worked. Most people liked it. Jazzmanian Devil was my first band in 1976. I had been playing with Jerry Jeff about four years, and I got sick and tired one day and quit. I had no idea what I was going to do. Friends said, "Let's get a band together." I was part of the Lost Gonzo Band with Jerry Jeff. I did not hang out with them when I was off the road. They were country boys and wrote pop songs. They were a group before I ever got into the gig.

HUDSON: What was the culture in Premont?

RAMIREZ: *Norteño*, country, and western.

HUDSON: What do you call *norteño*?

RAMIREZ: Accordion, *bajo sexto*.

HUDSON: I saw you playing with Los Cobblestones in Brownsville. They did a wonderful video with a focus on your face during a drum solo.

RAMIREZ: That was a nice bar. Brownsville probably has the best music in the Valley. McAllen has money, with a lot of Mexican nationals making money off trucking, but having money does not mean having taste. Some horrible music there. That part of the world is not really known for its musical treasures. Except for *norteño* music. And there is a lot of hard rock and head-banging music. Of course, the university there brings in a lot of acts.

I started off with the clarinet. But my uncle said that I needed to play sax because he needed one in the band. He got me a tenor sax, and I had a week to learn. He let me take solos. I had been playing clarinet for about a year. Here I was with these ancient guys . . . in their twenties. . . . [*Laughs*] I was in the sixth grade.

Back in those days, Mexican bands played everything from classic to top ten. And there were always sax solos in the songs. I thought that was pretty cool. They dressed me up. Back in those days you played private clubs (for the sale of liquor), and you had to become a member of the club. And the laws were strict on the age in the club, so they would dress me up, put a mustache on me, and tell everybody I was a midget. A strange midget.

HUDSON: I am staying over on Riverside in a condo that Townes stayed in. Enjoying his spirit.

RAMIREZ: There are some Townes memorial dumpsters here. [*Laughter*]

HUDSON: So, you left home in 1967. What caused you to get out of town?

RAMIREZ: I left and went to Del Mar in Corpus for two years and got married. In 1972 to 1976 I played with Jerry Jeff. In 1979 Jerry Jeff called me up to go back on the road. I ended up in San Diego for two years. We went to Australia. He was mega-famous by then, and it was a lot of fun. It was a trip playing with Jerry Jeff. I got to play with Carole King. The band then was Gary P., Freddy KRC, Jon Inmon, Bob Livingson, and Kelly Dunn on B3. I put out the third CD for INIO Music. So the idea was to put out a classic trio CD of sax, drums, and bass. The other trio we had was drums, B3 organ, and sax. The trio is traditional with jazz. The other trio is called an organ trio. INIO is out of Atlanta. I moved away from there a year ago and came back to Premont. Got a phone call from mom saying I needed to come back: "We are having a hard time." When your mom calls, you return.

HUDSON: Do you have a favorite band you have played with?

RAMIREZ: Mine!

HUDSON: And who is playing at the Elephant Room tonight?

RAMIREZ: Mitch Watkins, Michael Longoria, and a bass player I've never met before. A quartet.

HUDSON: Do you have any favorite songs?

RAMIREZ: "In a Sentimental Mood"—I love doing that. Miles Davis tunes in general.

I saw him at Montreux Jazz Festival, and he was playing. I was in the front row, and he came out and stood with his back to us. We had matching silver concho belts too. He held up his red horn and stood that way a long time. The soundman looked over at me and said, "He always does that. He makes them wait."

He does. And sometimes he kept his back to the audience the entire time. Nobody like him. He was a great champion of emerging jazz, when it emerged from one thing to the next. Everybody always said, "What is he doing now? That's just noise." Then everybody would be playing that sound in a few years.

HUDSON: Dylan is going to be in Texas in May, playing three times. I bought tickets for two of them. Austin and San Antonio. Charlie Sexton plays with him, and that's exciting. Dylan just keeps doing what he wants. Like Miles. I like the new Frank Sinatra stuff a lot. The idea of just being willing to be yourself. Looks like you have done that.

RAMIREZ: I didn't know what else to do. Either I fit in, or I didn't. My philosophy is what people in the business know me for. They realize you hire Tomás doing this thing this way. Either you like it or you don't. In many instances, I have had some pretty lean times.

HUDSON: I went with the Texana Dames to Switzerland, and I spent thirteen days with them, traveling.

RAMIREZ: I was there for the second one. I lost my passport and ticket in the first five minutes. I had to go to the embassy in another town to get another passport. Luckily, we had a newspaper clipping of me playing, and that really helped. And they had me prove I was me by playing sax for them. I think they were just bullshitting me, but it worked out.

HUDSON: I found out when talking with Charlene that this family had a lot more going on than met the eye.

RAMIREZ: They played a couple of gigs in Peru. I think I played with them about six or seven years. One of my longer stints—from '91 to '98. We had a great time touring Europe. I remember playing a gig in Carnegie Hall with a group of Texas bands—Redneck Rock at Carnegie Hall. Doug Sahm was on the bill. John Reed was there too. We were setting to leave the next day; he was in the lobby, pacing. I asked him what happened. He told me that they had been robbed in the hotel room. Then he got up and found everyone gone . . . so he came back home with us. Jerry Jeff said, "We'd better take him with us."

HUDSON: The Dames played a tribute to Jimmie Rodgers I did in Kerrville, and John Reed sometimes looks like Jimmie to me! Remember when we did that jazz show in the rain at the Point Theater and all ten people came up on the stage with us? So, switching gears, do any of the stereotypes people apply to Tejano apply to you?

RAMIREZ: Not sure about stereotypes. I am a musician, and that transcends all kinds of stuff. Any musician worth his salt can meet a musician worth his salt and play. As far as western music is concerned, we can all communicate. I try to bastardize everything. I would love to do a CD with Spanish on it. A lot of shortsightedness in this business. Guys with the purse strings are not exactly visionary.

HUDSON: Are you a reader?

RAMIREZ: Yes, and I'm a writer too. I have a bunch of short stories I put together when I was in the Valley. And I am writing micro stories because people have such short attention spans now.

HUDSON: Do you know the genre called flash fiction?

RAMIREZ: Found my niche! Five-minute stories. I am writing most of them on my iPhone . . . the notes section. Here's an idea. I'll let you read it. "Jazz Dog."

HUDSON: What kinds of things do you read?

RAMIREZ: I'm right in the middle of *Wuthering Heights* right now.

HUDSON: What? That's *my* book. I discovered it when I was sixteen, and it has had a profound effect on my life. Really. Cathy and Heathcliff. What made you decide to start writing these short pieces?

RAMIREZ: I had things to say, and a short story took too long. I just read a bunch of Hunter S. Thompson too. Great letters. And he is funny. Reading *National Lampoon* in the seventies led me down many trails. *Fear and Loathing in Las Vegas* blew me away. It was amazing and cool. Johnny Depp did a fantastic version of Hunter in film.

HUDSON: And on your culture?

RAMIREZ: I was called Tommy . . . and I looked in the mirror and saw Tomás! I gave that name on my driver's license, even though the birth certificate said Thomas.

HUDSON: I'm going to come hear you tonight at the Elephant Room.

RAMIREZ: Nine thirty to one thirty. Your name will be at the door.

TOMÁS RAMIREZ is a saxophonist; his style is a blend of fusion, smooth jazz, and Latin soul. He has toured all over the world with his own band, Jazzmanian Devil, and as a member of the Jerry Jeff Walker Band. He has been a studio musician for Walker, Carole King, Christopher Cross, Texana Dames, and Beto and the Fairlanes.

Roberto Sontoya Ramos

It's My World

I have been hearing Roberto play with Stephanie Urbina Jones each time she tours Texas. He brings a dramatic flair to the visual of the band, as well as a steady bass. Florin Sanchez also plays with her in Texas. The three of them present compelling music—dramatic music that calls to the heart. Roberto has his own creative flair, dressed in black with black glasses and a black hat. We sit down after an Austin gig on December 30, 2015, and talk about his life in Texas music. In 2019 Roberto was touring constantly with Little Joe y La Familia and was named the Texas State Musician.

HUDSON: "Roberto Sontoya Ramos!" as Stephanie Urbina Jones introduces you. And I love the Facebook page of your music and photography called *Nació Malo*: Born Bad. What a great photographer you are too!

RAMOS: Well, you know it has two meanings because my friend, Mike Bernal, the drummer with Dale Watson, is someone who told me it depends on how you say it. *Nacio* is like *Ignacio*. A shortened name. But, if you say *Nació* that means *born*. So, it depends on how you say it. I always just say it as a name because it's the name of the character in a movie.

HUDSON: So, you've just played with lots and lots of people, including Little Joe . . . and Stephanie Urbina Jones. I have an interview with her as part of this project. Do you have a band that you play with that feels like a home band? I mean you were just showing me the Tequila Rock Revolution. Is that home for you?

RAMOS: Most bands want more commitment. And it's totally understandable. But I call it somebody wanting me to fly their flag—run with their flag across the field into battle. Do gigs, get no money, do whatever it takes to win the battle.

HUDSON: Well, commitment often means that.

RAMOS: But I don't do that. I have my kind of semifavorites, but now it really is whoever gets to call first—and that's what a lot of people have to do. Now, it's like, "I'm already booked that day, I can't do that."

HUDSON: But, you played a lot with Stephanie, right?

RAMOS: Stephanie is playing a lot. That started only when she's here in the Southwest—you know, Texas. So, when she's here, it runs every two or three months. She'll be here because she's off doing her thing, and she'll roll back here and if I'm available, I'll play, but if I'm not, then something else happens. So, it's kind of amazing that I play with three or four different bands, and I've been pretty lucky that they haven't landed on the same days very often. I feel really lucky.

HUDSON: Let's talk about Tequila Rock Revolution. I see it's called "Mariachi and Metal."

RAMOS: Well, in particular, that genre is a really hard genre to book. If you're going for kind of a certain age group of Hispanics, and there's only so many of them that will go out and support that kind of music, and there's just not enough. I mean it's kind of the same challenge of trying to get that across overexposure so that people can appreciate it. But some of the songs are totally in Spanish, some songs are English and Spanish, some are in English. But once you have a song that's totally in Spanish, it's harder for a white audience who could not understand Spanish to get into the music.

HUDSON: Even with that really engaging music? The video is so exciting.

RAMOS: Yeah.

HUDSON: I mean Haydn Vitera—the lead singer who plays that violin.

RAMOS: Yeah. Haydn Vitera is a really good singer. And so is Dan, the guitar player, and the girl, Vanessa, is excellent also.

HUDSON: What kind of adjustments do you have to make jumping from playing behind Stephanie to playing behind a rock band?

RAMOS: I do what's appropriate for the style.

HUDSON: And you just do that automatically?

RAMOS: I just kind of slip into it. It's kind of like dealing with the general public. I can talk to a twenty-year-old drunk frat boy and understand and talk with him and move things along, and then I separate and then run into his grandparents. And then talk to his grandparents respectfully and also within the mindset of grandparents. Then, I turn around and then have a sorority girl or manager—the club owner. It's a constant evolution of people, and you just adjust. Well, the music is the same way of constantly adjusting, so I adjust to this band, young band, older band, jazz band, whatever it is. You just kind of fall into it, and I adjust because I've been doing it for so long.

HUDSON: But, how did you start off?

RAMOS: When I was younger, we all had kind of the band that we started with. I worked for years. But as time goes on, you do this, you do that, and you also realize that nothing lasts forever—like in a lot of things, nothing lasts forever.

So, I equate band years to dog years because if you can have a band staying together for four years, that's about the average before you start getting kind of bored, and you want new challenges. One example, when I was playing with Joe King Carrasco, we were averaging 270 days a year—270 days of one-nighters! I did that for four years. We had a road crew. All we did is go to the hotel. We go straight to the hotel, get ready, we show up in the green room about an hour before the show. We walk up onstage, and someone will put my guitar on me, tuned. We play for ninety minutes. Show is over, they come take the guitar off of me, and I'd walk off the stage, and I wouldn't see it again until the next day. And we did that every day.

And I knew that was going to end one of these days. That was a beautiful day. For four years, I've been doing that. That's a lot of work in one year—and then two, three, four years. If a band with the same people can stay together that long, it is quite an accomplishment—like the Rolling Stones. I don't know how they do it, but they're just really good friends. So, like I said, it's like dog years. It's a very intense living—you're living very compressed, and it just drives you crazy after a while. I got to go, I got to stop the arguments and boredom and stuff like that.

HUDSON: Well, 270 days. I knew he was a maniac, but how did he play that much?

RAMOS: We just did it. My first spring break down in South Padre Island, we—he was booked so often there, every time we'd play spring break, we did thirty days in a row without a day off, all in the South Texas area,

Corpus Christi, South Padre, all around there. We did thirty days in a row without a day off.

HUDSON: And so, that was because of his niche as a party band?

RAMOS: Yeah. Yeah. Joe was the perfect time at the perfect place with the perfect manager for everything he did. Joe Nick Patoski was his manager. He made all sorts of great deals for Joe. And then married his keyboardist on top of it. Anyway, they've been married for years.

When I first started playing with Joe is when we went to Bolivia for five-and-a-half weeks and that was . . . Bolivia is not really a great place if you're an alcoholic, and you like to do drugs [*laughs*] because we all do; there it was nonstop. It was basically twenty-four hours awake and then twenty-four hours asleep and twenty-four hours awake and twenty-four hours asleep. [*Laughs*]

HUDSON: So, on your wall, there's a sign from a magazine and it talks about Chicano, and we've talked about other labels: Hispanic, Tejano, Tex Mex, Mexican American, Latino. Who falls under the Chicano label?

RAMOS: Little Joe would kind of fall into that somewhat, but even though Joe has gone through that whole evolution because Joe has been directly involved in that music himself . . . even though, again, then you go into Tejano. You know Joe is Tejano. Joe is everyone. He came for Temple, Texas. He's been surrounded by Texas culture, American culture, his parents' culture, his grandparents' culture. And that's why in Texas you're able to do so many styles being Mexican because all this stuff is all around you. You have rock and roll. When I was a kid, my mom and dad had a Mexican radio station on, and they left the radio on that channel.

HUDSON: Was that right here in this house in Austin?

RAMOS: Yeah. We'd turn on the rock-and-roll stations, and my parents would come back in and change it back to Mexican radio, and then they would leave and we'd turn it back to rock and roll.

HUDSON: Did your parents come from Mexico?

RAMOS: No, they were born here in Texas. And my grandmother came from Mexico as a young girl. My great-grandmother brought my grandmother who was really young around eleven or twelve. I would say walking from the interior of Mexico to Texas during the revolution. And to raise her kids here and have them married, and when they got married, my great-grandmother went back to Mexico and lived out her life. She came here specifically to Texas to settle her kids, do it, get married, and she went back to Mexico, and that's where she lived the rest of her life.

HUDSON: And you heard the stories from your mother?

RAMOS: Yeah. And so, and consequently, the Indian that I have in me is Aztec. And, apparently, I have—I don't know how many great-grand-mothers. It's an interesting story that my mom told me about one of my grandmothers, who was picked by the Aztec Indian who met a Mexican guy from a village, and they got married. And so, the Aztec lady started living with a man in the village, but her—the Aztec tribe she was from did not like that. So, they came from where they were into the village and stole her and took her back, reclaiming her basically.

Apparently, she had a little piece of red cloth. And, without them knowing, as they were going back to where they were taking her back to, where she grew up, she left a little piece of cloth as a trail for them to follow to where she was because they didn't know where they were going. And so, the village people went and, seeing the trail, followed the trail, and in the middle of the night they stole her back. Then they left her alone. They never came back again after that.

HUDSON: That's so reminiscent of the stories in mythology. I teach my-thology class, and there's a story about a woman who leaves her peo-ple to go with other people. In the story, she goes with the bird people, but when she wakes up with this other tribe, they end up being snakes and she's not happy. There's something sort of archetypal about leaving your tribe and going back to it and being stolen—really ancient, an-cient stories about that. I love that with the red cloth, though.

RAMOS: So, that was an interesting thing. And, consequently, that's why my features are very American Indian, because every time I go to North Dakota or Oklahoma or anywhere there's American Indians, they al-ways ask me, "What tribe are you from?" Every time, they always ask me what tribe I'm from. So, I tell them I came from the Aztec Indians.

And when I used to play in some of the nightclubs out there, we have a lot of American Indians who were congregating that weekend. And, at the end of the night, when you walk to the parking lot, you can see these pockets of folks; they're all hanging out together. A Native American friend of ours would say, "Well, that's the so and so tribe, that's the so and so tribe, and that tribe doesn't like this tribe, and this tribe doesn't like that tribe." He'd just give us a rundown. . . . You would think they'd all just get together.

HUDSON: There's something about being human that has us separate and fear the other. I was listening to some kind of program on how we had the urge to be separate sort of, but we can also learn to be part of a community. But, we kind of romanticize that tribal stuff, and we think everybody is really loyal, but it's only within the small group, and then they're still "the other" and they're not you.

I mean, there's our basic instinct as animals. To me, our biggest challenge is that before there was any involved language, there was your basic instinct to protect and to survive. If someone threatened this, you react to it. You didn't really sit down and talk about it. We're intelligent, we have degrees, but are we any better? We still have that basic instinct of fear and of protecting our own territory. We live in a very hard world.

And, haven't you seen so many times when people do come together around music?

RAMOS: I see music as a great vehicle for so many positive things. Music is very . . . well, for me, it's therapy. It's very enlightening therapy, even in rehearsal. Just getting together with friends. It's a wonderful thing.

HUDSON: So, was music always a calling for you, or was there a time you were going to do something else?

RAMOS: There was a story when I was thirteen. My cousin was a saxophone player. He found out that I had wanted a guitar. I wanted a bass right from the very beginning. I saw my neighborhood friends about three houses down, playing in the backyard with two guitars and a bass, and they were playing Beatles songs. And I noticed that a couple of neighborhood girls were there paying attention, so that's what I want to do. Not only is it such a cool thing; it makes these cool noises, and it's the music, it's the notes, and girls too. I like the guitar. That whole scene is beautiful.

That's what I wanted to do, and so I started to gravitate. But, I wanted a guitar for two years before I got one. My parents could not afford to buy me one. My cousin was a saxophone player. He went to a pawnshop and bought a one-dollar, horrible, nasty guitar that just butchered my hands, but I played it for years and never stopped until I had a better guitar. So I played and played it. Finally, my parents gave up; it wasn't something that I was going to give up, so they bought me one.

My cousin who spent one dollar on that horrible guitar for me thought he was just giving me this guitar so I could learn to play guitar, but for one dollar he gave me a life.

HUDSON: I told you this—I had the same calling to teach. I didn't ever have to decide what I was going to do.

RAMOS: Really, for me, I didn't know for sure if I was going to do that, but I really liked it a lot. But they asked you in junior high school and stuff, "What do you want to be in your life, or what do you want to be when you grow up?" I have a friend of mine who told me her answer when they asked her that was "I'll let you know when I do."

HUDSON: So, you sound really positive to me, and you sound like someone who looks for what's positive, and you seem to be on that path. Has that always been your path?

RAMOS: Well, what helped me is when I quit drinking twenty-one years ago, because I was an alcoholic. I graduated to be an alcoholic slowly but surely, without even realizing it. I think that's all—not everybody is just a heavy drinker right from the beginning, but drink heavy and heavier, heavier, and before you know it, you're at the top level. And then, this is where you are.

Me, I wondered, "How did I get here? Where is my goal?" It started back in the Joe King days because we used to have beer endorsements, and we had two cases of beer at every show, iced down for us, from the beer company. This is 270 shows a year! [*Laughs*]

HUDSON: Yeah.

RAMOS: It's a lot of beer that we couldn't drink; we gave a lot of it away. But, I just graduated there, and then eventually I realized that kind of was really sad, stuff like that. Once I accepted the fact and realized I was an alcoholic, I was trying to think, "What am I going to do?" I was trying to figure it out, because all I've ever done is figure this stuff out myself. "I don't want doctors; I don't go get my head examined"—you know, all that kind of crap—like figure it out myself to the best of my ability, and that's what I've done all my life. That's it. And part of the extension of that was quitting drinking when I realized I had a problem. But I had never realized or even thought . . . it's like, "What do I do next? Because now I'm an alcoholic; this is what my life is. I don't want to do it." I never thought about quitting. That was my last solution. Then one day I just thought I'd like to quit. So, I did.

Well, I didn't do it right that moment. I said, "I'm going to quit. Yeah, it's just that simple. I will just stop drinking. And I'm not going to do it today, because right now at this moment is not the right time." I still drank for another two months after that, but I knew I was going to quit, and I knew when that was. That was in Fort Stockton, Texas, at nine-thirty in the morning in front of a La Quinta, checking in after we had driven and were about to go to West Texas. And beer helped me stay awake and I was driving late at night, so at four in the morning I started drinking and that kind of helped me wake up. But by the time I got to the La Quinta, the birds were chirping and people were going to work on this nice sunny day, and here I was in the middle of my third beer, and I thought like how disgusting it was. My buddy who was with me poured out that half a beer, and that was the last drink for me. Ever.

HUDSON: That's not usually the way people do it.

RAMOS: So . . . and it's funny because I drive by and I can see the parking lot right there in front of the lobby, the exact spot where I quit twenty-one years ago. So, that was my health insurance—another level up of like "I need to stop this." And I look at it all the time—look at beer and liquor right in front of me—that's no problem.

HUDSON: That's amazing. That's just not the way it usually happens.

RAMOS: And I've never been to that AA meeting. I've never even done that or don't know what those things were about. I've never been to one. So, I don't even think about it anymore. But I don't want to say I'll never ever do that.

HUDSON: Right.

RAMOS: So, my little clause to myself is that when I turn eighty, if I want to I can start drinking again—I might. But I figure by the time I'm eighty, I'll have done as much destruction as I am capable of.

ROBERTO SONTOYA RAMOS has toured throughout the United States and the world. He is a producer and composer of blues, rock, jazz, funk, and Latin for himself and multiple music icons.

Gilbert Reyes

Fount of Knowledge and Experience

I first met up with Gilbert at the Conjunto Festival in San Antonio. Then he showed up at various special programs about music at the Guadalupe Cultural Center. Chumbe Salinas, carrying her video camera, strongly recommended that I meet him and talk with him. What a storehouse of information he is as he travels the world representing Hohner. He is not only an ambassador for the instrument and the music, but he loves the performers.

HUDSON: Let's talk about your own story first. I know you represent Hohner in North America, and I know you also played accordion. And we can talk about the labels you hear regarding the music.

REYES: So many labels can lead to a lack of cohesiveness as well as confusion. Mexican American, Chicana, Tex ?Mex, and on the East Coast I hear "Latinos." I was a political science major, and Nixon coined the term *Hispanic*. I do know that a large majority share the same language (Spanish) and like similar music but are extremely different in world views and politics. I do, however, use "Latino" when trying to explain the market or when doing presentations. I am from South Texas, and my parents came to Texas from Nuevo Leon, Mexico, in the fifties. I played music from about age fourteen to eighteen and then decided to go to school in Austin. It was better than picking tomatoes in the fields. I had a scholarship to St. Edwards, but that became too expensive, so I moved to California and finished up at California State University. I was in California at the inception of the internet boom and started an online group called Reyes's Accordions: a platform to discuss accordions, learning how to play, repairing, and selling new and used accordions. We were the first to sell accordions online. We also sold instructional videos and contact info for artists and repair technicians in the US. The group grew from five to thirty thousand in a matter of a couple of years, all people who were interested in all things "accordion." This was before social media; all we had were forums and MySpace at the time. At first it was just about *conjunto* music, but it later grew to incorporate all genres of accordion music like Vallenato, *norteño*, zydeco, Cajun, and Irish. Kids were learning from this site. I met a young man in Monterrey, Mexico, who told me he learned to play accordion by being part of this online group. What I did not realize is that Germans were also looking at this forum online. As a matter of fact, I got a call from Horst Fausel, product manager for the German company, who said he was interested in exploring the Latino market, and he invited me to meet with him at the NAMM convention that is held in southern California every year. I was surprised at how little they knew about the market in the US. Still in their minds was the heyday of the piano accordion, which peaked by the mid-50s. Piano accordions outsold guitars 100 to 1. He told me about a new position being created for product management, and I was invited to go to the new office in Virginia for an interview. It was clear when I had my meeting with Hohner Germany, they were thinking more about the piano accordion market. They did want my insight into the Latino market, but this was not the direction they really wanted at first. I had other ideas based on the instrument that I grew up with and which is a big part of my community, the diatonic accordion. I told them about my background, passion in music, and the instrument I was familiar with, and they still hired me. I am not at all dismissing the piano accordion. It is still an important category that is a part of our product portfolio, but what I am referring to is sales. Today diatonic accordions outsell piano accordions 100 to 1. Obviously, this was not always the case.

HUDSON: And the rest is history! I know of your history with the product and the music.

REYES: I had the opportunity to create my position, and I am writing my own story about that journey now. I was the first Mexican American to work for this 160-year-old German company. In 2007 I went to Virginia and and did a presentation on demographics on the growing Latino population in the United States beyond Texas, California, and Florida. I also pointed out the buying power of this market. My business proposal included honoring the maestros with a signature series model: Los Tigres del Norte, Flaco Jimenez, and Esteban Jordan, to start off with. This was to show the community that Hohner never forgot our culture, community, and music. It worked! The market responded. Hohner has been in the community since the beginning and played a vital role with our music and the pioneers of *conjunto* and *norteño*: Los Alegres De Terán, Narciso Martínez, Santiago Jiménez Sr., Valerio Longoria, Don Pedro Ayala, Ramón Ayala, Juan Villarreal, Antonio Tanguma, and the list goes on.

HUDSON: Tell me how you did your work.

REYES: I visited dealers and noticed the accordions were sitting on the floor and the T-shirts were on nice, fancy display racks. I created colorful displays for accordions, to begin with. One dealer in Texas told me he could not sell them because he did not speak the language. That encouraged me to add some imagery—a photo of a community of musicians. I also used social media and got famous groups to use Hohners. We created a "pull" instead of a "push."

HUDSON: That sounds like smart business to me.

REYES: I also saw keyboards in colorful boxes stacked in stores, so we worked on unique packaging for our Panther edition—an entry-level accordion. We sold about fifteen hundred a year, and in three or four years, we were selling ten thousand. I have always followed Los Tigres del Norte from San José, California. I was invited to one of their concerts and saw firsthand the consumers that I needed to target. Before the event they invited me on their tour bus to talk about accordions. Jorge has always been a big fan of the Hohner Corona model; he has been playing one since the 1970s. His brother Eduardo, who also plays the accordion, prefers the large Italian accordion. It was clear after our meeting that we did not have the model that this market desires: Italian handmade accordions with registers. I went home after the concert, around 4:00 a.m., and was inspired to write a business plan to add a new premium category to our portfolio. It took some time to get Hohner Germany on board, but after many meetings and visits to different factories, we finally had our new line: the Hohner Anacleto Collection. To help us launch it, Los Tigres used the first prototype at the Latin Grammys in November 2011. It was a beautiful, red and black, five-register Anacleto with unique crystal designs, and the camera zoomed right in on the accordion during their performance onstage. It was a pre-launch, if you will, and the actual market launch took place at NAMM in January 2012. The phone didn't stop ringing: "What was that?" people were asking. We got calls from dealers and musicians. The exposure for our new Anacleto line had a halo effect on all our other products. It basically lifted our brand status in the market.

HUDSON: I know your life is special because of your deep appreciation for the musicians as well as the music.

REYES: Yes, I get to hang out backstage at the biggest concerts and again at the small dives. That is special to me! This is where I learn firsthand what is happening in the music scene.

HUDSON: And you bring your own personal South Texas history. Playing the accordion is also integral to your professional position, right?

REYES: Yes, I created that position. Hohner never had one like that before. When I arrived at Hohner, accordions were basically on life support; I had to figure out a strategy that was going to work. Even though I'm from Texas and grew up with Conjunto and Tejano, I had to look at the big picture and go beyond these genres. For example, in 2010, Gerardo Ortiz was booked in a hipster club in Richmond, Virginia, for the first time. Jokingly I told the promoter who invited me to the concert, "I am the only Mexican American in Richmond; you won't have an audience." To my surprise, the concert was sold out at $150 a ticket. I asked Gerardo's manager how they managed this. He replied, "Gerado has 50 million followers on social media. We announce where he is going to perform and quickly sell out venues all over country." They were already sold out for their concerts in Maryland and New York after the Richmond gig. What I am talking about here is regional Mexican music that is popular all over the US and Mexico. The accordion is an important part of this genre and its commercial success.

Gilberto agreed to send me some recommendations for this project and some more information about Hohner. He is known as a man of integrity and grace in this business.

GILBERT REYES began tuning and repairing accordions and became the innovator of the third button that extended the instrument's upper range. He worked for Hohner, where he created signature instruments inspired by greats such as Flaco Jiménez and Ramón Ayala, as well as a line of instruments for aspiring musicians. He was also responsible for the the Anacleto Collection premium line of accordions.

Lesly Reynaga

Dual Passport

I attended a gathering of scholars interested in the new Dylan archives at the University of Tulsa with Dr. Tom Palaima of the University of Texas at Austin. There, I met Gavin Lance Garcia, who impressed me with his work in Texas music—and we all loved Dylan. We met up again at the Dylan concert in October 2018 in Sugar Land. Then I received a message from Gavin, saying, "You will want to hear this young artist." I trusted his taste in music, and I called her immediately. The country was awash in conversations about borders, immigrants, and humanitarian behavior. My love for Mexico only made the political rhetoric even harder for me to bear. This young woman, who was honored with her own day in Austin in 2018, became a light in the darkness for me.

HUDSON: I'm going to Mexico tomorrow. San Miguel de Allende. I bought a place down there about twenty years ago. This time I'm just going for six days. So, talking to you right before I go also fits in with this semester. I'm teaching a film class I created on Mexican American directors and themes. So, my students have finally gotten around to talking about immigration and borders. And they just looked at me. After about the third week of school, I said, "How does this class relate to what's going on in the world? Because that's the only thing that matters." And dead silence. I said, "Does anybody watch the news?" Lesley and I took off from there.

REYNAGA: I have a lot of stories. And especially when you talk about borders. I grew up going back and forth between Monterrey and McAllen, because that's where my dad's family comes from.

HUDSON: That's actually where I wanted to start. I want to give you a chance to talk about the brilliantly named *Dual Passport*. In "American Girl," you said, "I'm from here, and I'm from there." I loved it. So, I thought you could tell me some things about how that feels to you. I do notice the fact of your influences and definitely want to have a little moment talking about Bob Dylan. One of my major guys. And you mention Shakira and Beyoncé. Let's talk about *Dual Passport.*

REYNAGA: It's very relevant to my life and from where I stand; it's been a very interesting year for me. I'm going to start with a little bit of background. I grew up very close to my family. My mom is one of eleven children. And I grew up very close to my mother's family. My parents got divorced when I was six years old. At that point, my dad stayed in McAllen, and my mom, and my siblings, and I went to Mexico like indefinitely. And this is kind of a complex story. We were trying to adjust to our new lives there, but it didn't work out for my parents. And the reason why we were in McAllen, by the way, is because my grandma, my paternal grandma, was born in Brownsville. And so, I have that connection to Texas that my grandma was born in Brownsville. And my dad and his siblings, they are American citizens, naturalized.

They were all born in Monterrey. And through my grandma's citizenship, they all became citizens. The last six months when my parents were together, we lived in McAllen. It didn't work out for them. So, my mom, and my siblings, and myself went back to Monterrey. It was going be very different for us to live in a house where it was just my mom, and my siblings, and I, and she was kind of starting from scratch. So, we went to live with my grandparents. And in my songs, I talk a little bit about my *abuelitos* because I was very, very close to them, both of my grandma and my grandpa. Growing up in the same house with them and with my mom being gone working so much—that just kind of opened up doors for me to spend a lot of time with my grandma, who by the way taught me my first song when I was four years old. She had an old songbook, and she pulled it out and taught me my very first song. It was a polka. It's called "Atotonilco."

It's funny that you happen to own a house in San Miguel because I just visited about a year ago. December of last year, my boyfriend and I just kind of borrowed my mom's car, and we drove from Monterrey to San Miguel. And we made a stop at Atotonilco. Let me tell you, that just totally filled my heart with joy. Of course, my grandma and my grandpa have been gone for years now. They've passed. And stopping by there was just so meaningful. And it brought me back to the start where I started singing, and that was really my introduction to music as a singer. That's how I started.

I did live in Monterrey until I was sixteen years old; then I moved to McAllen. And it was, to be honest, particularly to get my green card. I was under eighteen and talking to lawyers. They mentioned that it would be an easier path to citizenship if I became a US permanent resident before age eighteen. And at that time—by the way, this is in 2008—the violence in Monterrey was very, very strong. It started getting to the point to where we had really close friends who—children, and siblings, and brothers—were getting kidnapped and killed. So, that's where my mom said, "You know what? I think it's time. Go ahead and just go to McAllen. We'll get the paperwork process done, and then you come back." It was interesting because, at that time, I was going to a private high school in Monterrey, and I had almost a full scholarship for my high school, because obviously private school in Mexico is expensive. So, my mom was a little bit concerned that I would lose my scholarship. I was able to do my schooling.

Well, when I got to McAllen, I just decided I need to learn English. I mean, I'm already here and I barely know my basics—just numbers and ABCs. So, that's when I decided, "You know what? I think I just need to go to high school here."

HUDSON: And what made you want to be an American citizen?

REYNAGA: At that time, it was more about opportunity. I have that opportunity to move to the United States and find jobs. I was raised to be a really good student and to just strive for success. Mom worked so hard. Everything that she did her whole life—it was all about her three children growing up to be successful people. So, every move that we made was all about getting to a better place. And becoming a US citizen was a part of that process in our life.

My siblings also became US permanent residents; they were already over eighteen. So, for them, it wasn't as big as a priority as it was for me. So, that's it. I enrolled in high school in McAllen, and I didn't know English. So, I was supposed to start the eleventh grade, and they actually moved me back to the ninth grade. So, I had to start from freshman year. And I just started really somehow learning the language and just focusing on that. I excelled in all of my classes.

I did really well. I ended up moving to a school that allowed me to kind of move at my own pace. So, I graduated high school in two years instead of four years. And in those two years, I learned my English basics. And during those two years, I also discovered mariachi music. And my first elective class was a classical guitar class. So, when I started going to this class, the instructor also happened to be the director for their mariachi ensemble there at Nikki Rowe. And one day, he just kind of asked me, "Hey, you know, like do you sing?" I said, "Yes. I've been singing since I was very young." And he said, "Well, I'm the director of the mariachi." And I was just thrown off by the fact that there was a mariachi in high school, because coming from Mexico, that is not anything I'd heard of. And, of course, to be a part of the mariachi, you have to play an instrument. So, it worked out because I already had some basic guitar knowledge/skills. And I actually started picking up a guitar when I was fifteen.

My mom and my dad are both very musically inclined people. And they can both sing very well. And they can both play instruments. My mom had a guitar laying around for a long time. It was a beat-up guitar that my grandma gave her when she was a teenager. And one day, when I was home in Mexico, I just decided I wanted to pick that up and just figure it out. So, I did. Luckily, at that time, the internet was already prominent enough where I could look up how to play guitar. And so, I just started learning how to play chords. So, when it came to mariachi music, I started learning the different rhythms. And then, of course, with the mariachi music, you have so many different styles, from *huapangos*, to *ranchera*, to polkas, boleros. So, you have all these different styles as a guitarist.

When I first sang a mariachi song, I think it was "*Costumbres*"—it's a Juan Gabriel song. I surprised myself because I didn't know that I could sing like that. Growing up, I listened to a lot of pop music—really being influenced by an older sister who listened to Britney Spears and Christina Aguilera and then all the boy bands, like N'Sync and Backstreet Boys. And that was kind of like my upbringing in music. My mother, by the way, did listen to a lot of Rocío Dúrcal. That was her big-time idol. And I listened to a lot of that and also Shania Twain. And then my mom also listened to a lot of Shania Twain and the Carpenters. I had a very interesting musical upbringing.

And then, of course, I listen to a lot of Latin pop and what was playing on the radio. The people that came in my teens, we had bands like

Ha*Ash. They're two sisters who actually are from Louisiana, but they were singing in Spanish, and they became huge stars in Latin America. Again, it was a very wide range of genres that influenced me from when I was young and started singing, but always in the pop-music realm. That was really what I was listening to. So, when I started singing mariachi music, it really was a whole other world because the vocal technique is very different. And I just kind of started singing with a lot of power. I surprised myself that I could do mariachi music. My voice had a lot of power in it, and it was really getting people's attention whenever we would go out and play as an ensemble. And especially because mariachi music is played just outside—no PA systems, it's just acoustic instrument—my voice was able to project from long distances, and it would just kind of surprise people.

During the two years I played with the mariachi ensemble, I actually got to compete in McAllen. They had a festival, and I actually got a first-place vocal trophy. But the only thing that I can tell you is that I was just very surprised that all of this was happening because, well, first of all, trying to adjust to the system, the school system, and the new language and the new culture in a new home and everything else was overwhelming as is. But what got me through it was mariachi. That's absolutely what just kept me pushing forward because everything else was just very stressful, and I was trying to figure out what to do with what I had in front of me, especially because I started getting a lot of opportunities for scholarships and financial aid. And now, when we're looking at college.

My idea was to eventually go back to Mexico. And in Monterrey, we have a really big university. I grew up my whole life thinking that I was gonna go to school in Monterrey. But being in McAllen and going to high school there and talking to my counselors, they noticed that I was working really hard, and I was getting good grades, and I was just kind of pushing forward. And they told me there's a whole lot of opportunities with scholarships, and you can make that happen if you stay. And there's really no reason for you to go back to Mexico. So, that just kind of ended up being what happened. And luckily, my mom was very understanding. I stayed in Texas but moved up here to Austin. And my aunt and my cousin were living here. And my cousin was already going to UT, and she went to community college and was transferred to UT. So, I literally ended up doing the exact same thing. I moved to Austin. I enrolled in ACC. And I went there for a year before transferring to UT Austin.

HUDSON: I'm amazed at the work you did in school in your second language.

REYNAGA: Yeah. It was all about practice. I'm gonna say that 95 percent of the population in the Valley speak Spanish. So, you can easily get away without learning English, and it's fine, but that was just a part of my priorities. I wanted to learn English, and that was just the goal. And so, I started asking people not to speak to me in Spanish. And so at school, it just started getting really funny, where teachers were just kind of pointing at this new girl from Mexico who is doing better in US geography than all of you kids. "What's wrong with you? Well, how come this girl who is just learning the language and just moved to this country understands where states are located better than all of you?"

HUDSON: Were you getting deliberate about citizenship?

REYNAGA: Exactly this year (2018), I became a US citizen. But at that point, when I was in McAllen, it took about a year to get my US green card. So, I started as a green-card holder, and it was just this year that I made the move to become a US citizen. And I think something really important to bring into the equation here is that my mom had an immigration issue. And she had her visa taken away probably close to twenty years ago. And she hasn't been able to come back to the states ever since. My mom wasn't able to go to my college graduation. My mom has never seen me perform live with my band 'cause she hasn't been able to come to the states in all this time. So, everything that I've done is kind of like driving to just make my mom proud, but she's far away. So, she cannot really be there to see the success.

That's a really huge factor, especially when it came to writing my new material. It just touches on immigration a lot, and it's not just because I'm an immigrant; it's close to my life, but also my mom's experience and my family's experience.

When she goes and requests a US visa—which she has tried I believe four times or so ever since—they deny it every time. And so, most recently, she tried getting her visa before I graduated college, which was 2014. And they denied it on the grounds that "Well, your children live there," because my siblings now live here too.

HUDSON: So, there was like a fear that she wouldn't just be a tourist.

REYNAGA: Exactly. And I will tell you this, when it comes to the immigration system, very often it's about what mood the officer is in, what kind of person you're talking to. It's that biased and subjective to where the officer can make the decision on their own ground based on what their decision and what their opinion is. And she said that she was very close to getting through the process until she came across the woman who was looking at her paperwork. My mom had kind of ticked the box on the form that she filled out that said, "Have you ever had any immigration issues?" She checked "Yes." So, she said, you know, everything was going great until the woman saw that little box, and then she just kind of went back and just said, "I'm sorry. You have had a record and you have children there, so I have plenty of reason to believe that you are gonna move there, and you're just trying to get your tourist visa to overstay your visa," which is a little bit funny because she has all this paperwork that she brings with her to prove that she is established in Mexico and that she is married and has a life, but they didn't even bother looking at that. So, it's a very biased process. And so, anyway, that was the last time that she tried.

Gavin is very crucial in this story. I met him in 2014 when I was just about to graduate college—I didn't really finish my story about going to UT. So, I enrolled in communications school, and I majored in public relations at UT Austin. But while I was a student at UT, I also reached out to the mariachi ensemble, and I joined the ensemble.

So, I continued to do what I did in high school. And this time around, we got to play a little bit more in San Antonio. We got to play at fiesta. And it was just a really incredible experience. And through the UT mariachi, we did a little recording for their school of music and I met a producer, Michael Ramos. Whenever I went out there, and I sang a couple of songs for the project, he handed me his card and said, "Hey, if you're ever looking to do anything, any project, just reach out. I'd love to work with you." Well, it turns out that Michael Ramos works with people like Lila Downs. He has worked with and played keyboards and accordion for Paul Simon. So, he's kind of very well versed in the Americana world and has a really incredible reputation here in town. He's a really great musician. So then, it was 2014 and I'm meeting Gavin. It was the last gig that I played with the UT mariachi before I graduated, at the Mexican American Cultural Center here in Austin. And Gavin happened to be there. So, when I was walking out that night—I was on my way out— Gavin approached me, and we started talking. And from then on, we just kind of sat down for coffee and started talking about my career. And as you would know, Gavin is a huge Bob Dylan follower—and not just Bob Dylan, but music. I mean, he's been in the music industry for a long time. He plays music himself. But when it comes to music integrity, he has very strong opinions about what's good and what's not. And he has been a pretty big influence in my career ever since. So, I've known him for four years. In those four years, that's when I started writing music. I didn't write until I met Gavin, and I was twenty-two years old. I think I had written one song in college when I broke up with a boyfriend, and I never played it anywhere or shared it with anybody 'cause I thought it was dumb.

A really big influence of mine has been Linda Ronstadt. But I didn't know Linda Ronstadt's background. I didn't know anything about her other than her mariachi music in her album *Canciones Mi Padre*, which is her mariachi album. And in talking to Gavin, he kind of started there, asking me, "Do you understand what kind of impact she had in the music industry, being female and being Mexican American and with her background? Everything that she did set a precedent to what you're about to do." And he really brought into perspective the idea of respecting my elders and learning my history and just going back and figuring out things.

And everything that you're doing now has a cost. It has had a cost for many other people to just kind of open doors for you to do this. So, you have to learn your history. And at that point, we just kind of started working together very, very closely. And I've been learning my music history, especially when it came to American music, because, like I said, growing up in Mexico, I was all about pop music and that's just all I knew, but I never really understood that there was a whole world out there of songwriters—and that's really where Gavin came into the equation. Of course, Linda Ronstadt wasn't a songwriter, but her career was just an oddity crossing over so many different genres, starting in folk music and then eventually like jumping into more rock, having the Eagles as a backing band and bringing them together and then, you know, moving into more of a pop ballad field and then mariachi music. So, she did so many things. And, of course, it was inevitable that I was gonna be very, very influenced by her career.

But when it came to songwriting, Gavin said, "If you're going to have a music career, you cannot just go singing other people's songs. You can, but I think you have the potential to do more." And that's where Bob Dylan came into my worldview, because I had no idea who Bob Dylan was from years ago. And so, he took me to see my first Bob Dylan concert probably that year, 2014, in San Antonio. And, of course, I was just very confused as to what was going on because there's this old guy, and we're kind of far away from the stage and the stage is so dark. There's this guy who is like mumbling, and I can barely understand what he was saying.

HUDSON: That was during his sort of Frank Sinatra dark stage. I was there.

REYNAGA: Exactly. The Majestic. So then, we come back home and he started sharing Bob Dylan's catalog with me and just kind of like slowly introducing me to him. So, I will say it was a little bit overwhelming because he started from the very, very, very top. I mean, he just kind of threw me in there and said, "Read this. Do you get it?" I'm like "No." So, it's been a very interesting road just because it's been four years that I've been studying all of this. And, of course, I've been so fortunate that Gavin has kind of taken me under his wing. I call him my dad. So, we're that close. We're like father and daughter at this point. And he has undertaken this huge task, which is guiding me through a music career that is something that goes beyond just being a pop singer, which really when I was young and I used to sing in front of a mirror holding a brush, all I could think of when I saw myself and my reflection in the mirror was "I can be a huge pop star." I mean, that's what it's all about because that's what little girls dream of. And there was nobody there to tell me that there was this whole other world out there where I could actually write my own songs and share my stories and my perspective and just be OK with that.

HUDSON: Let's talk about role models.

REYNAGA: When it comes to Texas, ever since Selena Quintanilla, there really hasn't been a voice, a Latina voice, that reaches such a point that it's a national situation where they are looking at Texas and being like, "Hey, there is somebody there representing." So, most recently, there is Selena Gomez. And she's from San Antonio. And she's just a proud Texan, though she does not emphasize La Trinidad as much as I would like to see. And the reason I'm saying this is because I think there are a lot of little kids out there growing up and looking for influences who speak like them, and act like them, and look like them, and have a similar culture. And they're looking to connect with that person.

HUDSON: I hope I get a chance to invite you to Schreiner University someday.

REYNAGA: I'd love to. Absolutely. That would be such a great opportunity. But it is different when you talk about it and you share your experience. For me, it has been a very smooth ride just in general. I feel like I very easily adjusted to my new life here. And even though the most difficult part about it was the separation from my family, mostly being away from my home, that was just the hardest thing about the whole thing. But when it came to adjusting to the new system, and the new language, and the new culture, I didn't see it as a difficult thing. It was a good challenge, but it was more about reaching my goal and just getting there, rather than looking at it from a perspective of "This is really hard, and I don't know how to get there." It was more like, "Ooh, this is a challenge. Let's do it. I'm here now and I want to learn." So, especially when I moved to Austin, and I started going to college here, I started mostly hanging out with people who didn't speak Spanish, and I did that because I wanted to learn the language better. I wanted to learn English better. And I started hanging out with people in college who knew things, like sororities, and fraternities, and the Greek life, which honestly in my world was just a moment thing. I didn't understand that that was real. It's just little things that I had seen in movies that I had no clue were actually a real-life thing.

I had my first gig in Dallas Saturday night. And so, I took three guys out there—my band and myself. And we opened for Del Castillo at the Kessler.

HUDSON: Boy, you had a great audience.

REYNAGA: And the audience—oh man, that audience, it was just unbelievable. This particular experience has been mind-blowing, playing at the Kessler for the Del Castillo audience, because it was a bit of an older audience, probably in their forties and up, but they were so receptive to my music, which, as you know if you listen to the new material, is very pop driven. It's upbeat, and it's very current when it comes to the music, but the content, the lyrical content, was what they were able to connect to. And in between songs, I shared my story and talked about my roots and going back to Mexico, in the Valley, and then that just got them because most of these people had that connection to the Valley. Of course, Rick is from Brownsville. So, a lot of his followers are also from the Valley. A lot of the audience members approached me toward the end. I had this one particular woman who said, "I work in the entertainment industry in Las Vegas, and I came down here for my birthday visiting my brother. And I was here to see Del Castillo, but I didn't realize that I was here to see you, and what you just did up there and just giving your soul to the audience and just opening up and just giving it all you've got in your performance. You just reached so deep into my heart, and you made me cry. And this is exactly what the world needs to see. And I've seen people all over Las Vegas. Anybody. You name it. Bruno Mars— whoever. And I just haven't seen anything like what you just did."

Oh my gosh. And that just caught me off-guard because I was there to play my music. And I just released this material. So, it's been only a month that I've been playing this live, but that was the first time that I had many, many people approaching me and just talking about how connected they felt to what I did on the stage. And, of course, I threw in a couple of mariachi songs. I still incorporate that into my live set. And there was this other woman who approached me, and she said, "I'm from Brownsville. And hearing the story and seeing you out there and what you do, it made me feel so proud. It just made me feel proud, and I felt represented. I haven't seen that in so long." So, this was completely unprecedented for me because I didn't really understand what I was getting myself into with this crowd. I was mostly worried that they were gonna be a little bit thrown off by the pop sound, but it turns out that they were very moved by the content of my story, and my lyrics, and my message. And they identified and they connected, and that was something that just kind of made my whole crazy year worth it—the stress of questioning myself: "Am I doing the right thing? Are these lyrics fine?" Being just very critical of my own self, of course. I don't know if this is the right way to phrase it or word it or "What am I doing?," and then all the doubt, and all the stress of going into the studio, and I don't know if this is the right sound.

HUDSON: And so, your voice is part of what will inspire me, especially next week in Mexico as I just kind of absorb the cobblestones and the art and Atotonilco.

REYNAGA: Atotonilco—that town just made my whole trip. I mean, obviously, San Miguel is so beautiful, and we also stopped at Guanajuato, which is incredible. But to me, stopping at Atotonilco was magical. Every time you cross the border coming from Mexico to the United States, there is that little like knot in your stomach, like "What's gonna happen? Are they gonna be questioning me?" There's doubt every time. Though within me, I know that I'm following the rules and there's nothing that can go wrong. But it's always been very nerve-racking.

LESLY REYNAGA was born in Mexico but is now a US citizen. The UT Austin graduate writes, performs, and records bilingual songs. Her music style embraces pop, rock, urban, Americana, traditional Latin, and her roots in mariachi.

Frank Rodarte

I met up with this positive enthusiastic man in San Antonio. His name had come up many times in discussions of the music of San Antonio, and I had heard his soulful sax with some bands there. He brought me some tacos and a chest of drinks for the interview. It is Saturday, June 13, 2015, and we are sitting at my hotel on the river in San Antonio. His spirit is kind and generous, and he is eager to talk. I know I am going to enjoy this.

RODARTE: Communication is by burro. I would rather spend time with the grandchildren than learning to use new technology. You picked a great location. I went to school right across the street at Central Catholic. I graduated from there in 1960. All Mexican. I am seventy-two years old. I have been married to Beatrice for fifty-one years. And when she chases me off, I don't leave. When they tell you to leave, just go into the next room and shut up. That will keep your marriage together. It is no good to argue. I got my music training right across the street. I came from the east side, and my dad has a family business there. We are carpenters. My dad raised eight boys and two girls in the shop. We all started there as sweepers at eight or nine.

At first, I thought my first name was *Pendejo*. My dad had a bunch of workers there, and they might need some help. They said, "Hey, *Pendejo*, bring some water." I kid about that onstage now. I started playing music in the high school band. I kind of cheated my way there. I played by ear and never learned how to read. I still don't know how I do what I do. It's got to be the Holy Spirit. I can play just about any song.

HUDSON: I read a wonderful comment you made about playing the melody where people could feel it right along with you.

RODARTE: When you do a solo, you often have the melody in your head and just blow all kinds of notes. But when you play the melody, people join along with you. I want to record a lot of the songs in my hymnbook at church. Many great songs there.

HUDSON: I was raised in a Southern Baptist Church, and music was everything to me. My dad died last year at the age of ninety-one, and my mom died about a week ago, also at the age of ninety-one. They started singing at the end of their lives—even bedridden. And those old hymns were in there.

RODARTE: Remember what the apostles did by singing in jail. Sometimes the doors would open.

HUDSON: I have a book that has the stories of many of the old hymns. My foundation also does a tribute to Texas music each September, and we have added a beginning session that features gospel music. Very important in our culture, I think.

RODARTE: There is a recording made about thirty years ago that KEDA [radio station] plays every day at noon. It is called the noon prayer. The Davila family used to own the KEDA station, the jalapeño station, which is my nickname for it. Now that I am older, I am the mild one. I recorded this song written by Carlos Rosa, who was studying to become a priest. He decided that was not his profession, so he got married and had children. He is a wonderful parent. And he wrote this song called "*Virgincita.*" He was the choir director. I fell in love with this song. I called him and asked permission to record. He said yes, and I told him I would do him justice. By that time, Randy Garibay and his brother Ernie and Alfred Garcia joined me. And my daughter Edna joined me. I got a bunch of us together, and we recorded it. Joel Dilley was playing the bass. So I recorded this song, and I recorded a Christmas song, "*Niño Jesus.*"

I was taking a shower with my hair full of shampoo, and the Holy Spirit sent this melody to me. I had to turn the water off, wipe off the soap, stand naked, and write down the song. The Lord sent me the whole thing at one time. I have to be ready to accept it and take it in. [Frank sings me some of the song.] I decided to do a forty-five with my song on one side and "*Virgincita*" on the other side. A good combination. One morning at six-thirty I decided to take the master to the head DJ [at KEDA]. He went on the air talking about his father's [Mr. Davila's] seventy-eighth birthday. It's about ten in the morning. I wondered what I could give him for his birthday. I went to the bank and got a brand-new fifty-dollar bill, a brand new twenty, a brand new five, and three brand new ones. I put them in an envelope for him. I went to three different places to find the right card. I did. It said, "What do you give a person who has lots of money? More money."

He used to brag about how much money he had. I even asked him about giving 10 percent to the Lord. We would always talk like that. I showed up with the card. The family ran the station with an open-door policy. No other station did it this way. The Davila family did. I walked in, and Mr. Davila was at the front desk. I gave him the card. I went in and gave him the recording. He interviewed me, and we talked about the songs. I went back by the front desk. I thought Mr. Davila was pissed. "Son, come here. Sit down." "Oh shit, what did I do?" He gets behind me and starts rubbing on my shoulders. "Nobody's ever given me money. Everybody always fucks me. Who would think a musician would give me money? What can I do for you?" I thanked him for opening the door for me. "I really want to do something special."

"What is that you have there? Is that the song I just heard?" Then he asked me what I wanted to do with that. I told him I wanted that to be the noon prayer. "Consider it done," he said. He has even sold the station, and they still play that song to this day. On KEDA, the jalapeño station still plays this.

HUDSON: Let's have a conversation on the words used to describe the culture.

RODARTE: I am Mexican American, and I'm a jokester. I always tell people I'm a black man who lives in a brown body. I was raised on the east side. I'm like Steve Martin in that movie where he did not know he was white.

HUDSON: You brought me some great Tex Mex food.

RODARTE: I am not sure it is Tex Mex. But it is soulful.

HUDSON: I am not sure *Hispanic* is the right word.

RODARTE: People come from Mexico; we call them Mexicans. If people come from Spain, we do not call them Mexicans.

HUDSON: Does your heritage go back to Mexico?

RODARTE: Yes. My mother was from Saltillo, Mexico. My dad was an Aztec Indian. But I was born in America. My dad was an illegal when he came in, but he eventually became a citizen. I am Chicano. If you don't like that, I'll kick your ass. [*Laughter*] Pocho, Chicano, Mexican. *Pocho* is a guy that comes from Mexico and is Americanized.

HUDSON: Dagoberto Gilb does some great writing on the culture. He has written a book called *Gritos*. And he talks about his identity. His essays are fantastic and were used on NPR.

RODARTE: Sounds interesting. My upbringing separates me from the other brothers. My father had the financial means to send me to Central Catholic. I give my education a lot of credit for the life I have. I had to ride two buses to get to band practice early in the morning. It was not close to my house. It was a great formation for me, coming to this school. It took a lot on the part of my dad. I was one of eighteen Mexicans who came to this school. The discipline was strong. They would not take shit; they would kick your ass. Really. In 1958 we had some problems with a gang, and we regained some control and respect.

Sam Kenrick gave me my name, the Wild Jalapeño. And he hired me to write a column for years, "The Jalapeño's Corner." I used to write about people nobody wrote about. I used to love doing that. The west-side cats loved it. I got their story and a photo. You got to tell somebody. The devil wants you to be quiet. He don't want you to say shit; he knows it will do harm to the devil. Suppress you. Fuck you all up, man—that's what the devil does.

HUDSON: You are working on a book?

RODARTE: Starting a band is one story. Raising a family while you are doing this is one story. I don't want to leave my family out. They always traveled with me. We'd go to a gig in Chicago, and I would get us an apartment or a hotel room. We had a six-month gig in Hawaii; they went to school in Hawaii. I always had them with me. And that is the story I want to write. But it is confusing to tell both stories. I want to be inclusive; I don't want to leave nobody out who helped me. When I hit my father, that was the worst thing that ever happened in my life. My father apologized for putting me in a position to hit him. He was a minister, not a violent person. He lost his cool that one moment.

HUDSON: Maybe you should start your book with that moment. . . . It sounds like alchemy. Something happened in that moment.

RODARTE: The truth you cannot change. There are so many things that have happened when I tell a story. I dictate my story, and a friend types it. I wrote this so you could see what we are talking about; I kept that band together for seventeen years. No personnel changed. I have had a fun life. You won't believe it. I had a chance to party with great people. Elvis used to come in steadily to see us.

HUDSON: I am glad you are choosing to write about it.

FRANK RODARTE began playing saxophone in high school, and his R & B–style group landed a 320-week stint at the famed Sahara Hotel in Las Vegas. He still performs and uses his music to help at-risk folks with his Peace in the Streets concerts and ministry.

Florin Sanchez

Subtlety Speaking Volumes

I spoke to Florin Sanchez at the office of the Texas Heritage Music Foundation on November 20, 2014, at the Schreiner campus. He was the very first recipient of our Wayne Kennemer Scholarship. We named it after Wayne because of his heart—his heart was all about music.

HUDSON: As a recipient of your scholarship, you are in good company with Kristi Foster, Casey Hubble, John Christopher Way, and others, as you know. The first significant money we raised in 1996 with Merle Haggard and in 1997 with Willie.

SANCHEZ: I was there and played before Willie, but I had to leave for another gig and did not get to meet him.

HUDSON: I was listening to your album *Excursion*, produced in 1997, and I see that you sang all the songs, played all the instruments, and produced it. I was drawn to the eclectic nature of all the music. It does not sound like the same song over and over. You pulled many things from yourself. I know you used the scholarship money to do some work in a studio, and this was a result of that. Let's talk about this project.

SANCHEZ: I wanted to have something to showcase the various abilities that I have musically, and I wanted to have something that would show what I could do with various musical instruments, as well as my production skills. I wanted to put these songs together in a way that was cohesive. I wanted it to be a musical journey for the listener.

HUDSON: Did people around you encourage you to do this?

SANCHEZ: I have been playing all of my life, and I realized I wanted to do something more with that. I have been playing since before I can remember. I do have early memories, but I have photographs of me when I was little. Drums at age five.

HUDSON: What is the role of family for you? I know you had an uncle who played with Jimmie Rodgers.

SANCHEZ: On my father's side, I have a grandfather who was the leader of the Chamber of Commerce band in Kerrville in 1911. He was the only Hispanic in the band. He would be called here to Schreiner Institute to substitute for the band director here. His name was Florin C. Sanchez. His brother, Steve Sanchez, played twenty to thirty years with the San Antonio Symphony. My great uncle, Percy Bowles, was a hot-shot guitarist who played blues and ragtime. He was in the Legion Hospital at the same time Jimmie Rodgers was there. He later visited him at Blue Yodeler's Paradise, taking my father with him. My father was twelve and vividly remembers riding around town with them in a big car.

HUDSON: I met your father when I moved to town, and he told me that Jimmie Rodgers would give him a nickel to get him a Coke.

SANCHEZ: I heard these stories growing up in my family.

HUDSON: And your family has always had this barbershop?

SANCHEZ: It has been there since 1911, and we celebrated one hundred years a while back. My sister Paulette is a beautician, and my nephew Chris is a fourth-generation barber. Louis plays trumpet and cuts hair. I never got interested. The music was always my first love.

HUDSON: Did you finish a degree in school?

SANCHEZ: No, but I did finish a recording course I studied when I got the scholarship. I did go to college and study music theory and other things that interested me. When I thought I had what I wanted, I just moved on. I've always had a great interest in recording. I received a tape recorder when I was five years old. I've always been enamored and fascinated with it. When the time came, I decided to study engineering. That class gave me more focus for this.

HUDSON: Was there a point when you had a specific dream and fulfilled it?

SANCHEZ: As a kid, I remember wanting to play the guitar effortlessly. When I realized I could do that, I felt like I had accomplished a dream. Another was to have a recording where I did all the parts. It goes on and on. Being able to play professionally. Playing blues harmonica. I did work with the Trinidad Pan Masters for four years. Kim Loy Wong was one of the original steel-drum makers. Five were brought here by Pete Seeger in the early 1960s. He came down to San Antonio to work with a doctor who was working with troubled children. Before that, he had done some work with the Smithsonian and written a book on constructing steel drums. That was the original reason I became interested. I played guitar with them, and some bass on occasion. At times, I would sneak over and play the drums. We stayed in Texas, but we worked with producers outside of Texas.

HUDSON: Let's talk about what you are doing with music right now.

SANCHEZ: I am also still working on recording with a focus on singles. I am working toward putting more music on iTunes. I have about ten songs up there. Seems like that is one of the formats that will carry the music. I am looking toward doing things I can put online and sell individually. It seems that things are heading that way. And I see more writing ahead. I don't think I will abandon the idea of an album, either. I am still working on recordings where I produce, compose, and play. Stretching out with focus while being open to other influences.

HUDSON: Texas music is a separate label, it seems.

SANCHEZ: There are very few states that can claim a specific style of music. Texas is almost its own country, and we have our own music. I know Europeans admire the Texas model. It is a great experience to be in a state where music is such a big part of its rich heritage. Many people identify Texas music with the Americana style, including the polkas from the Germans and the music from Mexico. All different styles seem to exist here.

HUDSON: Have you heard people describe your music?

SANCHEZ: I have not heard a particular phrase that would solidify what I do.

HUDSON: Mostly I have watched you play an instrument, but I enjoyed watching you sing and play at our September tribute.

SANCHEZ: I don't put myself in the position of singing to be background music. I prefer to save that for a special presentation or a private party. I don't mind playing where people are partying, of course.

HUDSON: Your guitar work seems effortless, and it is exquisite. What is fulfilling for you is to play in a small club in Kerrville, like the Waterin' Hole gig on Thursday night. I see you playing for thousands in a huge arena, but this great band, SLY [Someone Like You], keeps rocking us here. I am glad too!

SANCHEZ: Musically that group allows me to explore different aspects of my guitar playing, and the group is pretty diverse. We have a varied set list.

SANCHEZ: I love all the instruments and styles.

SANCHEZ: People don't really expect to hear what we are doing. I get a lot of joy from people being surprised!

HUDSON: How is the writing process for you?

SANCHEZ: When it comes to composition, there are so many ways to approach it. Whatever it takes to go from a kernel of an idea to a song. I do have various methods. I have this thing where I write song titles down, and then I'll go over the list and look for the ones that start singing to me. If a phrase has a melodic character to it, I will go with it. Once I have a chorus developed, I develop the story, the verses. Then you start hearing it, and the song dictates how involved the arrangement will be. Some songs are very simple, and some demand more. And I sometimes start with a musical idea and then start singing words over it. It's always good to be inspired, but you don't have to wait for it.

HUDSON: Is there an autobiographical aspect at times?

SANCHEZ: Yes, you may have an idea from your life, and then alter it with some fiction. At times, you do have to bare your soul. Other times, I might see something that happens that leads to a song.

HUDSON: I have seen you more than once at the Kerrville Folk Festival, and you wander the campgrounds.

SANCHEZ: That is a central part of my life; my community is there. Each year when I return, I get that sense of coming home. Frank Hill is a memory there, and I played mandolin with him. Another great figure there is David Amram, another multi-instrumentalist. Watching him move from one instrument to the next without taking a breath is a great influence! This made me realize things. I did not realize I could learn from someone so accomplished. Even though he is a versatile conductor and composer, he is totally open and down to earth. To see someone of that stature just being down to earth—he was one of the driving forces to influence me.

HUDSON: He was always an encouraging voice for all that I did, and he inspired me to keep doing what I was doing. I have a couple of interviews with him, and I even read a bit of Kerouac as Amram played behind me. What a joyful moment in my life. What are some other influences on you?

SANCHEZ: I have a huge number of influences from composers, Bach and Mozart, to Debussy and Ravel and Shostakovich. Watching cartoons and hearing this orchestral madness was enriching. My folks listened to a lot of music at home, from big band to western swing.

HUDSON: Did you know Junior Pruneda? He lived in Kerrville at a time when he heard at a restaurant, "We don't need any Mexicans in here." Of course, he is a bit older. [*Laughter*]

SANCHEZ: Junior and Fritz Morquecho were part of this scene in Kerrville. When I was younger, one of the first bands I played was with Chuck Van Kirk. He is still here in Kerrville. He wanted to start a big-band orchestra. He played saxophone and many woodwinds. Occasionally, Junior would show up and play bass, and I was on drums. He was trying to fill out the horn section with guys from high school. But they were too interested in cars and girls, so we couldn't get them there every week. The core group would show up. We rehearsed at the VFW, and I was recommended by some people there to another group with Charlie Mann, who played on the Louisiana Hayride. I started playing professionally with them at twelve years old. I played every Friday to Sunday.

No one in the band was under thirty-five, so I was the youngster. I think around that time I decided to follow this road. My family supported me too, taking me to gigs or picking me up when late. I have been very fortunate that my parents have been so nurturing and supportive that I wanted to pursue music full-time. Coming from a strong musical family gave credence to the fact that I was going to play. My mother has been incredibly supportive of me and my music. One of my earliest memories is playing drums on pots and pans, and my mom would hold the lids so I could have cymbals.

HUDSON: I have seen pictures of her on Facebook thanks to your sister, Paulette Sanchez. Did you graduate from Tivy High?

SANCHEZ: I did not. My senior year, I ended up going to college, and I was on the dean's list that first semester. I got a GED to go on to college. At some point, I decided I was not going to pursue getting a degree.

HUDSON: What are some other interests in your life?

SANCHEZ: I have a penchant for reading, and I read a lot of music and art history. Earlier you asked about influences; aside from orchestral and big band, I am influenced by the arts and literature. I feel like those elements are influential in both subject matter and structure. I see the melody like an outline. I started noticing parallels among various forms of art. I do some photography, and I do love film. I have a music video online at the moment for a song called "*Todavia*" in Spanish. Go to You-Tube and put my name in. I haven't spent much time in Mexico.

HUDSON: *Hispanic heritage* as a term derives from origins in Spain, so I am struggling with terms here for this project. *Latino* doesn't quite work. Are you aware of being part of this culture?

SANCHEZ: I can definitely see the influence in my family. They are third-generation Hispanics who don't speak Spanish, but I was fortunate to have these influences and speak the language. We do speak Spanish at home, even now. I speak in Spanish to my mom. That plays a role in per-sonifying who I am. And in Texas, we have names of towns, food, and language that define who we are. *Tejas*. The Czech and German cultures also immigrated here. And the Irish.

HUDSON: Of course. Texas was once Mexico, and some people I know in Mexico will say that the land is still Mexico. History tells us that. I like the term *Tejano* for just that reason. We are all living on soil and breath-ing air that was also Mexico.

SANCHEZ: My mother is from Mexico, but I was born and raised Texan. And I do get asked about the blue eyes. That comes from my grand-mother. My great-grandfather was from Ireland. I have a fascination for Celtic music too. And I have some Native American blood in there too.

HUDSON: My family story is heavy on the Scotch-Irish roots, Tennessee to Texas. It is interesting to look back on all those family stories and know we are carrying that in us. What music do you listen to now?

SANCHEZ: It's a pretty eclectic mix. We have a good jazz station in San Antonio. I listen to that and the classical station. It is a matter of enjoy-ing it, and it being an education too. If you spend enough time listening to classical music, you understand the difference between Baroque and Romantic.

HUDSON: I tell my students that I discovered three musicians—Willie, Bob Dylan, and Leonard Cohen—in college and fifty years later I am still listening! I like to ask them, "Who will you be listening to in fifty years?"

Switching gears, what challenges do you face? You play with several bands right now.

SANCHEZ: Being able to let it ride. I accept that the work will come since I don't have a regular full-time job. I don't feel like I have too many hurdles, but as the music industry evolves, new challenges arise. How do you sell your music? Another might be staying relevant, not necessarily current. Ultimately, there is always an audience, but it is a matter of how you present it and make efforts to connect.

HUDSON: Do you have plans for the future?

SANCHEZ: I have some generalized plans. I would like to pursue the Les Paul method of taking it to the very end. He played until the very end. I want to be able to do that.

HUDSON: I have the same perspective about my teaching. No retirement ahead . . . yet.

SANCHEZ: Yes, I would like to reach a larger audience, and work with various projects that allow me the opportunity to use the skills I have acquired. I always wanted to work with Miles Davis or Frank Zappa. But they are gone. I would love to jam with George Benson, B. B. King, or Buddy Guy, just to have that musical conversation. I am open to jazz collaborations and orchestral work.

HUDSON: I want an album of you singing in Spanish!

SANCHEZ: That is not entirely impossible. Ultimately, I would like to have a collection of songs that I put together.

HUDSON: I admire your choice of words. I love visiting San Miguel de Allende, where I have a place. And I do love hearing the Spanish language all around me. Carrie Cameron and Rusty Henson produce a music festival there each March. I hope to get you there sometime with [your band] Someone Like You, or on your own to play with others.

SANCHEZ: I know that Doc Severinsen had a stint in San Miguel de Allende. I got to see Doc Severinsen a few years after his stint with Johnny

Carson. He was very modern, playing a lot of modern jazz. I don't think people were expecting that.

HUDSON: I would love to see you playing in Europe sometime.

SANCHEZ: I could go for that. It is good to get out of your comfort zone and see things differently. I would be open to that.

FLORIN SANCHEZ, barber, musician, classically trained guitarist, and jazz fan, conducted the local Chamber of Commerce band in Kerrville. He's known for the various styles he plays and records, as well as his original music.

Poncho Sanchez

The Heartbeat Is the Drumbeat

Previously, I had seen Poncho play in Fort Worth and Austin. Now I had the opportunity to see him again in San Antonio. Ramon Luera, the music aficionado who lived in Laredo, set up an interview for me after the show. He was friends with Poncho in Laredo, and they stayed friends as Poncho moved to LA. Poncho Sanchez is a big name in Latin jazz, and his prowess on those conga drums and vocals is a thrilling part of the musical experience for me. Not many people turned out on this cold night in San Antonio, but I stood in the front row and danced.

What a generous man. After the show, we talked with him briefly, and he showed his love for my friends Ramon and his brother, Polo. I had the experience of meeting the other bands backstage and watching Poncho interact with good friends. Those hands were taped for the conga, and his style is infectious. We talked by phone later on.

HUDSON: Was that the Pan American Jazz Festival in Austin where we met up?

SANCHEZ: I don't really get involved in the details anymore because I have a manager who handles that. Everything goes through my manager. Of course, you are calling me on my home line because of family, Ramon and Polito.

HUDSON: I want to give you a chance to tell me your stories. I would love to talk about Laredo and Texas. I also know you were raised in California. Let's talk about your time in Texas. Do you consider yourself a Texas performer?

SANCHEZ: Well, not really. I spent most of my life in California. But the way it worked out for me is that I am the youngest of eleven kids. I moved to California when I was three or four. I got here in 1954. But coming from Texas, my older brothers and sister got a hold of the radio and realized how many different types of music we could hear. Coming from Laredo, we had stations from Mexico with mariachi music and more traditional music. We didn't have a TV in Laredo, but here in LA we got a TV and my older brothers and sisters caught the first wave of the mambo and cha-cha music from the big dance TV shows. They were the ones who started buying the mambo or cha-cha music. It is now called salsa music. *Musica Latino. Muscia Tropical.* For them, they loved that music, and it ends up, as a little boy of five or six, watching my sisters dance to Tito Puente music, I loved the sound. I loved the rhythm and the way they would dance. They would shuffle their feet on the floor—those hard cement floors in Norwalk, a suburb of LA—and I would hear that rhythm. I thought, "Wow, this is great." And so that is how it happened to me.

I was exposed to many different types of music. They also liked pop music and black rhythm and blues music. There was only one black R & B program on TV at that time in the 1950s: *The Johnny Otis Show.* It was an all-black band, but he was Greek, and he married a black woman. My sisters used to love to watch that program. The pop music was Pat Boone and Ricky Nelson, but we learned they were copying the black artists. We learned that Elvis was copying Little Richard. As a little boy, I learned all this watching my sisters. That is how I was exposed to all this stuff.

Back to the original question. Yes, I am a Texan. That is in my blood. I got into a Tex Mex band out here, where all the band was from Texas: Little Jimmie and the Vagabonds. And two of the band members were from Marathon, Texas. They could copy Little Joe's Band and Sonny and the Sunliners. So, in high school, I played in this Tex Mex band. I was there because I was a singer at that time. So the story goes, I grew up in this neighborhood of Norwalk. I learned to play the guitar in about the sixth grade from a guy down the street. My father decided to move back to Laredo in 1964 because they were trying to buy our house to knock it down. Being raised here, having my friends here, I was going into seventh grade. And my brother did not like it, either. And I had six sisters. And Carmen was in her senior year in high school. They gave my father the money he wanted for the house. These brothers from Germany wanted to knock down the houses to put a shopping center in. These gentlemen came to our home and talked to my father about buying the property. I was in the kitchen listening. I was worried about moving; then my dad got the big idea to move back to Laredo.

He had a cleaners business, Hollywood Dry Cleaners, in Laredo. Anyway, I heard my dad argue with these German guys, and Dad held out. Then they said they would build a wall around his house and build the mall around him. And they started this wall. It was a nice brick wall, not a piece of junk. I am thinking, "What is going on here?" My dad wouldn't budge. My dad held out, held out. One day, they came back to the house and finally gave him what he wanted. Then they hired me and my brother to knock down the brick wall, brick by brick. We could sell them. So we packed up the car. Three of us had to go back to Laredo. We cried all the way back.

I went to Christian Junior High. My brother was in the ninth grade. My sister graduated at Martin High School. We were so used to the way things were done in LA. At that time, everyone was wearing continental-style clothes. We wore slacks and nice shoes to school. Well, back in Laredo, it was jeans and a white T-shirt. Nothing against that, but we were not used to it. It was too damn hot here. We were lucky because my father has always been in the dry-cleaning business. We could bring all the free clothes we wanted. We were always looking sharp in school.

HUDSON: You stood out a little bit in Laredo?

SANCHEZ: You got it; you see where I am heading. When we got back to Laredo, we noticed we were a little back in time. The "new" music on the radio was old to us. I would tell Paulo it was old. You know what I am trying to say. I was learning to play guitar at that time. I got to know Laredo when I was in junior high. During that one year, I got to know my cousins. We would go fishing at the river—catfish. Lake Casa Blanca. We enjoyed that part of it. Polito was playing guitar some, and he did not live that far from my house, and he lived by the bakery. We would strum and try to put things together. Ramon was older, and he would come in and out. Ends up that Polito was my best friend, and we would go to that bakery and get bread.

HUDSON: And that was just a year!

SANCHEZ: Yes, and I love the brothers. In that one year, I got to know them very well. You don't make many connections in life like that. I feel like I grew up with them. We share our life stories—our dos and don'ts. I think Polito thought I was cool from LA, and that helped. Some of the tough guys in my classroom would try and push me out of the way and most said in Spanish, "Weird guy wearing weird clothes." I had lost most of my Spanish, and I spoke English. LA has really changed now, and you hear lots of Spanish being spoken. It's not like it was in the fifties and sixties. When we got there, we spoke Spanish well. But we were laughed at during that time. In Laredo, you could always speak Spanish. I grabbed hold of Polo and another friend named Victor.

HUDSON: It sounds like this experience got woven into who you are, not in a negative way.

SANCHEZ: But I also lost sleep at times. It was a weird situation. My father bought a nice little home, and he made a back room into a dry cleaners in the house and had my sister run the front desk and had me and my brothers take the clothes back on bicycles. My father was keeping himself here to open a cleaners. He had a pretty good idea. It was right off of San Bernardo. But they were thinking about putting that freeway there and knocking down houses. Again!

After we all got out of school, we went to [my sister's] graduation, and we went home, packed up, and told Dad we were coming to California to visit our brothers and sisters. Of course, when we got here, my mother told my father, "We are not only on vacation, but we are staying here." My dad went off on her, but she said she was staying.

She was from Laredo too—well, they were both from Mexico, but they met in Laredo. But it bothered her that it bothered us. She used the vacation ploy to get us back to California. He stayed in Laredo another four months, sold the house, and the only thing left of our old home now is the fence that was between us and the next house. That was where the freeway came through. That's how I met Ramon and Polito. I never forgot about them, and I have returned there many times. And actually, as I got older, I became Poncho Sanchez; they were so proud of me. They knew me as a struggling kid learning to play. They were so proud of me. When I went back, we would go to Ramon's on Scott; we would have brisket and ice-cold beer, and Ramon collected records like I did. That's why I didn't interview with you in Texas, because I always just want to hang out with these guys.

HUDSON: You are an international and world artist now. Is there anything in your music or life you attribute to Texas?

SANCHEZ: For sure the Tex Mex food. My mother and father met as teenagers in Laredo. She had that Texas tradition—even the way she made tortillas. My mother made them toastier and crispier than the thicker ones out here. A lot of little things—the breaded steak thing. In Texas, they make a rue with meat and call it *carne guisada*. They don't have that here in California. Both my parents lived to eighty-seven. They were real old-school traditional style, going to church every Sunday. Mother took care of kids all her life and cooked all her life. She was great, and she made flour tortillas every day of her life for fifty years—except on Sundays. My father would take her to a church in East LA where mass was in Spanish, and they would go there. Even when we got older and quit going. Then they would go out to eat and go to a dance: *tardeada*.

Sunday was the day for my dad to take my mother out. It was a beautiful thing. Even after I got married, Sunday was my mother's day. Even after that, she helped raise all the grandkids. She had about sixty-five or seventy. I am the youngest of eleven. Everybody got married before me. She would babysit. And she was a great cook. In fact, when you called me earlier, I was making food like my mother did. I was making chicken with onions and tomatoes and chilies and garlic. We boiled some beans and rice.

HUDSON: You are sometimes called *Mexican American*. In Texas, there are many terms for this tradition—Tejano, Hispanic, Tex Mex, Chicano.

SANCHEZ: I am Mexican American, but when people ask, I say I am Tejano; I am from Texas. I say it all the time. In fact, people often come up to me and ask if I am Cuban. I say, "No, *yo soy Tejano*." I'm from Texas. I am a Mexican American from Texas. And they can't believe it. They are sure I am from Cuba or Puerto Rico. I was born in a hospital in Laredo. My father was from Jalisco, and my mother was from the north, in Nuevo Leon, Mexico, near Monterey. And both families migrated to Laredo during the revolution with Pancho Villa. A favorite story of my mother was a time when she hid under the bed at their small ranch when Pancho Villa and his band came to the house. They had a small ranch in Valle Cillo. They came to the house, and the young girls had to hide under the bed. And my father is from Matanzas in Jalisco.

HUDSON: Are you going to new places with your music at this point in your life?

SANCHEZ: I have been playing professionally since 1975 when I joined Cal Tjader's band. Latin jazz. I knew all about Latin jazz because my older brothers and sisters had all his records. I joined his band on New Year's Eve, and I have been playing and traveling ever since. I have been to Africa, Thailand, New Zealand, and across all the states. We played everywhere. For kings and queens. And that's no lie. I have played for presidents and prisoners. We have been nominated for the Grammy nine times, and I have won twice. At this point in my life, I am almost done with what I want to do. Now I want to be around family. I promised Ramon I would be back to hang out. I am an October baby, and they always have the parties for birthdays. I am not going to retire, but I might play just once a month in LA. It is painful to fly with ten people. And I have to include all the airline tickets in the price. It gets expensive.

HUDSON: You have had such a rich, full life. Can we have a short conversation about a song? Do you have a good old favorite?

SANCHEZ: There are so many great songs I could pick for different reasons. Something I have always liked that takes me back to Laredo, Texas. "Cien Años," one hundred years—I love that song. But the best I ever heard was from Sunny Ozuna and the Sunliners. I loved the horns. The way they recorded it in the sixties. That song takes me back to Laredo. I think it may be from Mexico. Javier Solís, or some of those big-name Mexican singers. It was a big popular song in the Mexican movies. Ramon will know all about that. I am thinking about recording it.

HUDSON: You have been very generous. Thank you very much. And I hope to see you again soon.

SANCHEZ: Tell Ramon and Polito I love them!

PANCHO SANCHEZ'S musical influences came from radio and television. Originally a guitarist, he auditioned for the R & B band Halos and became their lead vocalist. He taught himself flute, drums, and timbales. The Latin jazz bandleader and his ensemble won a Grammy for Best Latin Jazz Album in 2000.

Patsy Torres

Educating and Entertaining with Grace and Style

In December 2018, I went to El Mercado in San Antonio to see Patsy Torres perform. She engaged with the audience as if we were all her good friends, and she called up small children to sing and dance with her. I had seen her in Uvalde years earlier at a concert and watched her award-winning style then. The conversation we had by phone deepened my respect for her and her commitment to making a difference in life.

HUDSON: So glad to talk with you. I am impressed with all the work you have done in music, as well as all the talent you have. I met you in Uvalde once. I knew that we must talk. I have heard you introduced with several labels, and I wonder which one you identify with.

TORRES: I think you're right about the labeling because there's all those different labels out there, and some people get furious. They don't want to be called this or that. "Don't call me a Latino, or don't call me Hispanic, or call me Chicano, or don't you dare call me Chicano." Me, I like the *Latina* kind of label, if you will. You said label. When it comes to Tejano, all that is, all that means, is Texan. So, I'm both. I'm Latina and Tejano 'cause it's just like saying you're American and you're Texan. Yeah. So, Latina is more of a culture 'cause I'm American also. And I think that that's one of the main things that we consider ourselves. We were Americans, so, when they label you Latina, or you're Hispanic, why can't you just be American like everybody else?

HUDSON: There's a scholar out in El Paso, Dr. Yolanda Chavez Leyva, who alerted me that Mexican American without the hyphen was the word I needed to be using. We met at a conference on the border once. And I listened to her talk, and she said, "Hispanic is political, and it's Nixon era, and it's what we were called." She was very much against the word. So, when she came to my session, when she walked in the door, I marked out the word *Hispanic* on my poster. She got a kick out of that. I said, "Well, we're not going to be talking about *Hispanic* heritage here."

TORRES: I mean, it's like calling everybody Irish American, Swedish American, and Chinese American. Why the labels? Now, I am Mexican American because my father was Mexican and my mother was American. My father was from San Luis Potosi.

HUDSON: Oh, that's a good song.

TORRES: Oh yeah. It's the place I visited earlier this year for the first time in my life.

HUDSON: I stop there on the bus I ride down to San Miguel de Allende.

TORRES: Yes. And that's where my father grew up. They came over here to this country when he was, I think, thirteen—right around that age. He was thrown into the culture. He didn't know English.

HUDSON: Do you have opportunities in your career that go way beyond performing and entertaining because of your commitment to the world to make other things happen and your commitment to education? How would you describe your commitment? Because I think it's huge.

TORRES: It started with my grandfather. He was a medical doctor since the age of twenty-four, practicing medicine in Mexico. And he was one of the guys who was against . . . he was like part of the revolution over there. And they shot up his house, and they were out to get him. So, he came here to get away from getting shot over there for safety for his family, but he was a doctor. So, he got over here right away. He got work and was doing great. And I came along. I just love my grandfather, and I wanted to be just like him. I wanted to be Dr. Torres like him. And so, of course, he instilled education. You had to go to college. You have to do this. Yes, yes, yes. It wasn't if. It was yes. You're going to college. And my commitment was, "I'm going to be a doctor." And I studied. I interned during the summer at the hospital. I said, "Yes, this is what I wanna do. I wanna help people. I wanna help people with their pain and comfort them, especially pediatrics." It was my course. And music kinda threw me off.

HUDSON: Well, I would probably describe it as an added layer, an added feather in your cloak of many colors. I mean, it gives you other platforms to make a difference.

TORRES: Yeah. Because I never dreamed of being a singer or a musician. Not at all. I imagined myself in a white lab coat and working with kids, and helping, and giving comfort, and healing like my grandfather did. I know he's so excited that I decided—out of everyone that I was the one who was going to be a doctor like him. But then my sister started playing saxophone in middle school. She was passionate about music. By high school, she sounded really good. She was getting out of class all the time for pep rallies. I was like, "Hey, I wanna get out of class. I'm gonna play an instrument. I don't care what instrument. I'll just play anything just to get out of class and then hang with her." So, my grandfather had an old trumpet in his closet because he played many instruments also. He played classical guitar, piano, violin. He had an old trumpet, a flute, a sax. Oh, I think he had a clarinet in there. So, I picked the trumpet. I started playing trumpet in the school band. I practiced real hard. I got to the varsity band, marching band, concert band. And we just made a little group for a talent show. We made a little group and won the talent show—a bunch of friends in high school. I said, "Let's make some money doing this because we sound good." We thought we could do it anyway. And we started playing for the school dances. And we got better and more popular, but I was a trumpet player, not a singer. This was at Jefferson High School in San Antonio. That was just a little temporary thing. We didn't make a lot of money. We made some money.

But after graduation, I was like, "OK. Time to get serious." My sister got married. Some of the other guys went into the military. So, I was like, "OK. We're making money." And I kind of needed to make some money. I need to pay for college. I got a grant, and I had to pay my own way. I had a little apartment. So, I kept playing with the band. When these new people came in, older guys, they decided to cut the band down. They didn't need a big brass section. They could cut it down to like one keyboard player. But we didn't have a keyboard player. So then, we get one keyboard player and got rid of all of the brass players. So, that would save 'em one person instead of four. I was on the chopping block, and I was like, "Uh-oh. What am I gonna do?" I just got a job at Taco Bell and was starting at San Antonio College. I was on my own. I was estranged from my family. That's a whole other story.

HUDSON: Yeah. Well, estranged may say as much as we need. . . .

TORRES: I didn't get along with my father. He's an alcoholic. And I was the stubborn kind of person who fought back. And I ran away several times, but they always caught me. The last time I ran away, I never went back. So then, that's why I was on my own. But my father forbid me to talk to my mother and my siblings and told me I was dead. I didn't exist. I was just on my own. But my grandfather, I could visit him. He was like, "You can do this." He knew I was going to college. My grandfather was his father. So, there was a big problem.

HUDSON: That is tough. That's a big step from what you're telling me now to suddenly being this amazing voice of leadership. I mean, you're not just an award-winning performer. I've seen you perform, and sing, and dance, and bring all the elements of the history into it. You represent all the threads of the culture. All of them.

TORRES: For twenty years, I was so shy as a kid. Even when I started playing trumpet, I didn't want to be in the front. I'd stand in the back playing my trumpet. I'm trying not to confuse you, 'cause all this stuff was happening kind of at the same time—the battle with my dad, him keeping me away from my family. So then I gravitated more toward my grandparents. My grandmother had a stroke, and she was in a wheelchair. They had her living at home. They had a lady helping. I still visited them, but then the lady was in a car wreck and couldn't take care of her. They couldn't find anyone. So, I went in temporarily to help. I was living with them, but my father was furious and actually physically hit me when I was there when my grandfather wasn't there. And my grandmother—all she did was hear a bunch of noise. "What's happening? What's happening?" So, I came back in after the fight with him. "What was that?" "Nothing, Grandma. I'm OK. I'm OK." Well, she could have a stroke in a second. So, I told my grandfather, and my grandfather said my father couldn't come visit anymore.

I thought he hated me because I caused this break between him and his parents, especially his father. I was a rebel. I wouldn't listen to him. I was very stubborn growing up. It started in high school. Before then, I was like the little shining star for him. But in high school, I started developing and looking like a woman; he started getting real suspicious, like "Who are these boys?," because we were in a band. Everyone else was guys. He was just imagining me being with all these guys and stuff. I never was. I didn't do drugs. I didn't drink. I didn't hang out with the guys.

HUDSON: So, was there a turning point for you again that allowed you to step into the place you represent now?

TORRES: I guess it was being on my own, being with my grandfather, and when the group was gonna kick me out. I remember looking down at my feet, thinking, "What am I gonna do?" And they said, "Look, if you could sing . . . if you could sing, the band could keep you in a little longer." A bunch of the bands at that time were getting female vocalists. And they knew I wasn't a singer, but they were willing to give me a try because I was singing the backup harmonies. I was good at that. I never sang. So, I just said, "OK, I'll try." And I learned one song: "Ooh Baby" by Linda Ronstadt. And that was the first song I learned. On everything else, I would stand in the back and I would play the trumpet with the keyboard player. So, it would sound like brass. And I played my trumpet, sang background, and came up one time for that song. So then, we're singing at a wedding and there's a Tejano music promoter in the audience. I guess he sees me sing, thinking I'm the lead singer, and comes running up. "Oh, you guys are great . . . Any songs?" "That's the only song she knows, and she's not the lead singer." The guy says, "If you wanna be on a record, the girl can sing."

HUDSON: Wow.

TORRES: That's how it started. They put me on a record, and I remember hearing my voice for the first time. I was like, "Oh, I sound like a mouse. I sound horrible." It started getting put on the radio. They started calling me a singer. Next thing I know, they're offering me a record deal, and the band is just freaking out that their trumpet player is getting all the attention. It ended up finally splitting up the band. It wouldn't work. They went into the studio. They said, "Oh, no, we don't need you guys. We have professional musicians to do the music."

I wasn't pushing it 'cause I felt like, "Well, they signed me. I'm not a singer. Never had lessons. I'll go along with it this far. But, hey, I'm going to school." I've got 7:00 a.m. inorganic chemistry class. I got biology—I got health and English. I'm taking all these courses, pre-med courses. And I just saw this as a way to fund my education. I never thought it would last. When the band decided to break up, I was like, "OK. That's it—full-time school." After that it was, "No, Patsy. No. Let's do this. I mean, you've got an album. You've got people who wanna sponsor you.

Let's make your own band." I was like, "Really?" "Yeah, come on. You gotta pay for your school and everything." I was like, "What do you think I should name it?" I started to think of something cool sounding—a name that would sound cool in Spanish and English—and they came up with Patsy Torres Band.

HUDSON: Did you ever have any decisions to make about what language you sang in?

TORRES: In the beginning, I just kind of went with the flow because I just felt like any minute this is gonna end. This is not my future. I mean, then I got a sponsorship from Bud Lite and they gave me all this money. And they made free posters and they gave us outfits and jackets. Sponsored tours. Then I'm being splattered all over the magazines and radio interviews. I'm like, "Oh my gosh, my stuff's on the radio and all this is happening so fast." And I thought, "Oh, this is just the way it is." I mean, it happened so fast. The first time, you don't realize how lucky you are—especially now when you see people who can't even get airplay, can't get any attention.

HUDSON: And you're still going to school?

TORRES: I'm still going to school because of that. In the radio interviews, they say, "So, you're gonna be a doctor? Oh, well, gee, Dr. Torres and Dr. Patsy." And call me that. And it is like known. So then, I start getting calls from Say No to Drugs and the Stay in School organization for career days—"Come and talk to our kids"—'cause everybody knew that I was this new singer who was going to school to be a doctor. So, I started getting invited in these things, and I found out I had this rapport with the kids.

HUDSON: You found out you had rapport with these kids?

TORRES: I got called because of the music connection. And with the kids, I just had this rapport with them, and it was high school kids. This was all high school. Not the little ones. The big ones. And I guess I really connected with them because of being on my own and having this rift with my dad. All the other kids had rifts with their parents, one or the other, and were having family problems and pressures. I could totally relate, but I would do it in a positive way because I am faith based and I will always bring God into it. I remember the first time I did it was at Lanier High School. And they just had me go in and talk to the little classroom. And as I'm talking, now the teacher comes in and another one comes in, and they just started listening to me. The kids are just giving me their 100 percent attention and asking questions, which again is something I thought, "Oh, all students do that." I'm thinking this is what they do. I didn't realize that they're over there rolling their eyes at the other speakers, and talking, and being disrespectful, and not paying attention. I didn't realize that. I had all attention and cooperation. So, next thing I know, they said, "Aha, this is wonderful. Do you think you could come back and speak to our school again?" I said, "Oh yeah, sure." So, they invite me back and I show up. "OK, Ms. Torres, come this way. Come this way." And I'm walking down the hall.

Next thing I know, I'm walking out onto an auditorium stage. And this is an auditorium full of the whole school, including the balcony. I had no idea I was going to be addressing the whole school. So, I freaked out. I'm on the stage. So, I just stood up there and I just started talking—letting them ask the questions and talking. And, of course, they always ask me to sing something. And the teacher comes out with an out-of-tune guitar. "I know, '*La Bamba*'! Let's try '*La Bamba*.'" So, I would just sing "*La Bamba*" or sing something a capella that the kids knew. So, that's how I came up with the idea of having the band come and back me up during my speeches so that I could sing and talk at the same time. And that's how the Positive Force Tour was born, 'cause I talked the guys into donating their time just to set it up. HEB was the tour sponsor. Then we started touring not only all over San Antonio but all over South Texas. And the show just grew from that.

With the kind of action that they gave us, we could pay for everything. I bought new equipment, costumes for the guys. I added dancers and special effects. I made it a giant show; I put in hours and hours of work because I wrote out the script. It was a show that we put on. I didn't just go in and jam. I'd pick songs that had meanings, change the word if I had to, and during the show, I had topics between each song.

HUDSON: Was there any thought at that particular time about the language? Like I know you've recorded in Spanish. I mean, I love the Spanish songs, but did you make a specific choice?

TORRES: I would do the Spanish part at the end where I would talk about, "And this is our culture. This is what we do." And I would get teachers up to *cumbia* with me. I'd call up the audience and dance the polka with one of the kids. I'd get them all involved. I'd tell them about being proud of your culture and the color of your skin, and respecting others of different cultures and different colors. All these little different topics I would talk about. I played all-black schools, all-white schools. I played in an all-Apache Indian school in Arizona because I started touring all over. So, I wasn't playing for just Hispanics.

The students were there after the show to talk to me. I spoke through with the music, and then they listened. I consider myself an *edutainer* because I do edutainment. Whenever I perform, I'm always teaching something that has to do with some kind of awareness in the community or education. Because I understand that I have a responsibility not only to education, not only to higher education, but to the culture, and to the fact that this is how important diversity is and the old famous line that we're more alike than we are different. And now that I've traveled the world and traveled different states in our country, I've seen racism. I've seen through the different lenses how some people look at other races.

HUDSON: Right now [2018], the rhetoric of our culture is so inflammatory that it's such an important time to stand up and say what you're saying.

TORRES: I can feel it even in the store. I mean, just shopping in a grocery store, I feel this weird vibe I've never felt before, like you're the enemy. Oh my gosh, it's crazy.

HUDSON: Yeah. I get a chance to point it out in the classroom not as a political statement, but I said, "Let's talk about language. Let's talk about rhetoric." I pulled up eight news programs, and seven of them were talking about rhetoric. And I'm in a writing class, and I said words *do* matter.

TORRES: What's beautiful is that I found that the music does cross the bridges because I can go in and I can speak at these different organizations, whether they're black, whether they're all Anglos, whatever they are. OK? But once I start singing, everything changes, and I saw that overseas too. We were in Japan, in Turkey, in Korea. A lot of those countries don't like Americans. But when I would sing—oh, they love me. The music enabled us to cross the bridge. Music is an important part of it.

That's why I consider myself an *edutainer* because I entertain. I want to make people happy. I want to make them think. In fact, for most of my shows, there's one point in the show where I always make people cry because I feel my job isn't done until I see a tear. But it's a tear of making a realization, or happiness that they heard something they remembered, or something that touched their heart. It's not a sad type of tear.

HUDSON: Is there a song you like to talk about?

TORRES: Well, a song that seems to always get to people is when I sing "Hero," the song by Mariah Carey. I kind of do my own version of it where I speak in the middle, and it just always seems to get to people all the time. Now, if you talk about my recordings, just lately in the last albums I started really writing my own music. Because when I was with record companies, especially back when I started, they told you what you're gonna sing. They picked everything. You didn't have any choices. Sometimes I would hate the song I was recording, and I would never play it with the bands because I hated the song. But now, I record what I want. I write my own music. And I like my music.

HUDSON: Are there any specific consistent influences in your writing?

TORRES: In my writing, sometimes I'll mention God. I'll mention faith.

HUDSON: You have an album dedicated that way, right?

TORRES: Yeah. Called *Mi Inspiracion*. That's the album I've written the most songs on. And the new songs I'm writing too—they're always positive. I just finished my Christmas album. So, I'm gonna get that thing packaged, and I've got a song I wrote on it called "I've Got the Christmas Spirit." And there are many ways to distribute the music now. Because they can download your whole album, or they can download one or two songs, or they can order the actual physical CD online.

HUDSON: This is definitely what I wanted to talk about because, of course, no one else has this story to begin with, and you've really made such a strong statement I think with your life. And again, I didn't first know those things about you. I just stood in an audience and watched you sing and felt your presence when we talked briefly backstage. So, you're carrying your commitment with you. It's very obvious.

TORRES: I mentioned earlier about my faith, but my grandparents taught me about Jesus when I was a little kid, and then they made sure I went to Catholic school. So, of course, I was entrenched in the traditions of the Catholic Church. I went to church every day because that was part of it when you go to Catholic school. I had to go confession all the time over the same thing. "I lied to my father. I beat up my brother and sister." "All right. Do three Hail Marys and then—" I mean, I had no doubt who Jesus was and what he did for me. And I always asked him for everything, and he seemed to give me anything and everything I wanted. "Jesus, give me a home run. . . . Thank you, Jesus!" He just answered everything.

HUDSON: That's a great testimony to be able to share the different ways you do it.

TORRES: When you're young like that, you believe in Santa Claus, and the Tooth Fairy, and the Easter Bunny. I mean, that's how I believe in Jesus. The same way with that strong commitment, like, "Yes, of course." When I got older, I didn't—I only went till fourth grade and I started going to public school, so then I wasn't going to church anymore. I wasn't going to confession anymore, and then I hit high school. And that's when the battle started with my dad. And I was always fighting with him 'cause I used to always pray. I stopped praying. I think I felt ashamed that I was fighting with my dad all the time because I was always against him. That's the point that I was ready to fight with him. Ready to just stand up against him again. And I stopped praying. And then, when I left home, I barely prayed. And I got real cold, and nothing and no one could make me cry. And I felt like my God hated me. Then I started helping my grandparents because of my grandmother's stroke. Since then, there was that little softening about being with them and them needing me. And, finally, I started "My Prayer."

It's going to be on my next Christian CD. It tells the story of me finally breaking down after years and praying, and asking for forgiveness, and asking for help and guidance. And from that time on, he was there the whole time. He answered me. And my purpose came into focus: Just pray. Go out there and serve. Help your brothers and sisters, which is everybody—everybody is your brother and sister. Stop being so selfish, and stop feeling sorry for yourself. You've got lots of gifts and lots of blessings. Be positive. I woke up and started looking at things that way, and I made up with my father. I got my father back, my family back. I met the love of my life and got married.

I've been blessed in so many ways, and it was God who decided for me to go back to school to get my master's and my PhD. University of the Incarnate Word called me to do a commercial for them, but they could only pay me semester hours. So I continued to work and did perform every year. And when I got a 4.0 in my master's, a master's in education, they said, "You should go for a PhD. We'll give you a scholarship." It was like, "Oh wow." My thing was my bachelor's, but the master's and then that? And my professor was like, "Oh, Patsy, you've gotta keep going." I was like, "OK, God, I guess you want me to do it." "How long is it gonna take?" "Oh, between five and ten years."

HUDSON: Well, you were definitely being led, and the thing is you were aware of that.

TORRES: And I knew. I said, "OK. I'm gonna do this." Of course, I had to pass the exams. I had to do the work, and then I did. And I think the biggest realization was back when I got my first degree from San Antonio College, which was a science degree. I sat down with my grandfather and told him, "I can't do both anymore—these seven o'clock classes." That was just sad. "When I go into pre-med, that's going to be serious. I can't do both. I can't do music and that because I won't give justice to either one." He's the one who said, "*Chiquitita*, you have a God-given gift—your singing. You're helping kids. You're doing preventative medicine. You're being a doctor. So, you should sing." He has always told me to sing. I couldn't believe it 'cause I know how much he wanted me to be a doctor. That's how much he believed, and I think God was speaking to him because next thing you know, I'm about a year away from getting my doctorate. I'm completing my coursework, starting my dissertation. And one of my classmates said, "Hey, what's it gonna feel like when they call you Dr. Torres?" And I went, "Hmm, my dream came true the way my grandfather predicted. I'm gonna be a doctor of preventative medicine." "Yes, you are." And I said God knew what was really gonna make me happy and fulfilled and where I could do the most. He knew what was in my heart. He knew. And then it's like, "Wow!" Because all that time I never saw that. So, my classmate told me that.

HUDSON: That's beautiful.

TORRES: All my life, I wanted to be Dr. Patsy Torres, and here I am.

HUDSON: I'm thinking about how distinct your story is. Next week, I talk to a real young performer in Austin who came from Monterrey, Mexico. She became a citizen this year. And so, she's got a story about her citizenship and she's a very young college graduate. Lesly Reynaga. It just might be something you want to know. And then little Marisa Rose Mejia; she's twelve and singing like a monster and performing in festivals—a little Selena incarnate.

TORRES: So, Selena started when she was six.

HUDSON: Well, all of these interviews have a very positive, uplifting tone. I'm glad about that. Flaco, and Santiago, and Los Texmaniacs. Just a variety.

TORRES: Have you talked to Vikki Carr?

HUDSON: No. But she opened the theater in San Miguel de Allende.

TORRES: Well, she won a Grammy just a few years ago, and last I heard she was doing another album because she called me to ask me if I knew a good recording studio in this area. And I also connected her with a lawyer in Mexico because she was doing this other stuff in Mexico, and I connected her with someone. So, she called me for some advice here and there. Because she's got the whole culture thing. I mean, she had to use "Vikki Carr" instead of her real name, and she was recording in English and then later on in her life she started recording Spanish and had some big hits in Spanish. And all her albums now are Spanish. And she also for years, and years, and years, she would support the Holy Cross High School here in San Antonio. So, it was a lot of great music.

PATSY TORRES founded the Blue Harmony Band while in high school to raise money for college. Although she began as a trumpet player, she has become known as a world-renowned singer, winning multiple awards. Torres has returned to her initial calling and is studying to be a doctor of preventive medicine.

Ruben V

Life on the Line

Monday, June 27, 2017, at El Mercado on South First in Austin, Texas. I have been waiting for years to talk with Ruben V. I heard him once and was moved to invite him to the coffeehouse at Schreiner University. I watched him blow away the students here.

HUDSON: Let's talk about your family, your space in the world, and maybe a bit about your life of music.

RUBEN V: I was born and raised in Corpus Christi, Texas. I was a dead baby. Mom and I were both blue [dead] at the moment of birth. Dad was told to choose his wife or his kid. He refused. "I want them both," he answered. My mom used to call me every year on my birthday, like the scene in *City Slickers*, and say, "Do you remember the day you were born and we both passed?" She swears she saw Jesus; she saw the light. They named me Ruben Gerard Vela, after the patron for babies, Saint Gerard. I was raised Catholic. I used to say as a teenager, "Maybe I am not supposed to be here." But my mom said, "Why don't you flip it around and say you are supposed to be here?" It changed my outlook—from being a negative kid, blaming my birth, to someone who saw a different perspective. I just remember her saying that; it hit me pretty hard. I grew up thinking I was a mistake; I wasn't supposed to live. It gave me a new fire that made me look at life differently.

I started playing guitar when I was ten. Dad always had gear lying around. I tell this story all the time because it is one of my favorites. My parents had a club together in Corpus, and I was washing dishes to make some money. My mom was bartending, as was my dad. One time, the band was looking for my dad . . . to sing with the band. I said, "What? Does Dad sing with a band?" Mom said he did with a band before I was born. I didn't believe it. They found my dad, and they called him up. [*Tears arise; Ruben halts*] Sorry, I lost my dad three years ago, and I just tried to call him. It was the weirdest thing. A habit.

HUDSON: I understand that. I lost my mother two years ago, and she was the one who heard all my stories. I often pick up the phone to call her.

RUBEN V: Same with me! I was just dialing the number. OK . . . I was sitting behind the bar, and he started singing so beautifully. I looked up there, and I looked at the people who were watching, and I looked at my mom looking at him with adoration, a look that said, "That's my man," and I looked around. Every guy wanted to be my dad, and every woman wanted my dad. That was the coolest thing. He never forced us to play, but he left his instruments all around, like treasures to be found. I found the treasure. I never took lessons, and I did not learn to read music, even now.

I remember Willie saying, "There is music everywhere; you just have to reach up and grab it." It changed my life. It is just there, and if you listen, you can find it. Willie is not a huge influence on me musically, but he is a Texan who spoke to me. I had a metal band as a teenager. We packed the house, signed to a record label, and packed the house. I was gigging at fourteen or so. I moved to Austin, but it was hard for me here. In the 1980s it was hard. I didn't know a lot of Hispanic acts, and we happened to be the Hispanic in the room. I often heard, "Oh wow, you are Mexican? I didn't know you were Mexican." Not Latino, but Mexican. "You're the one I know. I don't even know any." That is weird. I come to Austin now [in 2017], and there are so many great Hispanic artists. With me, I hid from it, hid my heritage in my career. Being Hispanic in the eighties just didn't fly real well.

One of my favorite stories is Freddy Fender. I was friends with his son. I was fourteen or fifteen. One time, at his house, Freddy says, "You should learn to play 'La Bamba.'" I asked, "Why?" He said, "You are Mexican, and someone is always going to ask for that song." That seemed stupid to me. I am fifty-one today [but looks quite young], and at twenty-five, I didn't think I would see thirty. I was drunk and crazy. And sure enough, someone has to scream this out. He taught me the opening riff to the song. My brother and I had a band, actually called My Brothers and I, and it was hard to break in because we were the wrong color for the music we played. We played blues and rock.

I remember one time in East Texas hearing this racist remark made during sound check. I was wearing a cowboy hat because I had shaved my head and didn't like being bald then. I was probably hired from the picture. The owner, a big cowboy, came up, saying, "What the fuck? I don't get it. So you're a Mexican playing nigger music for white people? You need to get out. Straight up." For the first five minutes, I was pissed. Then he walked away, and I realized he was right. I am Hispanic playing black music.

RUBEN V taught himself the guitar and, as a teen, played and sang in clubs. His band is known for an assortment of Latin, blues, rock, and soul. The songwriter has released eight solo CDs and has collaborated on fourteen group albums.

Patricia Vonne

The Gypsy Dances and Sings

I talked with Patricia Vonne in February 2015, but I had heard her perform many times before that. She had also visited my writing class at Schreiner. Her performance art makes her performances each a work of art that includes castanets and dancing. Patricia recommended that I talk with Rick del Castillo, and then I saw her perform with him several times. This is a woman following her bliss in all ways, and she is an inspiration to all who are around her. In spring 2019 she headed to Italy with Rick to perform with Italian musicians who also came to Texas. International in many ways, Patricia carries joy with her.

HUDSON: Let's talk about your family first.

VONNE: Yeah. Well, I'm sixth-generation Texan. So, we go way back. My father is from Rio Grande City, Texas. And my mother is from El Paso, Texas. And my ancestors on my mother's side were from Northern Spain, and they migrated down to San Luis Potosi, Mexico. And one of my great-great-uncles was a poet in Mexico, and he wrote one of the famous Mother's Day poems. So we come from a family of writers and filmmakers.

HUDSON: Spaniards.

VONNE: Yeah. But my dad was one of eleven children. He came from very modest beginnings, but he put himself through college with a music scholarship as a drummer. And my mother loved to play—she was a psychiatric nurse. She worked the graveyard shift so she could be home when we got home from school. She loved musicals. She loved art. She learned how to play the guitar and her favorite mariachi songs. And she encouraged us all ten kids to harmonize with her. She taught us how to harmonize. And I remember her telling me specifically that she felt that the power lay in the artist who could write their own music. They had more longevity and they owned it. So, that really made an impression on me. We always had mariachis over to the house for anniversaries or birthday parties in San Antonio. After a certain hour, we had to go to bed, but we were upstairs. We could hear all the lively music downstairs and everyone getting into the mariachi music.

HUDSON: So, this is not only in your genetic blood, but it's also in your cultural upbringing.

VONNE: Exactly. I always had a connection to that, and my full name is Patricia Vonne Rodriguez. And the reason I use my middle name, Vonne, is because when I moved to New York to pursue the arts in acting and modeling, I could not find work as Rodriguez. Even the Hispanic magazines would tell my agent, "She does not look Mexican." And it really hurt my feelings. My sister goes by Lanza. She looks more Hispanic than I do. So, she said, "Well, I look more Hispanic. You're gonna have to do something with your name if you really want to pursue the arts in New York City, because they look at a list, and they see your name, and you walk in, and you're not gonna look like a Rodriguez to them obviously 'cause you're not getting these bookings." So, she said, "You should use your middle name. It sounds very European. They probably can't pigeonhole you. Just try it out." So, I did.

HUDSON: So, the name Rodriquez carried a stereotype, an impression. I mean, that wasn't anything negative. It's just that when you showed up, you weren't what they were looking for.

VONNE: Green eyes, Castilian features. Then I heard, "She does not look Mexican."

HUDSON: Sixth-generation Texan.

VONNE: Yes. So, I did. I altered my name. I used my middle name, and I was able to work in New York City for eleven years. I walk into the room, and they go, "Are you Greek? Are you French? Are you Italian?" And I go, "Pick one, man. Just hire me."

HUDSON: Don't worry about it.

VONNE: Yeah. Don't think too hard about it. What do you need? Sophia Loren Italian? Fine. I could play that. Or French. I could play that. I could play—and so, I just would. It helped me to be able to sustain work up there and save my life, or else what was I gonna do?

HUDSON: What number child were you out of ten?

VONNE: Fourth eldest. Second girl.

Through my music, when it came time for me to write—I decided to start a band and the decision was because I had always wanted to travel. What was gonna allow me to travel? Modeling, great. I tried modeling, and I found myself in Italy. I bought myself a one-way ticket when I was about twenty years old in 1991. And the Gulf War broke out. I had a one-way ticket, and I was stranded there for about five months. And when I finally earned enough money to come back, I said, "Well, gosh, that was very scary. I didn't think I'd make it out alive."

I had no credit card, and I bought a one-way ticket. So, I said, "I'm just gonna work hard to get back to America," and that really changed my focus. "If I'm not here tomorrow, what will I regret not doing?" And one of my passions was music.

So, once I got back to New York, I put an ad out in the *Village Voice*. I was determined to start my own band, and I did. And then when I decided, "Well, what am I gonna do? Is it gonna be covers? Is it gonna be country music?" I'm from Texas. I mean, we had to think about it. And I said, "Let's go back to my childhood. What really inspires me to write my own music if I can?" So, I learned the guitar—enough to write music. And I really made a decision that I would love to sing both in English and in Spanish. And because that's my heritage, and because I had to alter my name, through my music I could scream it out loud. People are gonna be, "Why is she singing in Spanish?" Well, because that's my heritage. Even though I don't use my last name, the music will speak for itself because it comes from me and I own it. And it really made me feel good to put my thumbprint on it. . . . I have five albums, all on my own record label. It's called *Bandolera*, which means "female bandit." Stand up for yourself. Stand up for your rights. Independent spirit of women. And I insisted that every album be bilingual because it just means a lot to me.

HUDSON: I love that in your music and your visits to my classroom.

VONNE: Oh, I love your classes.

HUDSON: Your ability to articulate your art as well as who you are in a classroom is very meaningful. This spring, we're starting a Texas studies minor. And I teach the Texas literature, culture, and song course. So, I think of the richness of your appreciation for how these threads weave together. Did you come by that just out of your family?

VONNE: The appreciation. Sure. I mean, my dad coming from . . . Can you imagine eleven children in a one-room house, third floor? For him to lift himself out of that . . . the first of eleven kids. He was the eldest. So, he paved the way for them, but music was his salvation. That's how he was able to graduate from college. He put himself through school.

HUDSON: And what's his name?

VONNE: Cecilio Rodriguez. He majored in music and also business. So, he was a salesman. And eventually sales were his forte. He was a traveling salesman door-to-door for thirty-nine years. Door-to-door salesman. It's not easy to raise ten children. And he sold cookware, and china, silverware. And that's where I get my work ethic. But he always encouraged music in the house. I know a lot of families that don't, but my parents always did and encouraged the arts. They always did emphatically enforce a second job—something to fall back on. My mother with nursing and everything. And my dad's a realtor now, and I am too. Always have something to fall back on.

HUDSON: Let's talk about that European thing you get to do.

VONNE: Oh my gosh, that is incredible. Germany is our best market. And how I started over there was my favorite band, which is now called Tito & Tarantula—they were formerly known as the Cruzados—and my brothers and I were big fans of theirs in the eighties when they first came out. Well, they only had two albums, but I mean they always had a Spanish song on the album. And it was like a Mexican rock band from East LA, although the lead singer/songwriter was from El Paso, but that was a great impression on me too with the rock—'cause my music is rock. It's roots rock. And theirs is rock, but they always had that—again, that thumbprint. A Spanish song like "We're *Mexicanos*." And, woah, that impacted me also to make my albums bilingual. Maybe three or four songs. And they ended up scoring my brother's films. Many of them. 'Cause he was such a fan also. So, on *From Dusk till Dawn*, *Desperado*, and *Machete*, he used their music.

HUDSON: And your music ended up there too, right?

VONNE: *"Traeme Paz"* was chosen for *Once Upon a Time in Mexico*, the trilogy of *El Mariachi*. And it was Tito. I had written a song for him when I met him in Mexico on the set of *Desperado*. He was like our Sixto Rodriguez. Where did he go? Where did they go? They kind of made their albums and then disappeared. And my brother found them in New York or LA and said, "I want you to not only act in my film but also compose the score for *Desperado*." So, when I met him on the set, I was like, "Oh my gosh, you're our hero." I wrote the song "*El Cruzado*," which is on my debut CD, and then he invited me to join him on tour with him for eight weeks in Europe, which was opening night in Paris, France, and then there was Italy, and Belgium, and Switzerland, and Germany. And I kept the itineraries for when it was time for me to go and bring my band over. And I was able to find a booker to help me. And I incorporate the castanets when I perform.

HUDSON: Yes, and I am so happy to have my collection, which started with a set you brought me after traveling in Spain. Let's talk about that spectacular part of your show.

VONNE: My mother put me in ballet when I was nine, and I always loved dancing and watching the MGM musicals. So, when it was time to do my music, I couldn't stay still onstage, especially when I sing in Spanish. I'm like, "Wow. I should take flamenco classes or Spanish dance classes to really incorporate." 'Cause my background is ballet. And so, like I thought with the castanets . . . My mother had a pair in her armoire when I was a child, and I remember finding them. I remember always playing with them. I didn't know how to use 'em, and she caught me one time. She said, "OK. I'll teach you." And then later on, when I was taking classes, I thought, "This would be so cool to incorporate in a live performance," because in New York there were many venues where you can only see the heads up 'cause they're standing room only. Mercury Lounge—we played there all the time—and you can't see the bands playing from [the chest] down. It was very frustrating. So, I'm like "Well, castanets are way over your head, and at least I can get a little theatrical."

HUDSON: Well, I think the dance, and the rock element, and the songwriting, and the bilingual lyrics—I mean, I just think you've got something that's very one of a kind. You're not in any niche except maybe *glamorous*. It seems to me like you get to expand into cultural places, different kinds of festivals.

VONNE: Yeah. Overseas, we play festivals, cultural centers, pubs, clubs. We were talking about the cultural aspect, in places. We played Poland. We've played Ireland. We played many, many times in Germany—those three particular places. We haven't been to the Czech area yet. But yeah, I definitely remind them. . . . I say, "Gracias for your influence because you all brought the music to us, like in my hometown of San Antonio." The Tejano, Tex Mex sound was very much influenced by German polka music, and the people understand. I try to speak slowly, and I've heard their reactions in the audience. I said, "You know, between Austin and San Antonio are a lot of German towns, and villages, and stuff still, and great influences in my hometown with the King William District. And you'll be very surprised to see the German influence there." So, they are so thrilled to hear that 'cause they would tell me after the show I was from another planet. "You Texans are not just from another country or a state. You're from another planet to us." And they say, "We can't understand the words in Spanish, but the music speaks to us." And they will say, "Thank you for bringing us culture."

HUDSON: Did you ever incorporate the accordion?

VONNE: Yeah. In fact, Michael Ramos is on our albums. As far as live shows when we are in Europe, our booker in Switzerland plays the accordion. So, he would join us for some of our shows. We usually do a four-piece band over there. But it would be nice to incorporate more.

And then just recently, I did get to work with Flaco> and Max Baca. My Italian booker arranged it, and he called me and said, "There's a band here that wants to hire Flaco. If you can just oversee it, go and be there. And he likes your music. He wants to meet you anyway." So, I went to San Antonio and then they ended up asking me to sing on the project. And I got to see Flaco work. He brought three accordions and pull them all out. And he says, "What style do you want? Traditional? Or do you want this?" And he was so on his game. I was like a fly on the wall. And he was asking them, like, "In Italy, what is the song—what kind of songs portray your culture the best?" He really was hungry for knowledge, their cultural aspect.

HUDSON: Well, I had the privilege of talking to him three days before he received the Lifetime Heritage Grammy and just lucked out. We canceled our talk two to three times, and it just turned out that I got in on that Wednesday before he was leaving town. And so, it's really exciting to see him accepting that award right after I had been in his living room listening to him talk about the music. Your performance is so visual with the castanets and dancing. Unique.

VONNE: And I bring people in just by simply . . . bringing them in just by seeing somebody. And then over here bring the left—the whole left part of the stage, you can cover with just one wave of the hand. And the whole right part, and then the whole middle, and then take the—I like to take the scarf and whip it around and then maybe whip a person in the front. They're so far away, but they see it's toward them. And really, it's just bringing people in. Hard to describe what I do onstage!

HUDSON: So, for you, part of the excitement in performing is bringing in the audience.

VONNE: Yeah. Totally. Totally.

HUDSON: Like you're not separate onstage—just doing your thing.

VONNE: No.

HUDSON: So, what are the challenges now for you in the performance world?

VONNE: I think the fact that I'm an independent artist—that's the difference. I did try in the beginning when I was in New York to sell it to a record label, but they just didn't get it. Roots rock doesn't sell. We can't put it on the radio. For the sake of trying to be who they wanted me to be, one company wanted me to be the next Celine Dion—Mexican Celine Dion. Like I love her, but I'm not her. I do not have a voice like her. They didn't even present any contracts or anything written down. It was just their ideas, and I just wasn't connecting with their ideas. They wanted to get a new band, new songs, new songwriters. So, I just decided from that first album to just put it out myself. I like the journey, and you have to just be happy you're on your journey and wherever it takes you. And what did I ever want? I wanted to travel, and that's what I'm doing. So, I'm content. I get to live close to my parents, who are still alive, and see them on weekends. I'll be there this weekend. And the people. I love living here because on my last album I got to write with my heroes. I got to choose my cowriters. Doyle Bramhall, and Alejandro Escovedo, and Rosie Flores. Like all the other albums, it's a hybrid mix of what I was used to listening to in San Antonio. It's not just one genre.

I was able to cowrite with some of my favorite Texas artists, like Rosie Flores. We wrote this song called "Cats in the Doghouse." Doyle Bramhall, we wrote "Dark Mile." Johnny Reno took the title track, "Rattle My Cage." And Alejandro Escovedo, we wrote "Ravage Your Heart." This was just my dream album because I love to incorporate Castilian, Mexican influences with American rock and roll. My music is very much roots rock with an emphasis on melodies. It's acoustic driven. And I love all my albums to be bilingual because that's my heritage. Patricia Vonne Rodriguez is my full name. And yes, it really meant a lot to me to be able to cowrite with a lot of my favorite artists on this album. For me to choose using them as my muse for the music and the mood. And so, like Doyle Bramhall is very drum driven because he was a drummer and a writer. And Rosie Flores sounds very rockabilly inspired.

HUDSON: And how did you choose? I mean, Austin's big, and you have lots of friends and lots of musicians. So, how did this come about?

VONNE: When you're playing in Austin and there's a double bill, for me, personally, it's about who goes well with you. I always say, "Hey, if Doyle Bramhall ever plays at Continental, put my name in the hat. It's a double bill." And it started to happen that way, and then we became friends, and then we started talking about songwriting together. And I got right to it. And so, this is the song that came out of it, and we were able to also make a really brilliant music video out of it, which is like my homage to that spooky movie *The Hitcher*. So, I think Doyle would have been proud.

And it's about new beginnings. It's about the end of a relationship, but with a new beginning. Very hopeful at the end. And then Johnny Reno, we've done many double bills together. We've cowritten many, many songs. "Hot Rod Heart." I wrote a song for him. It's called "The Sax Maniac" because his band from Fort Worth was the first band I ever saw in my hometown of San Antonio.

HUDSON: Johnny Reno, the Sax Maniacs, the Juke Jumpers, Stephen Bruton, Delbert and Lou Ann Barton, and Ray Sharp are from Fort Worth. Like me, they have the Fort Worth gene. So, when I saw you were doing something with Johnny Reno—I mean, Fort Worth has a sound. These cities have sounds. Fort Worth has a sound.

VONNE: Yeah. And it was just like I wanted to be his protégé, and I was like, "Man, I love your music and I still listen to it to this day. And whenever I'm getting ready for a gig, what do I put on? Johnny Reno music, you know, to get ready for the show."

HUDSON: So, what's ahead for this album?

VONNE: *Rattle My Cage* will be released probably in March, this coming next month. And it was recorded in Austin during this Hot Rod Fest because my favorite club to play is the Continental Club. And the owner is so gracious in having us play there. That's where we got to do double bills with Alejandro, and Doyle, and Rosie, and everybody that's on this album. And so, it takes place during the Hot Rod Fest. So, yeah, in the song, I'm a cowgirl coming down and zapping very handsome men into my spaceship. 'Hey, come and rattle my cage.' But all of my albums being from San Antonio, Texas, as Rosie is from San Antonio, as Alejandro Escovedo is from San Antonio, there are so many different artists like Steve Earle, Charlie Sexton, Flaco Jiménez, Doug Sahm, and how our music is so different. There's always nuance lines of San Antonio because it's a hybrid mix of music.

HUDSON: *Hybrid* is a very key word.

VONNE: Very proud, and it's who I am too. Patricia Vonne Rodriguez—a sixth-generation Texan paying homage to my ancestors. In New York City I would go to auditions, and they would turn me away. And my agent finally asked, "Tell me why you're turning her away." They said, "She does not look Mexican enough." And it really hurt my feelings. I can understand how the Native Americans felt—I mean, changing their names, and their religion, and their everything. It's an ongoing thing. And so, I decided to use my middle name, not a foreign name. It allowed me to live and work in New York.

HUDSON: So, it wasn't about covering up the heritage. It was about dealing with the expectations other people had.

VONNE: Music is an experience. And for me, to be able to have all my albums original—this is my imprint. This is my legacy. And I'm proud of it. And I'm an independent artist. I don't have any help, except from my fans. And that makes me proud. Because of them, I'm able to keep putting albums out myself, and they're for my fans.

HUDSON: I think it's absolutely beautiful that you are courageous and willing to say, "This is who I am" and not have other voices try to shape you.

VONNE: Once I was quoted as saying, "They tried to take away my heritage, but through my music, I get to scream it out loud." And I believe that. Through my music, they can't stop me because I'm the writer. And I can put on my shows whenever I want. It's not like an acting job where it's up to the casting director. I can put on my show whenever I want. I can tour Europe now.

HUDSON: Yeah. There you go. So, one last bit of this conversation about the words: *Tejano, Tex Mex, Latina.* I know Tish mentioned that she sometimes saw herself as Chicana, which has overtones of political resistance, I think. But do any of those words resonate with you?

VONNE: I've been called all of them.

HUDSON: Well, *Hispanic* is pretty accurate for you because it does go back to Spain.

VONNE: I'm not offended by any of them. It's like, I am Mexican American. And you know who I miss the most? Selena. I wish she was still here, 'cause she would have been an advocate. Like she would have said, "Call me whatever you want. I am Selena. One word. That's my name. Whatever you want." But she also did the hybrid mix, but it was who she was. Her very essence spoke to so many people. I miss her so much. I never met her. I wish I did.

PATRICIA VONNE'S musical and acting career started in New York City, where she formed her own band and appeared in commercials and movies. Her songs have also been featured in films, including *Once Upon a Time in Mexico*. She has recorded seven albums and tours extensively around the world.

Part 2

Other Voices

Flaco's Eightieth Birthday: A Reminder of How Far Conjunto Can Go

Hector Saldaña

Nearly a month after Flaco Jiménez's eightieth birthday, the celebration was still going strong in San Antonio for the good-natured conjunto music legend.

He didn't seem to mind the third birthday cake in as many weeks, or accolades from the mayor—this time at a private gathering at the Squeeze Box, a tiny cantina on the St. Mary's Strip where a florist shop once operated. In the hip bar's dim light, he easily blew out all eighty candles on a white-icing cake decorated with a sugary-drawn button accordion—a three-row-button Hohner just like his.

It's as if Flaco's hometown didn't want to let go of the moment for an enduring musician who ranks as our Satchmo of conjunto. Like Louis Armstrong, Jiménez became a beloved music ambassador to the world for a distinctly American music form he helped pioneer—music intertwined with region, culture, and ethnicity.

Armstrong did so with his trumpet and smile; Jiménez with a squeeze box and a *grito*.

And if one stops and thinks about it, Flaco's eightieth represents almost the entirety of the history of conjunto music.

The music genre, born in Texas, California, and New Mexico, combined elements of German beer-barrel polka music, folkloric Mexican ballads, and cowboy songs, emerging in the late 1920s and early 1930s.

He didn't invent it. It predated him.

Leonardo "Flaco" Jiménez, born March 11, 1939, took it farther than anyone else.

That's because many wanted to add a taste of Flaco's *alegre* (happy) magic to their music—Doug Sahm, Ry Cooder, Willie Nelson, Buck Owens, Bob Dylan, Dwight Yoakam, Carlos Santana, Texas Tornados, and the Rolling Stones.

And Flaco could hang.

"My music is a rainbow," Jiménez told a TV reporter at his most recent party, describing the various music styles he plays: conjunto, Tex Mex, rock and roll, country, and blues.

"I'm just me—that's it."

Minutes later, he was sipping a cold longneck beer and laughing about his genuine, in-the-moment answer. "It just came to me," he said.

It reflects his instinctual approach: listen first; then react. Don't edit. Onstage and in the recording studio, Flaco's fingers respond to his auditory nerves almost instantaneously.

That—sometimes lost to outsiders distracted by the good times, self-deprecating humor, and a complicated personal life—is at the heart of his artistry, a trait shared with his father and his brother, Santiago Jiménez Jr.

He is an unlikely genius—a self-taught musician born in a Mexican *colonia* of quarry workers, a shanty neighborhood on a street that no longer exists near the San Antonio Zoo.

The sounds of lions roaring and hyenas crying in the distance at night was as much a musical education as watching the thick fingers of his father, Santiago Jiménez Sr., working the buttons on his squeeze box, or listening to German music on the radio, or watching Gene Autry movies.

Wonderfully poetic, he once described the sound of twentieth-century Mexican American singer Lydia Mendoza and her twelve-string guitar "like the stars falling from the sky."

As a teenager, he was receptive to the sounds of Elvis Presley too—secretly dreaming he could make a record with the future king of rock and roll.

Jiménez remains as humble as his roots. That he would become music royalty—he's a Lifetime Grammy recipient, he was bestowed a National Endowment for the Arts National Heritage Fellowship, and his photo graced the National Portrait Gallery of the Smithsonian Institute—was no certain destiny.

His first recordings were made in a garage studio on the west side under the guidance of Salome Gutierrez and José Morante.

Flaco's first hit came in 1955 with *"Hasta La Vista"*/*"Pobre Bohemio."* Twenty years later, *"Un Mojado Sin Licencia"* would combine social commentary with satire and unapologetic *vato* humor.

He's been a regional star since the mid-1950s. His reputation as a straight-up conjunto badass grew throughout the sixties and seventies.

The album covers are classic—from posing with a horse for *El Gran Flaco Jiménez* to the colorful *Battle of the Decade*, depicting both he and Esteban "Steve" Jordan as boxers in the ring.

He might've remained under the radar to the world had Sir Doug not plucked him for his 1973 solo album *Doug Sahm and Band*, and more importantly, if he had never been showcased in Les Blank's and Chris Strachwitz's 1976 documentary *Chulas Fronteras*.

The mainstream caught up to the possibilities with the Grammy-winning Tex Mex super group Texas Tornados, with Jiménez, Sahm, Freddy Fender, and Augie Meyers.

At the height of his powers, Jiménez was a convulsing electric jitterbug onstage. Musicians Josh Baca, Michael Guerra, Alex Meixner, Dwayne Verheyden, and Juanito study and recycle his licks and his moves.

These days, Flaco needs a little help climbing the steps onto the stage, and he plays his Hohner Corona II while sitting on a stool to ease the pain of an increasingly creaky back. Still, he says music keeps him young. And he still rocks it effortlessly.

Flaco's legacy: "The heart doesn't get old."

HECTOR SALDAÑA is the curator of the Texas Music Collection at the Wittliff Collections at Texas State University.

Freddy Fender's Voice Could Console and Comfort

Christine Granados

Dallas Morning News, October 18, 2006

"I'll be there before the next teardrop falls."

And Freddy Fender was there for me, for us all. His nasal twang comforted me during the worst and best times in my life.

He was there during my first high school crush and for the heartbreaking end of that puppy love. He was a comfort to me during the separation of my parents. He was there with me during my dollar dance on my wedding day and through the birth of my first and second child. He was there during my uncle's funeral and countless times in between.

The Bebop King was not just a country music or Tejano crossover star. He was a part of my family, a part of everyone's family.

My parents talked about his stint in Angola like they talked about all my uncles who had served time. He was one in the same—a wild-haired, wild-assed *tío* of mine. I prayed for and rooted for him like a member of the family.

I grew up watching him play the Fiesta de Las Flores in El Paso. He'd come most years, and he was always good. We never tired of seeing him, and he never had an off night that I can recall.

He was a living symbol of what a Mexican American can accomplish through hard work, humility, and a sense of humor. His star began to rise back when there were few Mexican American symbols for us to root for, the ultimate underdog.

I got to see to Freddy perform again in 2004, his first show after his liver transplant. When he walked onto the stage at the Paramount Theater in Austin, he looked tired, sick, and small. But when he sang he was transformed, and so were we.

I sat in my chair and cried and cried through the first ten songs. My husband said I was like the women in the 1960s who were seeing the Beatles. But it was different because my tears came from the pride I felt for him and the relief of knowing he was with us for a while longer. It was like seeing a family member again.

I cried because, like so many Tejanos, he held a special place in my life. I cheered his success because he was one of us, because his music brought so many happiness and because I wished him all the best.

His bilingual ballads reminded everyone that being Mexican is just another way of being American. It brought cultures together and continues to do so on the dance floor.

His faults were like those of our family members—entirely forgivable.

And when I heard about his death on Saturday, I just wanted to crawl into bed with my mother like I used to when I was kid, have her wrap her arms around me as we both listened to "When the Next Teardrop Falls."

"Freddy Fender was mom's cure for aches—stomach, head, or heart." Only this time he won't be able to dry away all the teardrops that are being cried for him throughout Texas.

Pride

Dagoberto Gilb

It's almost time to close at the northwest corner of Altura and Copia in El Paso. That means it is so dark that it is as restful as the deepest, unremembering sleep—dark as the empty space around this spinning planet, as a black star. Headlights that beam a little cross-eyed from a fatso American car are feeling around the asphalt road up the hill toward the Good Time Store—its yellow, plastic smiley face bright like a sugary suck candy.

The loose muffler holds only half the misfires, and, dry springs squeaking, the automobile curves slowly into the establishment's lot, swerving to avoid the new self-serve gas pump island. Behind it, across the street, a Texas flag, out too late this and all the nights, pops and slaps in a summer wind that, finally, is cool.

A good man, gray on the edges, an assistant manager in a brown starched and ironed uniform, is washing the glass windows of the store, lit up by as many watts as Venus, with a roll of paper towels and the blue liquid from a spray bottle. "Goodnight, *mijo!*," he tells a young boy coming out after playing the video game, a Grande Guzzler the size of a wastebasket balanced in one hand, an open bag of Flamin' Hot Cheetos in the other, its red dye already smearing his mouth and the hand not carrying the weight of the soda, his white T-shirt, its short-sleeve arms reaching halfway down his wrists, the whole XXL of it billowing and puffing out in the outdoor gust.

A plump young woman steps out of that car. She's wearing a party dress—wide scoops out of the top front and back, its hemline way above the knees. "Did you get a water pump?" the assistant manager asks her. "Are you going to make it to Horizon City?" He's still washing the glass of the storefront, his hand sweeping in small, hard circles.

The young woman is patient and calm, like a loving mother. "I don't know yet," she tells him as she stops close to him, thinking. "I guess I should make a call," she says, and her thick-soled shoes, the latest fashion, slap against her heels to one of the pay phones at the front of the store.

Pride is working a job like it's as important as art or war, is the happiness of a new high score on a video arcade game, of a pretty new black dress and shoes. Pride is the deaf and blind confidence of the good people who are too poor but don't notice.

A son is a long time sitting on the front porch where he played all those years with the squirmy dog who still licks his face, both puppies then, even before he played on the winning teams of little league baseball and city league basketball. They sprint down the sidewalk and across streets, side by side, until they stop to rest on the park grass where a red ant, or a spider, bites the son's calf. It already swells, but he no longer thinks to complain to his mom about it—he's too old now—when he comes home. He gets ready, putting on the shirt and pants his mom would have ironed but he wanted to do it himself. He takes the ride with his best friend since first grade. The hundreds of moms and dads, *abuelos y abuelitas*, the *tios* and *primos*, baby brothers and older married sisters, all are at the Special Events Center for the son's high school graduation. His dad is a man bigger than most, and when he walks in his dress eel-skin boots down the cement stairs to get as close to the hardwood basketball court floor and ceremony to see him—"*Mijo!*"—he feels an embarrassing sob bursting from his eyes and mouth. He holds it back, hides the tears that do escape with his hands, wipes them with his fingers, because the *chavalitos* in his aisle are playing and laughing, and they are so small and he is so big next to them. And when his son walks to the stage to get his high school diploma and his dad wants to scream his name, he hears how many others, from the floor in caps and gowns and from around the arena, are already screaming it—could be any name, it could be any son's or a daughter's: Alex! Vanessa! Carlos!

Veronica! Ricky! Tony! Estella! Isa!—and he sees his boy waving back to all of them.

Pride hears gritty dirt blowing against an agave whose stiff fertile stalk, so tall, will not bend—the love of land, rugged like the people who live on it. Pride sees the sunlight on the Franklin Mountains in the first light of morning and listens to a neighbor's *gallo*—the love of culture and history. Pride smells a sweet, musky drizzle of rain and eats *huevos con chile* in corn tortillas heated on a cast-iron pan—the love of heritage.

Pride is the fearless reaction to disrespect and disregard. It is knowing that the future will prove that wrong.

Seeing the beauty: Look out there from a height of the mountain and in front of and after the Rio Grande, to the so far away and so close, the so many miles more of fuzz on the wide horizon, knowing how many years the people have passed and have stayed, the ancestors, the ones who have medaled, limped back on crutches or died or were heroes from wars in the Pacific or Europe or Korea or Vietnam or the Persian Gulf, the ones who have raised the fist and dared to defy, the ones who wash the clothes and cook and serve the meals, who stitch the factory shoes and the factory slacks, who assemble and sort, the ones who laugh and the ones who weep, the ones who care, the ones who want more, the ones who try, the ones who love, those ones with shameless courage and hardened wisdom, and the old ones still so alive, holding their grandchildren, and the young ones in their glowing prime, strong and gorgeous, holding each other, the ones that will be born from them. The desert land is rock dry and ungreen. It is brown. Brown like the skin is brown. Beautiful brown.

Having Recently Escaped from the Maws of a Deathly Life, but Not That Life Sentence Called Death, I Am Ready to Begin the Year Anew

Sandra Cisneros

For the New Year I will buy myself a chocolate éclair filled with custard.

Eat it slowly, with an infinity of joy, without concern of woe and tight-underwear.

Susan's mother was directed by her doctor to cut down on salami or risk death. "But, doctor," she said, "Is life worth living without salami?"

For my new year I will sit down in the sun and dunk in my coffee a little knob of bread hard as my elbow, and on it, without concern for cholesterol, I will spread delicious butter, the kind that reminds me of Mexico City's Café La Blanca on Cinco de Mayo Street or the clinking glasses of El Gran Café de la Parroquia in Veracruz.

I will snooze with my dogs till I radiate love, for they are life's true gurus. I will wake gently so as not to disturb the dreams that have alighted overnight on the branches of sleep, and before they flutter away on soundless wings, I will examine and admire each.

This season of my escape, I will push my foot down on the accelerator of my life, vámanos vobiscum, and hurry to sit under a tree with a book thicker than a dozen homemade tamales. Henceforth, I will read only for pleasure or transmogrification.

All toxic folk are to be excised from the remaining days of my life, the chupacabras and chupacabronas, who are a purgatory of pain.

I will allow myself the luxury to laugh daily and in liberal doses to overbalance the bitter compost called the news.

I will cease waiting for someone to do something about the war, the walls, the guns, the drugs, the stupidity of leaders, and ally myself with citizens who practice the art of tossing their shoes at heads of state.

There is much I know and much I do not know as a woman at fifty-six, but I am certain I know this. Life is not worth living without salami.

Manuel's Destiny

Stephanie Urbina Jones

Generations ago he came from Mexico to the promised land
One night in the dark he followed his heart across the Rio Grande
He walked from El Paso alone on a dirt road with the sun shining
down from above

To old San Antone where he found his home and someone to love
Through the doubt and the dust from dawn to dusk
He worked hard and he prayed
Every border he crossed brought him closer to God
And the freedom he'd find someday

Like a bird in the sky with his heart open wide and the faith to fly
Like an unbridled horse on an uncharted course to a better life
With hope in his soul his *corazón* made of gold he believed he could do
    anything
That was the story they told when I left home at twenty years old
Manuel's destiny

So I got in my car with my Spanish guitar bound for Tennessee
As I drove through my fear I felt his spirit near it was guiding me
I was strong I was able I waited on tables said, "Yes sir, no man" 'cause I
    knew
I'd get the chance for my dreams to dance and do what I was born to do

Like a bird in the sky with my heart open wide and the faith to fly
Like an unbridled horse on an uncharted course to a better life
With hope in my soul his *corazón* made of gold I believed I could do
    anything
His story it lives on in me I'm so grateful to live and be free
Manuel's destiny

Like a bird in the sky with his heart open wide and the faith to fly
Like an unbridled horse on an uncharted course to a better life
With hope in his soul his *corazón* made of gold he believed he could do
   anything
That was the story they told when I left home at twenty years old
Manuel's destiny

Generations ago he came from Mexico to the promised land

CONCLUSION

This collection of voices points to the rich textures in the Texas music tapestry with a focus on our connection with Mexico . . . *la tierra, la familia, el corazón,* and *la musica.* My love for the heart of this culture is unexplainable when looking at my childhood in the suburbs of Fort Worth, Texas (Richland Hills). My mother took me shopping when I was a teenager, and we went to the Mexican Inn downtown. I was immediately hooked, and the rest is history. That was in about 1961. I now own an apartment in San Miguel de Allende, and at the age of seventy-three in 2019, I walked across the border at Laredo and caught a first-class bus to Querétaro. Twelve hours later, I arrived and took another bus for the last hour to San Miguel. Something about the road still calls to me. Everything connects.

Index

Abilene, TX, 73, 142
accordion: Bacas on, 11–14, 17–19, 26–27, 30; *conjunto*,1; del Castillo on, 42, 49; Durawa on, 51, 54; Escobar on,59–60; festival, 68; Flores on, 69–70; Gomez on, 75–77; Guerra on, 78–80, 114; Hinojosa on, 90, 93; Hohner, 160–63, 223, 225; Italian, 162; Jiménez on, 13, 51, 54, 68, 77, 98–99, 102, 109–113; Jordan on, 119–121, 123, 126–27; Morquecho on, 140–42; *norteño*, 147, piano, 161, Ramos on, 170, 215; squeeze box, 223–24
African American, 87, 90, 178, 190, 202, 209
albums: *20 Corridos,* 29; *American Groove,* 25; *Amor y Dolor,* 108; awards for, 11, 29, 71, 194; *Bandolera,* 212; *Battle of the Decade,* 225; *20 ; Borders y Bailes,* 28–29; *Canciones Mi Padre,* 171; *Chulas Fronteras,* 225; covers, 52, 93, 225, *Cruzando Borders,* 11; *Crying Over Your,* 68, *Del Castillo Live,* 45, 49; *Destiny's Gate, 92;Doug Sahm and Band,* 225; *Dreaming in the Labyrinth,* 91; *Dual Passport; El Gran Flaco Jimenez,* 225; *El Jefe,* 52; *Excursion,* 181; Flores, 69–70; Hinojosa, 94–96; Jiménez, 102, 110, *Labyrinth of Solitude,* 93; *Mi Inspiration,* 230; *Midnight to Moonligh*t, 70; *Rattle My Cage,* 218; Roddan, 46; Sharp, 75, 77; *Simple Case of the Blues,* 71; Sanchez, 183, 187, Smithsonian Folkway, 26; *Souled Out,* 86;*Texas Towns and Tex-Mex Sounds,* 29; Torres, 199, 203, 206, *Tularosa,* 78–79, 118; *Voodoo Lady,* 82, Vonne's, 212–13, 215–19
Albuquerque, NM, 11–12, 15, 17–18, 23, 27
Alice, TX, 26, 57–58, 141
Allen, Dalis, 29, 94
Amram, David, 33, 184–85
America, Americans: artists, 1; citizen, 134, 165–66, 195–96, 202; culture, 48, 89, 91,155, 227; ideals, 94; music, 74, 86, 119, 135, 171, 217, 223
Americana music, 42, 70–71, 78, 171, 175, 183
American Indians. *See* Native Americans
Arciniega, Armanod, 7–10
Arizona, 85, 202
Atotonilco, Mexico, 165, 175
Austin, TX: Music Awards, 40, 71; musicians on, 37–40, 43, 47, 52–54, 72–74, 95, 132, 155, 160, 168, 173; University of Texas at, 146, 164, 168–71, 175; venues in, 41, 51, 146, 148, 151; 217–18; 164, 169–73, 189
awards: Ameripolitan, 70, 130; appreciation, 30; Austin Music, 40, 71; *Brownsville Magazine* Music, 139; Grammy, 11, 24, 29, 31, 55, 77, 88, 102, 113, 162, 194, 206; lifetime, 88, 215–16, 224–25; National Heritage, 87, 113; Peabody, 65; Regional Mexican Music Album, 11; Tejano ROOTS Hall of Fame, 141
Ayala, Pedro, 110, 162
Ayala, Ramón, 58, 162–63
Aztec, 3, 156, 178

Baca, Josh: in China, 19–23; family, 17–18; and Grupo Vida, 13, 24; and Los Texmaniacs, 9,11, 14, 16, 19, 24; and Tex-Mex music, 12–13, 15–17, 225

Baca, Max, 9, 25–31

bajo sexto. See guitar

bands: Alabama, 130; Backstreet Boys, 167; Bad Habit, 34; the Beatles, 58, 95, 128, 157, 226, Black Sabbath, 35; Blue Harmony, 206; Chingon, 40, 43; Credence Clearwater, 16; Deep Purple, 34–35; Del Castillo, 32, 36–41, 43, 47–50; Grateful Dead, 36; Gypsy Kings, 41; 194; Jefferson Airplane, 36; Juke Jumpers, 217; Little Jimmie and the Vagabonds, 190; Los Lobos, 25, 37, 39, 43, 80; Los Lonely Boys, 100, 116; Lost Gonzo Band, 147 Metallica, 16; Milhouse, 37; My Brothers and I, 208; N'Sync, 167; Restless Heart, 130; Rolling Stones, 25, 80, 154, 223; Santana, 36, 41–42, 74, 101, 223; Sax Maniacs, 217; Skatalites, 81; Sunny and the Sunliners, 63, 90, 190, 194; Tito & Tarantula, 213. *See also* groups

Bauer, Hans, 98

Beatles: Harrison, 45; Escobar on, 58; in Germany, 95; Mata on, 128; music, 157, 226

Bernal family, 58, 152,

Black. *See* African American

Blue Cat Studio, 25, 75, 77, 78–80, 114

blues, bluesman: Baca on, 15, 17, 28; del Castillo on 36–37; Durawa on, 51–54; Flores on, 71; Gomez on, 76; Gutierrez on, 86; Guy, 137; Jiménez on, 101, 224; Urbina Jones on116; Jordan on, 125; and King (BB) 187; 130; Ramos on, 159; Ruben V on, 208–09; Sanchez on, 182, 190; Waters, 50; and Wills, 130

bolero, 95, 167

border, 2–3, 81, 84–85, 92, 95–96, 112, 164, 175, 195, 235

Bowles, Percy, 35, 182

Boxcar Fritz. *See* Morquecho, Fritz

Bramhall, Doyle, 216–18

Brownsville, TX, 34–41, 46–48, 80–81, 92, 139, 147, 165, 174

Bruton, Stephen, 54, 217

Buddha, Buddhism, 43–44

Bush, Johnny, 129, 131

Cajun, 15, 26, 101, 161

California: culture, 17, 91, 102, 104, 119, 189, 192–93; roots, 60, 63; scene, 36, 106, 120, 223; State University, 160, 192–93, 223

Canales, Laura, 63, 141

Carino, Rick, 81, 83

Carnitas Uruapan, 7, 88, 102, 109

Carrasco, Joe King, 41, 154, 158

Cash, Johnny, 30, 71, 128, 129, 137

Cash, Roseanne, 69

castanets, 32, 40, 53, 210, 214, 216

Castillo, Juanito, 120, 225

Catholic, Catholicism: Baca on, 23; del Castillo on, 43, 48; Gomez on, 76; Guerra on, 82; Hinojosa on, 91; Mata on, 128, 133, Rodarte on, 176, 179; Ruben V, 207; Torres on, 204

CDs. *See* albums

Chavez, Caesar, 89, 91

Chaves, Carlos, 112

Chicago, IL, 53, 58, 179

Chicana, Chicano: 3, 87, 92, 155, 178, 193, 197. *See also* Hispanic, Latin, Latina

China, 11, 13, 19–22, 25–26, 29–31, 95

Chingon, 40, 43

Chittlin Circuit, 72

Christianity, Christians, 43–44, 61–62, 77, 191, 204

Christmas music, 177, 203

Cinco de Mayo, 114, 117

Cisneros, Sandra, 114, 231

Coal Miners, 144–45

Cohen, Leonard, 65, 91, 98, 187

Cole, Nat King, 128, 137

conga, 15, 189

conjunto: definition of, 15, 17, 26–28, 30, 98–99, 105, 112; festivals, 7–9, 12–13, 56,75, 87, 102–04, 119, 160; influence of, 25, 51, 58–62, 66, 76–78, 81, 95, 109–10, 225; instrumentation in, 1, 9, 121; Jiménez (Flaco), 223–25; and Jordan III and, 122; Mata and, 135; Reyes and, 161–63. *See also* norteña norteño

Continental Club, 217–18

Cooder, Ry, 98, 111, 223

corridos, 47, 49, 95

Corpus Christi, TX, 9, 42, 58–59 146, 155, 207

Coryell, Muryali, 53–54

country-western music: Baca on, 15–17, 30; Benson, 29; del Castillo on, 33, 39, 42, 44, 46; Durawa on, 54–55; Escobar on, 62, 65; Flores on, 68, 70–71; Friedman, 119; Gill, 68, 118; Gomez on, 76–77; Griffin, 71; Haggard, 35, 181; Hancock, 93, 113; Jiménez on, 99, 101; Urbina Jones on, 114, 116–18; Kraus, 71; Lynn, 70, 144–45; Lovett, 70; Mata on, 129–32, 135–37; Owens, 223; Pruneda, 145; Ramirez on, 147; songs, 88, 130, 146, Strait, 134; Tillis, 129; Twain, 167; Twitty, 130; Tubb, 144; Vonne on, 212, 215; Wells, 70, Wynette, 70

cowboy poetry, 2, 16–17, 51, 66, 99, 146, 223

Crowell, Rodney, 69, 71

Cuba, Cuban, 43, 54, 193

culture: American, 48, 89, 91,155, 227; California, 17, 91, 102, 104, 119, 189, 192–93; Czech, 49, 90, 186, 215; Mexican, 85, 90–91, 101, 115, 125, 144; Tejano, 155, 163, 193, 227. *See also* heritage

cultural centers. *See* museums

Czech heritage, 49, 90, 186, 215

dance: flamenco, 214; 106; performance, 46, 66–67, 190, 226–27; polka, 27–28, 54, 90, 99, 109–10, 130, 165–67, 183, 201–02, 215, 223, 231–32; school, 197; *tardeada*, 193

dance halls, 30–31, 33, 57, 119, 130, 132

Davila Family, 8, 177–78

Davis, Miles, 149, 187

Del Castillo (group), 32, 36–41, 43, 47–50

del Castillo, Bernal Diaz, 48; Juan, 48; Mark, 36–37; Rick, 32–50

Desperado, 37, 213–14

drums, drummers: Baca on, 14–19, 22, 26–27; Bernal on, 152; Bramhall on, 217; del Castillo on, 37, 40, 49; Durawa on, 51–55, 121, Escobar on, 59–60; Flores on, 66–68; Guerra on, 79; Jiménez on, 104, 110; Jordan on, 120, 123, 127; Mata on, 130; Puig on, 141; Ramirez on, 147–48; Sanchez on, 185, 189, 194; steel, 182–83

Duncan, Tommy, 136–37

Durango, Mexico, 8, 90

Durawa, Ernie, 51–55

Dylan, Bob: Baca on, 25; celebration of, 138, 223; del Castillo on 33, 46, 49; and Garnier, 97; Guerra on, 80; and Gutherie, 91; Jiménez on, 97–100; Mata on, 135–36; Ramirez on, 149; Reynaga on, 164–65, 171–72, Sanchez on, 187

Eagle Pass, TX, 9, 112

Earle, Steve, 69, 218

Elephant Room, 146, 148, 151

El Mercado, 51, 195, 207

El Paso, TX, 3, 27–29, 84–87, 112–14, 125, 195, 210, 213, 226, 232

Escobar, Eligio, 58, 60–61

Escobar, Linda, 7, 9, 30, 42, 56–64

Escovedo, Alejandro, 216–18

Europe, European: festivals in, 113;

Gilb on, 230; Hudson on, 1, 46, 188; musicians on, 43, 49, 87, 89, 96, 106, 149, 183, 211, 213–15, 219

families, family: Arciniega on, 7–10, Baca, 9, 12–15, 17–24; 26–31, 225; Beall, 141; Cash, 30, 69, 71, 128, 129, 137; Davila, 8, 177–78; del Castillo on, 32, 35–36, 39, 47–48; Durawa on, 51; Escobar on, 56, 59, 64; Flores on, 65, Garza; 141; Gomez on, 75–76; Gutierrez on, 84–87; Hernandez, 141; Hinojosa on, 89–94; Jiménez, 97, 101, 104–05, 108, 113; Urbina Jones on, 117; Jordan on, 119–20, 123, 126, 129, 133–34, 138; Morquecho on, 140–42; Nelson, 16, 28, 33, 35, 98, 100, 118–19, 223; Reynaga on, 164–65, 169, 173, 176; Rodarte on, 179; Rodriguez, 66; Sanchez, 181–83, 185–86, 189, 193–94; Torres on, 196–200, 205; Vonne on, 210, 213; Williams, 71, 75, 99, Wills, 6, 28, 99, 130, 135–36, 143–44
Fear and Loathing in Las Vegas (Thompson), 150
Fender, Freddy, 52, 68–69, 208, 225–27
Fernández, Vincente, 36, 63
festivals: accordion, 68; Chihuahua, 84; in China, 29; Conjunto, 7–9, 12, 56, 75, 87, 102–03, 119, 160; cultural, 108, 131, 138–39, 206, 214–15; European; 113, 118; folk, 28; Hot Rod, 218; Kerrville Folk, 29, 33, 88, 112, 184; Lucerne Blues, 53–54; Magic Town, 114; McAllen, 168; Memphis Folklife, 30; Montreux Jazz, 149; New Orleans Jazz, 31; Pan American Jazz, 189; in San Miguel de Allende, 115, 146, 187; Smithsonian Folklife, 24, 28–29; songwriters' 94; Tejano, 7, 68; Texas Heritage Music Festival, 114; Veterano Conjunto, 61; Western Swing, 132
flea market, 7–8, 12, 49

Flores, Bobby, 75, 77, 216–17
Flores, Rosie, 42, 65–71
flute, 15, 120, 125, 194, 197
folk music: Baez, 91–92; Cohen, 65, 91, 98, 187; Collins, 33; festivals, 28–30, 88, 92, 112, 184; songs, 28, 71, 96; style, 118, 172, 223; traditional, 16, 31
Fort Worth, TX, 33, 91, 132, 135, 145, 189, 217, 235
France, French, 48, 211, 214
Fredericksburg, TX, 24, 114–15
funk, 146, 159

Garcia, Gavin, 164, 170–72
Garza, David, 72–74
Garibay, Randy Sr., 51, 177
German, Germany: Hinojosa in, 89–90, 94–95; Hohner in, 161–62; immigrants, 26, 186, 190–91; music, 49, 99, 109, 135, 213, 223–24; polkas, 130, 183, 215; touring in, 214
Gilb, Dagoberto, 114–15, 125, 179, 228–30
Gill, Vince, 68, 118
Gomez, Al, 30, 90
Gomez, Henry, 75–77
Gordan, Kirpal, 146–47
gospel, 61, 135, 177
Grammy: ceremony, 11, 24, Latin, 162, lifetime, 88, 215, 224; nominees, 113, 194, 206, 225. *See also* awards
Grand Ole Opry, 117–18
Green, Bill, 130–31, 136
groups: Carpenters, 167; Cigarettes After Sex, 87; Grupo Vida, 13, 24; Halos, 194; Light Crust Doughboys, 36; Little Jimmie and the Vagabonds, 190; Little Joe y la Familia, 35, 119, 152; Los Cobblestones, 147; Los Guadalupanos, 57; Mills Brothers, 67; Peter, Paul, and Mary, 98; Sir Douglas Quintet, 55, 83, 98; Westside Horns, 30, 54. *See also* bands

Guerra, Michael, 26, 75, 77, 78–83, 114, 225

guitar/?guitarist: accompaniment, 82, 86, 92, 95, 110, 129, 139, 167, 207, 224; *bajo sexto*, 9, 17, 19, 26–28, 59–60, 81, 88, 120, 126, 147; del Castillo on, 32, 34, 37–42, 48–49; Flores on, 66–67; *guitarrón*, 75–76; Jordan on, 121, 126–27; Morquecho on, 140–42; Ramos, 153–54, 157–58; Sanchez on, 182–84, 188, 190–91; styles, 28, 36, 54, 72, 74, 93, 143, 197; Vonne on, 210–12

Gutierrez, Ruben, 84–87

Haggard, Merle, 35, 181

harmony, harmonize, 26–27, 39, 73, 75, 120, 125, 182, 199, 210

Hancock, Butch, 93, 113

Hartman, Jimmy, 40–41

heritage: Hispanic, 12, 42, 65–67, 114–15, 140, 178, 195, 212, 217–19; Texas, 25–26, 56, 116–17, 138, 146, 181–83; Spanish, 186, tributes to, 97, 100, 114, 215. *See also* culture

Hidalgo, David, 25, 43, 69–70

Hinojosa, Tish: Baca on, 30; del Castillo on, 47; Destiny's Gate, 92, family, 91–93, Flores on, 66; in Germany, 89–90, 94–95; songs, 88, 96

hip-hop-17–19, 139

Hispanic, 3, 12, 16, 49, 55, 59, 66–69, 85–87, 96, 101. *See also* Chicana, Chicano, Latin, Latina

Hohner, 11, 160–63, 223, 225

Holly, Buddy, 16, 66–67, 69–70

honky-tonk, 65, 70–71, 130–31

Houston, TX, 14, 58, 60, 72

huapangos, 27, 167

Hurdlow, Paul, 38

immigrant, immigration, 95, 164, 169–70, 186

India, 30, 44–46, 73, 95

Indians. *See* Native Americans

Ireland, Irish, 106, 186, 161, 186, 196, 215

Italy, Italian, 32, 54, 162, 210–12, 214–15

Jalisco, Mexico, 76, 193

Japan, Japanese, 59, 202

Jasper, Pat, 29, 92,

jazz: Armstrong, 86, 223; Baca on, 28, 31; band, 154; Bobo, 120; collaboration, 187–88; Davis, 149, 187; Durawa on, 51–55; Flores on, 67, 71, Gutierrez on, 84–87; Jordan on, 120, 125, 127; Latin, 189, 194; radio, 186, Ramirez on, 146–51

Jews, Jewish, 48, 66–67

Jiménez Don Patricio, 105, 109, 112–13

Jiménez, Flaco: and accordion, 13, 51, 54, 68, 77, 98–99, 102; and Baca, 13–15, 27–28, 101; Dylan on, 25, 49, 80, 97–99; Hinojosa on, 88, 93, 95–96; influence, 124, 141, 161, 215, 218, and Nelson, 100; Saldaña on, 223–25; sons, 103–13, songs, 224

Jiménez, Gill, 103–08

Jiménez, José Alfredo, 27–28, 63

Jiménez, Santiago Jr., 109–13, 124, 162, 206, 224

Johnson City, TX, 88, 96

Jones, Stephanie Urbina, 78–79, 86, 114–18, 152, 232–33

Jordan, Esteban III, 119–27, 161, 225

Jordan, Steve, 119, 123, 127, 225

Kennedy, Rod, 35, 88, 94, 96, 113

Kerrville Folk Festival, 29, 33, 88, 112, 184

Kessler, the, 173–74

keyboards: musicians, 19, 36, 68, 84–86, 119–20, 170–71, 197–99, influence, 9, 93

King, Joe, 41, 154, 158

King Carole, 148, 151

Korea, 202, 230

Little Jimmie and the Vagabonds, 190
Little Joe y la Familia, 35, 119, 152
Lomax, John, 2, 146
Longoria, Valerio, 27, 80, 102, 110, 162
Los Angeles, CA, 11, 24, 58, 68, 80
Los Lobos, 25, 37, 39, 43, 80, 87
Los Lonely Boys, 100, 116
Los Texmaniacs. See Texmaniacs
Luera, Ramon, 75, 189
Lynn, Loretta, 70, 144–45

magazines. See newspapers, periodicals
"Manuel's Destiny" (Urbina Jones), 114,
    117, 232–33
Maple, Lynx. See Garza, David
mariachi: bands, 76, 114–15, 117, 141,
    Hinojosa on, 90, 93; influence of, 62,
    81–82, 86, 118; Reynaga on, 167–68,
    171–75; traditional, 19, 27, 189–90;
    Vonne on, 210–11, 213
Martinez, Lorenzo, 17, 19
Mata, Billy, 128–137
Mavericks, 78–79, 81, 83
McAllen, TX, 58, 147, 164–66, 168–69
McClinton, Delbert, 53–55
Mejia, Marisa Rose, 138–39, 140, 206
Memphis, TN, 29–30, 36, 39, 47–48
Mendoza, Lydia, 9, 92, 95, 224
Mexican American, 55, 86–87, 92,
    115, 155, 160–63, 171, 178, 193–96, 219,
    224–26
Mexico/?Mexican: Arciniega on, 7–10;
    artists, 84; culture 85, 90–91, 101, 115,
    125, 144, del Castillo on, 35–36, 43,
    48–50; Durawa on, 51–52; Escobar
    on, 62–64; Flores on, 66–68; Garza
    on, 72–74; Guerra on, Hinojosa on,
    88–96; Hispanic, 208; history, 95, 100,
    186; influences, 12, 118, 183, 217, Mata
    on, 133–34; Monterrey, 161, 165, 167–
    68, 193, 223; movies, 63, 194, music,
    11, 19, 27–28, 75–76, 130, 145, 148, 163,
    189–90, 223–24; Ramos on, 155–56;

Reynaga on, 165–74, San Miguel de
    Allende, 33, 72, 75, 91, 114–15, 146, 164,
    187, 196, 206, 235; Saltillo, 178; Vonne
    on, 210–13, 218–19
Meyers, Augie, 27, 90, 98, 225,
Michael Guerra, 26, 75, 78–83, 225
Mi Tierra, 75, 138
Monterrey, Mexico, 161, 165, 167–68, 193
Morquecho, Fritz, 131, 140–42, 185
Montreux, Switzerland, 49, 97, 100, 149
movies: The Border; 98; A Chance to Say
    Goodbye, 83; City Slickers, 207; Chulas
    Fronteras, 225; Del Castillo Live, 40;
    Desperado, 37, 213–14; El Mariachi,
    Fear and Loathing in Las Vegas, 150;
    From Dusk till Dawn,213; The Hitcher
    217; Killing Snakes, 41; Machete, 213;
    Once Upon a Time in Mexico, 213, 219
music genres: blues, 3,15–17, 28, 36–37,
    51–54, 71, 76, 86, 101, 116, 121, 125, 130,
    159, 182, 190, 208–09, 224; folk, 16,
    28–31, 71, 96, 118, 127, 172; funk, 146,
    159; jazz, 28, 51, 53–55, 65–67, 71, 76,
    84–87, 120, 125–27,146–51, 154, 186–88,
    194; hip-hop, 17–19, 139; mariachi,
    19, 27, 62, 76, 81–82, 86, 90–95, 99,
    114–18, 141, 167–68; 171–75; 189–90;
    210–13; norteña, norteño, 7–9, 27, 90,
    147, 161–62; pop, 70–71, 151, 190; 216;
    reggae, 81; rock and roll, 9, 18, 21–22,
    34–37, 41–42, 49, 54, 66, 85–87, 99,
    114, 155, 213–17, 224; ska; 17, 81–82;
    swing, 28, 71, 132, 137, 145, 185; Tejano,
    7, 9, 13–17, 26, 62, 68, 29, 85–97, 90,
    105, 115–16, 119–25, 141–42, 155, 186,
    193–95, 215, 227; tropical, 139, 190. See
    also music styles
music styles: Americana, 42, 70–71, 78,
    171, 175, 183; Ameripolitan, 70; bolero,
    95, 167; Cajun, 15, 26, 101, 161; Celtic,
    186; conga, 15, 189; conjunto, 7–9,
    12–15, 17, 25–28, 30, 51, 56, 58–62,
    66, 75–78, 81, 87, 95, 98–99, 102–05,

109–12, 119, 122, 135, 160–61, 223–25;
corridos, 47, 49, 95; country and
western, 15–17, 30, 33, 39, 42, 44, 46,
54–55, 62, 65, 68, 70–71, 118–19; cumbia, 9, 27, 78, 201; gospel, 61, 135, 177;
honky-tonk, 65, 70–71, 130–31; polka,
27–28, 54, 90, 99, 109–10, 130, 165–67,
183, 201–02, 215, 223, 231–32; metal,
72, 153, 208; rockabilly, 65–68, 70–71,
217; Tex-Mex, 7, 12, 17, 28–30, 51,
68–70, 80–82, 90, 108, 112, 190, 224–25
world, 15, 42, 87; zydeco, 15, 127, 161.
See also music genres
museums, 24, 26, 28–30, 76, 101, 141–42,
160, 171, 183, 224
mythology, 44, 97, 156

Nashville, TN, 68, 70, 130
National Heritage Fellowship, 97, 113,
224
Native Americans, 12, 17, 91, 133, 156
Nelson, Willie: del Castillo on, 33, 35;
family, 16, 73; influence of, 181, 223,
181; music, 28, 91, 98, 100, 116, 119, 136,
187, 223, songs, 33, 100
New Braunfels, TX, 99, 109
New Mexico, 8, 11–12, 17, 27–28, 30, 223
New York, NY, 54, 65, 80, 87, 211–12, 214,
216, 218–19
newspapers and periodicals: Browns-
ville Magazine, 139; *Dallas Morning
News,* 226; *Rolling Stone,* 42; *San
Antonio Express-News,* 52, 138; *Village
Voice, 212*
Nicholas, Johnny, 3, 24, 54
norteña, norteño, 7–9, 27, 90, 95, 99, 147,
161–62. *See also* conjunto
Nuevo Laredo, Mexico, 2, 76
Nuevo Leon, Mexico, 9, 160, 193

Once Upon a Time in Mexico, 213, 219
Ozuna, Sunny, 141, 194

Panco Villa, 2, 35, 41, 117, 193
Paredes, Americo, 47, 67
Patoski, Joe Nick, 155
Pedrazine, David, 78, 83
periodicals. *See* newspapers and
periodicals
percussion. *See* drummers, drums
piano. *See* keyboards
piano accordion, 161
polka: dance, 201–02, rhythm 27–28;
song,165, 223; style, 15, 54, 90, 99,
109–10, 130, 167, 183, 215
pop music: Bennett, 128; Boone, 190;
Carr, 206; Cole, 128, 137; Cross, 151;
Dion, 216; Gomez, 173; lang, 70; Nelson (Ricky), 190; Sinatra, 128
Presley, Elvis, 58, 66, 180, 190, 224
Price, Ray, 33, 102, 129, 131, 137
Pruneda, Junior, 132, 141, 143–45
Puerto Rico, Puerto Ricans, 43,86, 193

quinceañeras, 81, 140
Quintanilla, Selena. *See* Selena

radio: music on, 15, 57–58, 91, 129, 167,
189, 191, 224; shows, 65, stations, 8, 90,
92, 99, 155, 177–78; shows, 29; Torres
on, 199–200; Vonne on, 216
Ramirez, Tomas, 146–151
Ramos, Michael, 68, 170, 215
Ramos, Roberto Sontoya, 152–59
rancheras, 76, 167
record labels: A&R, 69; Akashic, 34;
Arhoolie Records, 30; Atlantic, 74,
98; Bernal; 58; Disco Corona, 110–11;
Hightone; 70; Ideal; 141; Mono Mundo 91; Rounder Records, 91; Smithsonian Folkways, 29–30, 142; Thirty
Tigers, 79; VMB Music, 38
recording studios: Abbey Road, 41; Bill
Worrell, 3; Blue Cat, 25, 75, 77, 78–79,
114; Fire Station, 52; garage, 224; Max
Baca, 13, 15; Santiago Jiménez, 109

Reed, John, 149–50
Reno, Johhny, 217–18
requinto. See guitar
Reyes, Gilbert, 160–63
Reynaga, Lesly, 164–75, 206
rivers, 3, 20, 76, 176
rhythm: dance, 9, 27,190; hip-hop, 19;
  del Castillo on, 35, 39–41, 49; polka,
  27–58; tempo, 54, 90, 101, 142, 167, 190
Richmond, Virginia, 23, 163
Robbins, Marty, 29, 137
rockabilly, 65–68, 70–71, 217
rock and roll: Baca on, 18, 21–22; del
  Castillo on, 34–37, 41; early 66, 85–86,
  99; hard, 147; Hendrix, 36; Holly, 16,
  66–67, 69–70; indie, 87; Latin rock,
  42, 49, 114; Lewis, 70; Plant, 71; Pres-
  ley, 58, 66, 180, 190, 224; radio, 155;
  roots, 213–17; rhythm, 9, 54
Rondstadt, Linda, 171, 199
Rodarte, Frank, 176–80
Roddy Tree Cantina, 11, 143
Rodgers, Jimmie, 35, 86, 97, 117, 119, 140,
  150, 181–82
Rodriguez, Robert, 39–40, 42–43, 50
Rolling Stones, 25, 80, 154, 223
Ronstadt, Linda, 171, 99
Rudy Gazelle and the Jury. *See*, Prune-
  da, Jr.
Ruiz, Alex, 32, 37

Sahm, Doug, 27–28, 51, 55, 68, 90, 98,
  100, 149, 218, 223–25
Saldaña, Hector, 111, 223–25
Salinas, Chumbe, 11, 25–26, 56, 97, 103,
  160
San Antonio, TX: Baca on, 14, 25;
  Conjunto Festival in, 12–13, 56, 75,
  160 Durawa on, 51–54; Escobar on,
  57–58, 60; Flores on, 65; Gomez on,
  76–77; Guerra on, 80–81; Hinojosa
  on, 88–96; history of, 30–31; Jiménez
  on, 97–98, 103, 106, 109–12; Jordan on,

119, 124; Mata on, 132–33; Reynaga
  on, 170, 172–73, Rosedale Park, 119;
  Sanchez on, 182, 186, 189; Symphony,
  182; Tejano festival in, 68; Torres on,
  195–97, 201, 205–06; Urbina Jones on,
  115; Vonne on, 211, 215–18; Zoo, 224
Sanchez, Florin, 33–35, 152, 181–88
Sanchez, Paulette, 182, 185
Sanchez, Poncho, 189–93
San José, CA, 120, 162
San Luis Potosi, Mexico, 196, 210
San Marcos, TX, 64, 74
San Miguel de Allende, Mexico, festival
  in, 114–16, 146; performers in, 187,
  retreat, 2, 33, 72, 74–75, 91, 164–65,
  175, 196, 235; theater in, 206
Santana, Carlos, 36, 41–42, 74, 101, 223
Sathya Sai Baba, 43–46
saxophone, 9, 121, 125, 146–47, 157, 180,
  185, 197
Schreiner University, 9, 11, 24, 84, 114,
  117, 140, 173, 207
Seattle, WA, 36, 477
Selena, 85, 93, 139, 173, 206, 219
Sexton, Charlie, 71, 149, 218
Shakira, 139, 165
Sharp, Terry, 25, 75, 77
Simon, Paul, 91, 171
Sir Douglas Quintet, 55, 83, 98
ska, 17, 81–82
Smithsonian Institution, 24, 26, 28–30,
  101, 142, 183, 224
Solis, Javier, 36, 194
songs: "Atotonilco," 165; "Blue Eyes Cry-
  ing in the Rain," 100; "*Cancion del Ma-*
  riachi," 37; "*Cien Años*," 194; "*Collar de*
  Perles," 92; "*Corazón Loco*," 35, 45, 50;
  "*Costumbres*," 167; "Crazy Winds," 88;
  "*El Cruzo*," 214; "El Paso," 137; "*El Veter-*
  ano," 61; "*Frijolitos Pintos*," 58; "*Hasta*
  La Vista," 224; "Hot Rod Heart,"
  217–18; "*La Bamba*," 201, 208; "Laredo
  Rose," 52; "Me Gusta," 111; "Midnight

to Moonlight," 69–70; "*Niño Jesus*," 207; "*Oye Como Va*," 74; "*Paloma Negra*," 111–12; "*Pobre Bohemio*," 224; "Rattle My Cage," 217; "*Revolucion en mi Corazón*," 116; "Ring of Fire," 128–29, 137; "*Rosa tan Hermosa*," 107; "*Sabor a Mí*," 55; "San Antonio Rose," 29, 130; "Smokey Mountain Memories," 130; "Something in the Rain," 89; "This Time I've Hurt Her More than She Loves Me," 130; "*Traeme Paz*," 213; "*Un Mojado Sin Licencia*," 224; "*Virgincita*," 177; "*Viva Felice*," 112; "*Viva Seguin*," 112; "*Volver, Volver*," 88; "*Vueltas y Vueltas*," 139; "The Westside of Town," 96

songwriters, 27–30, 53, 67, 71, 74, 78, 88, 91–95, 103, 107, 171, 213

South Padre Island, TX, 34, 154–55

Spain, Spanish: Baca on, 12, 17, 25; del Castillo on, 35, 41–42, 46–50; guitars, 93; heritage, 186, music, 17–18, 94–95, 116, 130–31, 146, 150, 206, 215; songs, 67, 72–74, 78, 96, 111–12, 139, 153, 201, 83, 176–78, 201; Vonne on, 210, 212–15, 219

Spanish language, 52, 81, 85–86, 91, 101, 160, 168–69, 173, 186–87, 192–93

squeeze box. *See* accordion

studio. *See* recording studio

Sunny and the Sunliners, 63, 90, 190, 194

swing, Texas, 28; western, 71, 132, 137, 145, 185

Switzerland, 49, 53–54, 97, 118, 149, 214–15

SXSW (South By Southwest), 42, 68

Tequila Rock Revolution, 152–53

Tejano: album, 29, bands, 26, 85–87, 90; culture, 155, 163, 193, 227, definition of, 9, 16–17, 51, 81–82, 91–93, 115, 124–25, 186, 195, 219; festivals, 7, 68,

119; influences on, 215; modern, 13–15, 62, 105, 121–22; museum, 141–42

television shows: *Austin City Limits*, 53; dance 190; *The Hollywood Palace*, 158; *The Johnny Otis Show*, 190; *Saturday Night Live*, 53; *Solid Gold*, 53; talk, 116; *The Voice*, 16, 116; *telenovela*; 74; variety, 128

Texana Dames, 146, 149, 151

Texas Folk Life Organization, 29, 92

Texas Heritage Day, 56, 117, 138

Texas Heritage Music Foundation, 2, 25, 116–17 146, 181

Tex-Mex: heritage 3, 12, 52, 65–67, 73, 78, 86, 101, 193, 215, 219; music, 7, 17, 28–30, 51, 68–70, 80–82, 90, 108, 112, 190, 224–25

Texas Tornados, 27–28, 51–55, 68, 83, 100, 223, 225

Texmaniacs: albums, 25, 29; band, 9,11, 14, 16, 19, 24, 27–28, 31 53–54, 83, 206

Tequila Rock Revolution, 152–53

Tigres del Norte, 161–62

Trevino, Joe, 25, 75, 77, 114

trumpet, 9, 141, 182, 197–99, 206, 223

Tubb, Ernest, 144

University of Texas, 8, 39, 47, 84, 87, 146, 164, 168–71, 175

V, Ruben, 100, 136, 207–09

Valens, Ritchie, 16, 67

Valley, (Texas), 58, 60, 147, 150, 169, 174

Van Zandt, Townes, 148

venues, 38–39, 51, 57, 88, 131–32, 140–41, 146–49, 183, 195, 207, 214

violin, 75, 77, 86, 139, 142, 153, 197

Virginia, 11, 161, 163,

Vonne, Patricia, 32, 40, 42–43, 53, 65, 124, 210–19

Walker, Jerry Jeff, 147–48, 150–51

Watson, Dale, 71, 152

Warner Brothers, 68–69, 91, 94
Watson, Dale, 71, 152
western swing, 71, 132, 137, 145, 185
Westside Horns, 30, 54
Whalum, Kirk, 55, 147
Williams, Hank, 71, 75, 99
Wills, Bob, 16, 28–29, 99, 130, 135–36, 143–44
Wills, John Lee, 143–44

world music, 15, 42, 87

Ybarra, Eva, 7, 9, 63
Yoakam, Dwight, 70, 223
YouTube, 11, 16, 52, 87

Zappa, Frank, 187
zydeco, 15, 127, 161